THE LIBRARY OF ECONOMICS

SECTION TWO: *New Works*

4. A Study in the Theory of Inflation

THE LIBRARY OF ECONOMICS

Section One

AN OUTLINE OF THE SCIENCE OF POLITICAL ECONOMY

by Nassau Senior

AN INQUIRY INTO THE NATURE OF THE PAPER CREDIT OF GREAT BRITAIN

by Henry Thornton

Section Two

STUDIES IN THE THEORY OF MONEY AND CAPITAL

by Professor Erik Lindahl

OVERHEAD COSTS

some Essays in Economic Analysis

by Professor W. Arthur Lewis

APPLIED ECONOMICS

by Professor A. J. Brown

Third Impression

WELFARE AND COMPETITION

The Economics of a Fully Employed Economy

by Professor Tibor Scitovsky

VALUE, CAPITAL AND RENT

by Knut Wicksell

SELECTED PAPERS ON ECONOMIC THEORY

by Knut Wicksell

A STUDY IN
THE THEORY OF
INFLATION

by

BENT HANSEN

The University of Uppsala,
Sweden

LONDON
GEORGE ALLEN & UNWIN LTD
MUSEUM STREET

FIRST PUBLISHED IN 1951
SECOND IMPRESSION 1953
THIRD IMPRESSION 1961

PRINTED IN GREAT BRITAIN
BY BRADFORD AND DICKENS
LONDON, W.C.1

PREFACE

This book is not a treatise on war-economics, and it does not pretend to provide any general theory of inflation; it is a theoretical study inspired by some central economic problems which have appeared during and after the second World War in many countries, including the Scandinavian countries.

The inflations of the second World War were almost everywhere marked by a considerably greater use of measures of direct control than had previously been applied, and the war and post-war inflations had to develop within this frame of direct control; the inflations thus became repressed inflations, the problems of which have been subject to only sporadic investigations. Of course, a good deal has been written about repressed inflations, most of which is purely descriptive or political in character. Investigations of the social and welfare aspects of the control measures are also to be found. But the monetary or "total" economic problems connected with repressed inflation have not been the subject of any thorough theoretical analysis.

I think, therefore, that it is useful to try to develop a monetary theory for repressed inflation. This is done in Chaps. IV, V, and VI. In order to develop such a theory, Chaps. I, II, and III give a number of definitions and concepts, discuss in a more or less tautological fashion the connections between the concepts thus defined, and examine the question of whether it is reasonable to use just these definitions.

This introductory discussion is carried out in such a way that it is also relevant for open inflation. Furthermore, during the course of my work on this book it became evident to me that it may be an advantage to consider repressed inflation as a special boundary case of open inflation, that is, it is possible to consider the models used for the study of repressed inflation as a simplified version of a special type of model for open inflation, which is developed in Chap. VII. Thus, quite apart from any significance they may have in themselves, the investigations of the problems of repressed inflation serve as an introduction to the study of open inflation.

The emphasis throughout the present study is on the interdependence of commodity and factor markets in an inflationary situation. Therefore, it is only natural to attempt to fix the connection between the models used and the general theory of interdependence as it is formulated in a Walrasian system of equations; this is done in Chap. VIII where an inflationary dynamic Walras system without static equilibrium solution is investigated.

Finally, in Chap. IX, the theory of the preceding chapters is used to draw up some conditions for the maintenance of monetary equilibrium, that is, equilibrium with full employment.

The fact that the conditions of the second World War have inspired the present study has also caused certain factors which usually occupy an essential place in writings on inflation to be more or less neglected. These factors are concerned with the significance of the rate of interest for the inflationary process and the effects of foreign trade. However, the analysis is given in such a way that it is not difficult to include the problems arising from changes in the rate of interest and from the circumstances of foreign trade.

The analytic equipment used is not new, but neither is it out-moded. It employs the terminology and technique of the Stockholm School, as presented by Erik Lindahl, and some of the lines of reasoning of that school of thought whose pioneer is J. R. Hicks. Naturally, there are traces of influence from J. M. Keynes, but the analysis of this book can hardly be described as "Keynesian".

When one is working with several magnitudes and relationships, it is often useful, and sometimes necessary, to introduce mathematical reasoning. This has been done in the present study to some extent; but I have found it appropriate, as far as possible, to put the mathematics into small type when it goes beyond elementary algebra and differential calculus. At the same time, the main text is written so that these parts in small type may be omitted without losing the thread of the argument.

Since I began writing this book early in 1948, I have had the benefit of Professor Erik Lindahl's interest in my work. He has discussed with me the greater part of the book, and, as a consequence, much of the text has been rearranged and rewritten several times. Without his encouragement, this book would never have been written.

Among others who have helped me and with whom I have had the opportunity to discuss my ideas, I would especially like to mention Professor Erik Lundberg of Stockholm University, Professor Tord Palander of the University of Uppsala, Docent Tor Fernholm of the School of Commerce, Gothenburg, Docent Göran Borg of the University of Uppsala, and Ralph Turvey B. A., of The London School of Economics. Professor Trygve Haavelmo of the University of Oslo read through a preliminary draft of Chaps. VII and VIII.

The translation was done by Reginald S. Stedman B.A., who also helped with the reading of the proofs. The diagrams were drawn by Mr. Wladimir Tiit. The costs of translation and drawing of diagrams were met by a grant from Statens Samhällsvetenskapliga Forskningsråd (The State's Council of Social Research) in Sweden. My original manuscript in Danish was typed by Miss Ingierd Aurén of the School of Commerce, Gothenburg, and the English manuscript by Miss Litta Fryk and Mrs. Barbro Svensson of the Institute of Economics of the University of Uppsala.

I would like to express my thanks to all these, and all others who have helped me in my work in one way or another.

A stencilled preliminary version of Chaps. I to VII was circulated privately in the autumn of 1949. Sections 1 to 5 of Chap. VII comprise the main argument of an article published in the *Nationaløkonomisk Tidsskrift*, Copenhagen, 1949.

Uppsala, April 1951.

Bent Hansen

CONTENTS

CHAPTER I

GENERAL SURVEY
OF THE CHARACTERISTICS OF INFLATION

1. Two main treatments of the theory of inflation

On considering the history of theories of inflation, it is possible
to distinguish two main treatments, of which the one seems to have
had its origin far back in the past, while the other is only half a
century old.

The first of these is based on some form or other of the quantity
theory of money, and regards an increase in the quantity of money
as the cause and characteristic of inflation. According to this way of
thinking, if the quantity of money increases, prices rise and inflation
exists as a consequence—other things being equal. Thus inflation is regarded as actually identical with an increase in the quantity of money.
Undue concentration upon the changes in the quantity of money often
leads to peculiar results. For example if the state finances public works
with central bank credits during a severe depression, this might be
called inflation, as was done sometimes during the thirties. From the
same point of view, it has also been argued that during the German
hyper-inflation in 1923, there was in reality no inflation at all.[1] These
are just a couple of the strangest examples of what this approach to
inflation theory may lead to. But even apart from that, it is generally agreed that this use of the quantity of money (in one sense or
another) as the starting-point for the study of inflation has not shown
itself to be very appropriate.[2]

---

[1] C. Bresciani-Turroni, *The Economics of Inflation, A Study of Currency Depreci-
ation in Post War Economy*, George Allen & Unwin Ltd., London, 1937, p. 155 et seq.

[2] An author who has attempted to set the quantity-theoretical approach on its
feet once more during the second World War is Clark Warburton. See his various
articles in the *American Economic Review*, 1942, 1943 and 1944.

Even if this approach is very commonly taken, in economic journalism and in so-called "common-sense" argument, the discussion in more recent years has consistently stressed other aspects of inflation, and that will be done in the present study also. This does not imply a denial that changes in the quantity of money may be of important causal significance in the course of inflation: the period since the second World War has witnessed several interesting monetary reforms, which seem to have been effective to a certain degree in combating inflation, although the interrelationships have certainly been rather too complicated to be explained by a simple quantity theory of money. What matters is that we will try to find a more general approach to the theory of inflation, in which the effects of changes in the quantity of money can be incorporated if necessary as one among many other (probably more important) features of significance in the process of inflation.

The second main treatment of the theory of inflation dates back to Wicksell's famous model in *Geldzins und Güterpreise*[1] and his later more general presentation of the theory of the price-level in *Lectures on Political Economy*.[2] It is irrelevant here that Wicksell's personal wish was to rescue the quantity theory of money from all its difficulties; the important thing is his view-point that, just as the price of any good is determined by the demand for it and the supply of it, so also is the general price-level determined by the total demand for and total supply of the group of goods concerned, the prices of which determine the price-level. Thus the foundation was laid for an integration of the micro and macro-theory in this field, so that it subsequently becomes the task of inflation theory to analyse the factors determining the relation between the demand for and supply of those goods which are of interest for some reason, and the consequences of this relation for anti-inflationary policy. "Swedish" inflation theory, if it may be so called, is to a large extent built on this Wicksellian approach, and the same applies a good deal to the whole of Scandinavian and Anglo-American discussion during and after the second World War. In the same way, the present study can be regarded

---

[1] Knut Wicksell, *Geldzins und Güterpreise*, Gustav Fisher, Jena, 1898.

[2] Knut Wicksell, *Föreläsningar i nationalekonomi*, Första delen: Häft. II, Stockholm, 1906. (English translation 1934, *Lectures on Political Economy*).

as an attempt to develop a theory of inflation with Wicksell's general way of thinking as a background.

2. The concept of excess demand

As soon as our attention is turned to the relation between the demand for and supply of goods, the concept of *excess demand*[1] comes to the fore. If we consider an ordinary partial demand-and-supply diagram with a demand curve and a supply curve drawn for a particular good, and perfect competition assumed, then the excess demand is the difference between the quantity demanded and the quantity supplied at a certain given price. Such a simple demand-and-supply diagram does not exist when perfect competition does not hold sway, but the concept of excess demand is easily formed, as the difference between the quantity which is in demand and the quantity which is supplied at the price chosen by the monopolist (monopsonist). The excess demand at a certain given price may be positive, zero, or negative. It is at once possible to understand the analogous expression, *excess supply*. Both concepts, with due regard to appropriate signs, can be used to express one and the same difference between supply and demand. Where misunderstanding does not seem to be possible, no sign is used in what follows.

3. Open and repressed inflation

When we speak about inflation, we usually associate with it increases of prices and/or increases of income, and it is clear that, in so far as an excess demand can be taken as the cause of a rise in prices, we can take inflation to mean (amongst other things) a situation where "extensive" excess demand exists in the markets for the many individual goods.

However, a distinction between *open* and *repressed* inflation confronts us in the consideration of the economic policies pursued by many countries during the second World War, and to a lesser extent the first World War. Repressed inflation is characterized by the fact that prices and possibly wages, are fixed by the institution of direct controls; whereas such controls are not in operation under open inflation. That inflation is still referred to in spite of fixed prices and wages in

---

[1] J. R. Hicks, *Value and Capital*, Clarendon Press, Oxford, 1939, p. 63.

4

a situation of repressed inflation, is due to the fact that there exists a shortage of goods and labour-power in the economy, i.e. there is a predominant excess demand. Accordingly, if control of prices and wages is given up, it can be expected that the level of prices and the level of wages will move upwards. It was precisely with the intention of preventing an excess demand from finding expression in rising prices that so many countries introduced price control during the second World War.

Thus, by concentrating on the relation between demand and supply, we come across a phenomenon which seems characteristic of both open and repressed inflation, namely, the existence of extensive excess demand.[1] The analysis of the following chapters deals with systems in which an extensive excess demand exists. However, to say that there exists an extensive or dominating excess demand is altogether too vague an expression to be used as a basis for an exact analysis, and we shall therefore in the following section define more precisely what is to be understood by "extensive excess demand".

4. The pressure of inflation

In carrying out the analysis of inflation as a macro-economic analysis, as is done in the greater part of what follows, where we work with aggregates, the money value of the demand and of the supply, and consequently of the excess demand, must be used. Otherwise we are liable to sum incommensurable magnitudes. This is, of course, also true when quantity-indices are used. We then have the problem of determining such value totals of excess demand as will be of special interest, and that becomes a question of which way the goods dealt with shall be grouped together.

Now it is a well-known consideration that, if in an economic system we consider every demand for a commodity, factor or claim as an equivalent supply of money of the same value, and conversely every supply of a commodity, factor or claim as a demand for money, the following identity is valid.[2] The value of the excess demand for commodities and factors and claims is equal to the value of the excess

---

[1] A. P. Lerner, "The Inflationary Process, 1. Some Theoretical Aspects"; with comments by S. E. Harris, Fritz Machlup, Harold M. Somers and Henry H. Villard, *The Review of Economics and Statistics*, Vol. XXXI, 1949.

[2] In Chap. VIII, Section 3, the validity of this identity is discussed.

supply of money. Or, as the identity can also be written, the value of the excess demand for commodities, factors, claims and money is zero. There is nothing gained by working with such a comprehensive value total of excess demand, for it is identically equal to zero and includes all economic goods, so that there is nothing to which it can be related. It is also apparent that, as a consequence of introducing a special fictitious market for money[1], in which there is this excess demand for money, it is impossible in the foregoing broad sense to have excess demand in every market at one time. There must always be at least one market in which there is excess supply, if excess demand exists in any of the other markets; but simultaneous excess demand in each one of the commodity, factor and claim markets may quite well exist.

It is clear that in order to talk about inflation we do not in general require either an excess demand for money or an excess demand for claims. We say that a system is in a state of inflation even if the rate of interest is increasing. This means that it is possible to confine our attention to the excess demand in the various individual commodity and factor markets. Furthermore, there are obvious advantages in distinguishing at least between the commodity and factor markets, for one reason because it is the interrelationship between the excess demands in just these two groups of markets that is of considerable significance. In so far as we can take excess demand as an indication of the tendency of prices to rise, it will also be important to distinguish between the upward pressure on commodity-prices and the upward pressure on factor-prices.

We will now say, by way of definition, that *monetary excess demand in the composite commodity-market* exists if the sum of the values of excess demand in all the individual commodity-markets is positive, and that *monetary excess supply in the composite commodity-market* exists if this sum is negative; if the total value of excess demand in all commodity-markets is precisely zero, we will say that there is *monetary equilibrium in the composite commodity-market*. In the same way we may say that *monetary excess demand in the composite factor-market* exists if the sum of the values of the excess demand in all the in-

---

[1] This market is, so to speak, a mirror-image of all the other markets in one, but this does not imply that it is without interest to work with such a "money-market". Cf. J. R. Hicks, *Value and Capital*, Part III.

dividual factor-markets is positive; *monetary excess supply in the composite factor-market* if this sum is negative, and *monetary equilibrium in the composite factor-market* if this sum is zero.

These summations in themselves raise no problems, as they only signify that certain fixed money sums—that such fixed sums are involved is evident from the fact that the concept of excess demand itself assumes that given prices exist—are added together to give wider aggregates. But it is clear that the existence of monetary excess demand in the composite commodity-market for instance, does not prevent the existence of excess supply in individual commodity-markets. We are only sure that there exists excess demand of such a value that the total market value of the excess demand in those individual markets which exhibit excess demand is greater than the value of the excess supply in those individual markets which exhibit excess supply. So it is this we mean when we say, for example, that an "extensive" or "predominant" excess demand exists in the commodity-markets; but it must be emphasized that no unambiguous expression is thus given for a quantitative excess demand in the composite commodity-market (factor-market). Such an unambiguous expression can only be given in the special cases where there is either an excess demand in each individual commodity-markets or where there is only one commodity in the system considered. This last special case is of interest, since in Chaps. IV to VII we work with models for which it is assumed that there is only one commodity and one factor.

We are now able to define what is to be meant by the existence of a monetary pressure of inflation in the commodity and factor markets. We say that a *monetary pressure of inflation* exists if there is monetary excess demand in either the composite commodity-market or the composite factor-market, or in both these composite markets, so long as neither of them exhibits monetary excess supply. So we will not say that a monetary pressure of inflation exists, if, for instance, the monetary excess demand in the composite factor-market should be negative, even if there simultaneously exists a positive monetary excess demand in the composite commodity-market which is greater than the monetary excess supply in the composite factor-market.

If we suppose that there are n commodity-markets, where for the ith commodity the difference between the quantity demanded and the quantity supplied, i.e. the excess demand, is x_i and the price p_i, and that there are m factor-markets where for the jth factor the excess demand is X_j and the price P_j, we can briefly describe the situation where there exists a *monetary pressure of inflation* as follows:

$$\sum_{i=1}^{n} x_i \cdot p_i + \sum_{j=1}^{m} X_j \cdot P_j > 0 \qquad (\text{I}:1)$$

with the subsidiary conditions:

$$\sum_{i=1}^{n} x_i \cdot p_i \geqq 0 \qquad (\text{I}:2)$$

and

$$\sum_{j=1}^{m} X_j \cdot P_j \geqq 0. \qquad (\text{I}:3)$$

It is clear that an analogous definition of *monetary pressure of deflation* could be made, simply by changing the inequality signs in (I:1), (I:2), and (I:3). This is equivalent to saying that a monetary pressure of deflation exists if there is a monetary excess supply in either the composite commodity-market or in the composite factor-market or in both these composite markets, so long as neither of them exhibits monetary excess demand. Finally we may say that *monetary equilibrium* exists if there is monetary equilibrium in both the composite commodity-market and the composite factor-market. In applying these definitions certain "open cases" will appear, where there is neither monetary pressure of inflation, nor of deflation, nor monetary equilibrium; but that is of no importance, however, since there is no reason why every imaginable economic situation should precisely fit one of these three headings.

This limitation of the concept of monetary pressure of inflation is of course to a great extent arbitrary. It is, however, most easily seen that it is appropriate to occupy ourselves with such a state of an economic system, if we consider a system where (I:1), (I:2), and (I:3) are fulfilled and where there is only one commodity and one factor. According to (I:3), there cannot be excess supply of factors (labour-services) either quantitatively or in value, i.e. that there cannot be unemployment. In other words, there must be at least full employment. This is generally regarded as something characteristic of inflation, both open and repressed. According to (I:2), there must not be an excess supply of commodities either quantitatively or in value;

2

this also may be regarded as a characteristic of inflation. According to (I: 1), paying due regard to (I: 2) and (I: 3), the excess demand must be positive, both quantitatively and in value, for at least one of the markets concerned. If there is excess demand for both the commodity and the factor concerned, then (I: 1) is of course fulfilled; but it should be noted, that we also speak of a monetary pressure of inflation where there is excess demand only in the commodity-market, while there is equilibrium in the factor-market, and, similarly, where there is excess demand for factors only, and equilibrium in the commodity-market.

When there are several commodities and several factors, a monetary pressure of inflation can also be taken as identical with what might be called a *quantitative pressure of inflation* if we interpret the sums of values which enter into (I: 1), (I: 2), and (I: 3) as indices of the quantitative excess demand in the composite commodity-market and the composite factor-market.

Let us consider the commodity-markets. If d_i and q_i denote the demand for and supply of the ith commodity, we have $\sum x_i \cdot p_i = \sum d_i \cdot p_i - \sum q_i \cdot p_i$. It follows at once that $\sum x_i \cdot p_i \gtreqless 0$ may be rewritten as $\sum d_i \cdot p_i / \sum q_i \cdot p_i \gtreqless 1$. The expression $\sum d_i \cdot p_i / \sum q_i \cdot p_i$ is an ordinary quantity-index of demand for the moment (period) considered, the quantities supplied at the same moment (period) being taken as basis, and the prices of the moment (period) as weights. In this sense, but only in this sense, the statement, $\sum x_i \cdot p_i \gtreqless 0$, may be taken as equivalent to the statement that the total quantity of commodities in demand $\gtreqless$ total quantity of commodities in supply. Analogous reasoning applies to the factor-markets.

It is seen that by limiting the field of investigation to that determined by (I: 1), (I: 2), and (I: 3), we have also limited the sum of the value of the excess demand for claims and money to a negative value. On the other hand, nothing is implied about the value of excess demand for claims or the value of the excess demand for money. Both may be negative, or one positive and the other negative. From this it becomes apparent, too, why it is inappropriate to take an increase in the quantity of money (or the velocity of circulation), i.e. an excess supply of money, as the starting point for the analysis of inflation. For, it is quite possible to have simultaneously an excess supply of money and excess supply for each individual commodity and factor, if only there is a sufficient excess demand for claims.

5. *Changes in the pressure of inflation*

It is, of course, often necessary to compare two different states of an economic system, for instance, at two different points of time between which a certain development has taken place, or a system with and without a certain measure against inflation, in order to be able to say whether the development or the measure against inflation have brought the system nearer to or farther away from equilibrium. Here we speak of "equilibrium" only when the monetary excess demands in both the composite commodity-market and the composite factor-market are zero, i.e. when the commodity-markets and the factor-markets are in monetary equilibrium. If we are considering only one commodity and one factor, this of course means that equilibrium exists in both the commodity and the factor-markets.

It proves necessary here, even in this simplest possible example where there is only one commodity and one factor, to distinguish between the monetary excess demand and the quantitative excess demand. We shall first illustrate this with the case where there is only one commodity and one factor (labour-services), this example being used in Chaps. IV to VII.

We consider two situations, 1 and 2. The commodity price in situation 1 is p^1 and the excess demand for the commodity x^1, while in situation 2 we have respectively p^2 and x^2. Now, if $p^1 \cdot x^1 < p^2 \cdot x^2$, the monetary excess demand in the commodity-market has of course risen from situation 1 to situation 2, and the system has moved monetarily farther away from equilibrium in the commodity-market. The excess demand need not have risen quantitatively, however, even if $p^1 \cdot x^1 < p^2 \cdot x^2$, for if the price has risen relatively more strongly than the excess demand has fallen, this inequality will be fulfilled, in spite of the fall in the amount of the excess demand. If we therefore compare the quantitative excess demands in situations 1 and 2—and wish to make the comparison in value terms—we may compare either $p^1 \cdot x^1$ and $p^1 \cdot x^2$ or $p^2 \cdot x^1$ and $p^2 \cdot x^2$. It is immaterial whether we use the prices of the one situation or the other (or even a third situation), when we are only considering one commodity. The main thing is that the same price is used throughout the comparison. The development of the monetary and of the quantitative excess demand can thus proceed in different directions, and since both aspects are of interest in themselves, they must both be considered, when we wish to express whether or not the system has approached or receded from equilibrium, i.e. whether the disequilibrium has become smaller or greater.

When we now consider the *monetary* aspect of the matter, it is evident that because we have defined the situation in which a monetary pressure of inflation exists by inequalities (I: 1), (I: 2), and (I: 3) in which two independent subsidiary conditions apply to commodity and factor markets, we cannot lump together the monetary excess demand in the commodity and factor market and say that this pressure of inflation has risen, if only the monetary excess demand in the commodity and factor markets taken together has exhibited a rise. For we should run the risk of talking about a rise in the monetary pressure of inflation in a situation in which this pressure, as defined by inequalities (I: 1), (I: 2), and (I: 3), has disappeared. For example, if there was in situation 1 a monetary excess demand in the commodity-market to the value of $ 1.0 billion, and in the factor-market of $ 0.5 billion, and in situation 2 $ 2.5 billion and $ — 0.5 billion respectively, the sum of the monetary excess demands for both markets taken in one has risen from $ 1.5 billion to $ 2.0 billion. Nevertheless, in our sense there is no monetary pressure of inflation in situation 2, because the monetary excess demand in the factor-market is negative (cf. (I: 3)). Such a result is obviously meaningless, and consequently here too the two markets must be kept apart in estimating whether the monetary pressure of inflation has risen or fallen.

If the monetary excess demand in situation 2 is greater than in situation 1 in both commodity and factor markets, it is clear that the pressure of inflation has risen monetarily from situation 1 to situation 2. Conversely, if the monetary excess demand in each market has fallen, the pressure of inflation has fallen monetarily. And if the monetary excess demand in each market is unchanged, the pressure of inflation is also unchanged monetarily. We can, however, progress a little further by analogy with a well-known method of reasoning in the theory of consumption, where we say that the total utility obtained by a person—tastes remaining unchanged—has definitely increased, if he consumes more of at least one commodity without consuming less of any other commodity. For we can say that, if the monetary excess demand rises in one of the markets without falling in the other, the monetary pressure of inflation has definitely increased; and conversely, if the monetary excess demand falls in one of the markets without rising in the other, the monetary pressure of inflation has definitely decreased; and lastly, if the monetary excess demand is unchanged in both markets, the monetary pressure of inflation has remained definitely unchanged. This is the closest we can come to an unambiguous answer to the question, with those reservations we have made (inequalities (I: 1), (I: 2), and (I: 3)) about the possibility of speaking of a monetary pressure of inflation. But it is clear that cases may arise, where we cannot decide whether the monetary pressure of inflation has risen or fallen, e.g. if the monetary excess demand in the commodity-market in situation 1 is smaller than it is in situation 2, whereas the monetary excess demand in the factor-market is greater in situation 1 than in situation 2. When such cases arise we shall call them "open" cases. This is of course a deficiency in the concept of monetary pressure of inflation as chosen, but that cannot be remedied without changing the definition of monetary pressure of inflation, and it is hardly suitable to do that.

A more or less analogous discussion can be used in considering the quantitative pressure of inflation (provided that we continue with only one commodity and one factor). The nearest we can come to answering the problem is to say that the pressure of inflation has definitely increased quantitatively, if the quantitative excess demand has increased in at least one of the markets without simultaneously falling in the other. Decreased and unchanged quantitative pressure of inflation can be treated in a similar manner.

Now we can go on to the general case where there are several commodities and several factors, and say that the pressure of inflation has risen (fallen) monetarily from a situation 1 to a situation 2, if the monetary excess demand has risen (fallen) either in the composite commodity-market, or in the composite factor-market, or in both, without falling (rising) in any one of these two groups of markets. Also, the pressure of inflation is unchanged monetarily if the monetary excess demand is unchanged in both the composite commodity-market and the composite factor-market.

If we use a notation similar to that used before, so that excess demand for commodities in situation 1 is denoted by x^1, and for factors by X^1, and prices respectively by p^1 and P^1, and the corresponding symbols for situation 2 are x^2, X^2, p^2, and P^2, we can write the condition for a monetary rise (fall) in the pressure of inflation thus:

$$\sum_{i=1}^{n}(p_i^2 \cdot x_i^2 - p_i^1 \cdot x_i^1) + \sum_{j=1}^{m}(P_j^2 \cdot X_j^2 - P_j^1 \cdot X_j^1) > 0 \quad (< 0) \qquad \text{(I: 4)}$$

with the subsidiary conditions:

$$\sum_{i=1}^{n}(p_i^2 \cdot x_i^2 - p_i^1 \cdot x_i^1) \geqq 0 \quad (\leqq 0) \qquad \text{(I: 5)}$$

and

$$\sum_{j=1}^{m}(P_j^2 \cdot X_j^2 - P_j^1 \cdot X_j^1) \geqq 0 \quad (\leqq 0). \qquad \text{(I: 6)}$$

(I: 5) and (I: 6) by themselves express the fact that the pressure of inflation is unchanged monetarily, when only the sign of equality is valid in both.

It should be remarked that the presentation of (I: 4), (I: 5), and (I: 6) does not in itself raise any problems of aggregation, since all that we sum, and wish to compare, are certain amounts of money expressed in the prices of the situations compared.

However, if we wish to formulate similar inequalities, in the case of several commodities and several factors, in order to define whether the pressure of inflation has risen or fallen quantitatively, we encounter the intricate problem of index-numbers. In fact the problem here is equivalent to the problem of determining quantity-indices for the development of the excess demand in commodity and factor markets, and subsequently investigating if these indices provide sufficient basis for determining whether the quantitative pressure of inflation has become definitely greater (or smaller), the condition for this being that at least one of the indices of quantitative excess demand exhibits a rise (fall), and neither of them exhibits a fall (rise); also, if both the indices remain unchanged, the quantitative pressure of inflation is unchanged.

If, from among several possibilities, we choose as weights the prices of the first of the situations compared, we arrive at the following expression for whether the quantitative pressure of inflation has risen (fallen):

$$\sum_{i=1}^{n} p_i^1 (x_i^2 - x_i^1) + \sum_{j=1}^{m} P_j^1 (X_j^2 - X_j^1) > 0 \quad (< 0) \tag{I:7}$$

with the subsidiary conditions:

$$\sum_{i=1}^{n} p_i^1 (x_i^2 - x_i^1) \geqq 0 \quad (\leqq 0) \tag{I:8}$$

and

$$\sum_{j=1}^{m} P_j^1 (X_j^2 - X_j^1) \geqq 0 \quad (\leqq 0). \tag{I:9}$$

(I:8) and (I:9) by themselves express the fact that the pressure of inflation is unchanged quantitatively, when only the sign of equality is valid in both.

6. *The problem of aggregation*

The use of such summations of values of excess demand as occur in the previous sections implies, as has already been mentioned, that the so-called aggregation problem crops up. Generally speaking, the aggregation problem has not yet been solved; even the problem itself has not, according to Marschak, been generally formulated. Only in entirely special cases has it been stated and solved.[1] We shall not in any way attempt to formulate and solve the general problem; we shall only attempt to give what might be called a partial solution. What is meant by this will become clearer as we proceed, but, to begin with, we can say the following:

When it comes to answering the question of what significance is really to be given the summations with which we are concerned here, it is convenient for our purpose to distinguish between their purely "definitional" significance and their "functional" significance.[2] The "definitional" significance is that associated with the way in which

[1] Lawrence R. Klein, "Macroeconomics and the Theory of Rational Behavior"; Kenneth May, "The Aggregation Problem for a One-Industry Model"; Shou Shan Pu, "A Note on Macroeconomics", and Lawrence R. Klein, "Remarks on the Theory of Aggregation"; all in *Econometrica*, Vol. 14, 1946.

[2] Some authors have denied outright that any definite meaning can be given to such aggregates in general, for example, Bertil Ohlin, "Professor Lindahl om dynamisk teori, Reflektioner kring 'Studies in the Theory of Money and Capital'" ("Prof. Lindahl on Dynamic Theory, Remarks on 'Studies in the Theory of Money and Capital'"), *Ekonomisk Tidskrift*, Stockholm, 1940.

14

these summations occur in the budget equations (definitional relationships) for a system; these budget equations apply, in a period
analysis, within the single period. This question is treated in Chaps.
II and III and does not involve any difficulties of principle. The
"functional" significance, on the other hand, refers to another and less
clear question; if we consider a period analysis we can say that the
problem we have to deal with here is the question of the causal importance of the summations of values of excess demand for the development from period to period, especially the significance of a certain
value-sum of excess demand for the development of the price-level.
I have found it convenient to delay the treatment of this problem to
one of the last chapters—Chap. IX—of which the first three sections are,
however, written so that they may be read in conjunction with this
chapter.—The impatient reader is invited to do that.

7. *Induced and spontaneous changes of prices*

In the previous sections we have tried to find a general characteristic of the inflationary situation in the existence of excess demand,
from the commonly held point of view that the existence of excess
demand implies a tendency of prices to rise. However, it has gradually
been admitted that this does not always sufficiently account for the
possible tendencies of prices to rise. In *A Treatise on Money*, J. M.
Keynes worked on a very significant distinction between "spontaneous
income-inflation" and "induced income-inflation" in connection with
his "fundamental equations".[1] The distinction between what is there
considered as "induced", and what is considered as "spontaneous" rise
in factor-prices (Keynes's E) depends on whether the rise in factor prices
takès place in. a situation where quantitative equilibrium prevails in
the factor-markets, or one where quantitative disequilibrium prevails.
In the terminology used by Keynes in the *Treatise*, the distinction is
whether the rise in factor prices happens as a result of investment exceeding saving, or happens in a situation where investment and saving
are equal. In considering spontaneous rises in factor prices, Keynes

---

[1] J. M. Keynes, *A Treatise on Money*, MacMillan & Co, London, 1930, I, Ch. XI.
See also Myrdal's distinction between "internal" and "external" causes of price-
changes, G. Myrdal, *Monetary Equilibrium*, William Hodge & Co., London, 1939,
p. 152 et seq.

had in mind the fixing of wage-rates and such raising of the wage-rates as is forced by the trade unions without regard to the conditions of demand in the labour-market. However, the distinction can be extended to other factors, as well as to the fixing of commodity prices and the tendency for these prices to change.

What is of importance here is that we cannot assume that there is no tendency to price increases even when the excess demand—actual or expected—in the market for a certain good is zero. For, as Keynes emphasizes, price increases may quite well appear, without there being any excess demand as driving force behind them. However, if we distinguish, as does Keynes, between *induced price increases* which appear as the result of an excess demand, and *spontaneous* or *autonomous price increases*, which appear without having an origin in an excess demand, then we can of course say that there is a causal connection between excess demand and tendency to induced price increases. If there is a tendency to induced price increases, then excess demand must exist. It is to be noticed, however, that it is never possible to decide whether a price increase is induced or spontaneous without investigating whether there is simultaneous excess demand or not. While we can be sure that any tendency of prices to rise is quite spontaneous if the excess demand for the good in question is negative or zero, we cannot decide at once if a tendency to price increases is wholly induced or partly spontaneous, when the excess demand is positive. Of course, induced and spontaneous rises in prices can quite well coexist. Whether a given tendency to price increases is to be regarded as induced, or partly induced and partly spontaneous depends, therefore, on our being able to find independent criteria for whether a tendency to spontaneous price increases exists when a positive excess demand prevails.

To arrive at an independent definition of the size of the tendency for prices to increase spontaneously, we must begin by stating that this magnitude is equal to the tendency of prices to rise which would exist if the excess demand for the good considered were made zero, other things beeing equal. A very important category of price increases now comes to be included among this spontaneous group, namely the price increases of those goods, the prices of which, singly or in groups, are automatically determined by the price development for another good or group of goods. The most typical case is that of wage-rates regulated according to a cost-of-living index. Where there is such index regulation of wage-rates, wages must tend to rise in accordance with a predetermined relationship when prices (index-numbers) rise, without regard to the relation between demand and supply in the labour-market. The rise in wage-rates which actually does occur will of course be influenced by the size of the excess demand in the labour-market. When there is a positive excess demand wage-rates will tend to rise more steeply than if they were only subject to regulation according to a cost-of-living index, and conversely when a negative excess demand for labour-power exists at the same time as regulation according to cost-of-living index. Of course, it might be said that the rise in wage-rates is "induced" by the rise in the prices of the cost-of-living index goods, and that these price increases themselves can be induced by an excess demand in their markets; but what is important is that the rise in wage-rates occurs without being necessarily connected with the relation between demand and supply in the *labour-market*. In an actual inflationary process, induced and spontaneous price increases will in all probability go hand in hand in this way. This does not, however, make the distinction any the less useful.

Another important field in which spontaneous price increases play some part is that of export and import prices in foreign trade. Although such price increases may be induced by excess demand in the world market taken as a whole, they must as a rule be regarded as spontaneous when seen from a small country's view-point.

It will often be extremely difficult to measure the forces behind a tendency to spontaneous price increases. Where there are legally binding contracts (possibly laws) as a basis, e.g. in agreements about the regulation of wages according to cost-of-living index, such contracts give complete information, of course. It is more difficult where such contracts or laws do not exist. The attempt has been made to use the inequality of distribution of income as an indicator, because such social groups as have had their living-standards impaired will be especially anxious to force rises in their money incomes. A fall in real wages has also been used as an indicator for the spontaneous upward pressure on wage-rates, since it can be assumed that the trade unions will always endeavour to maintain the workers' real wages at least intact, by raising money wages, and the more the real wages sink below the customary level, the harder the trade unions will work to raise the money wages. Many other relationships contribute as well, such as the strength of the unions and their fighting spirit, political connections and things of that sort, which can be put under the heading of "factors in the class struggle".

It should be clear from the foregoing that considerable difficulties are connected with the distinction between induced and spontaneous price increases, and that in an actual case it can be difficult to decide whether to call the price increases of a good induced or spontaneous. But in spite of that the distinction may be regarded as very useful and sometimes necessary. Similar distinctions have been used in several attempts to explain the war inflations and post-war inflations[1], and it will be utilized in this study. It is perhaps of minor significance for the formal analysis of repressed inflation, but it cannot be neglected in considering open inflation. Its most typical occurrence—when wage-rates are regulated by a cost-of-living index—is therefore included in the model in Chap. VII illustrating open inflation. Apart from the spontaneous price increases in foreign trade, the other forms of spontaneous price increases originate essentially in the existence of economic organisations of various types[2], and are conditioned by monopolism (monopsonism) in the markets. They will not be dealt with in any detail in this study.

Finally, it is to be remembered that where we have explained in the preceding sections what is to be understood by the existence of a (monetary or quantitative) pressure of inflation, and by changes in this pressure, we have disregarded that pressure on prices which is a

---

[1] E.g. I. Grünbaum, "Inflatoriske foranstaltninger og inflationistiske systemer" ("Inflationary Policies and Inflationary Systems"), *Socialt Tidsskrift*, Copenhagen, 1940; A. C. Pigou, "Types of War Inflation", *The Economic Journal*, 1941; Anders Östlind, *Svensk samhällsekonomi 1914—22 (Swedish National Economy 1914—22)*, published by Svenska Bankföreningen, Stockholm, 1945, Appendix I; Erik Lindahl, "Några synpunkter på inflationsproblemet" ("Some Aspects of the Inflation Problem"), *Nationaløkonomisk Tidsskrift*, Copenhagen, 1948; Jørgen Pedersen, "Sanering af pengevæsenet" ("Reconstruction of the Monetary System"), *Nationaløkonomisk Tidsskrift*, Copenhagen, 1949, and James Duesenberry, "The Mechanics of Inflation", *The Review of Economics and Statistics*, Vol. XXXII, May 1950, No. 2. Duesenberry distinguishes between "the 'ortodox' theory of inflation", by which expression is meant the excess demand analysis, and his own "mark-up" hypothesis.

[2] A price increase which occurs merely as a consequence of a changed price policy on the part of an enterprise, with costs and demand relationships unchanged, must be reckoned among the spontaneous price increases.

result of the tendency to spontaneous price increases. We might very well distinguish between an induced and a spontaneous pressure of inflation, and this should be borne in mind in what follows.

8. The relation between this analysis and earlier theories of inflation

It will not be out of place now to go into the relation between the attempt at a theory of inflation which will be put forward in this study and other recent investigations of inflation theory. This can be done quite briefly with the concepts of the previous sections as a background.

The reason we have laid so much stress on the explanation of what is to be understood when we say that a monetary pressure of inflation exists is simply that this concept brings us at once into contact with the Swedish (and Austrian, and *Treatise*-Keynesian) theories of inflation, which are ultimately based on Wicksell's model in *Geldzins und Güterpreise*. Although these theories of inflation work with a difference between investment and saving as the driving force of inflation, the crux of these theories is, however, that this difference is taken to be identical with the existence of an excess demand which forces up both commodity prices and factor prices alternately. We shall go fully into the way the difference between planned investment and saving is connected with excess demand in the next two chapters, and show that it is not of quite the simple character that has been assumed in these theories. Here, however, it is important to note that these theories take the factor-markets and their excess demands as an essential link in the chain of causation which leads to rises in commodity prices and factor prices. Further, that what is thus dealt with is clearly what we have called induced price-increases. The inflation analysis of the following chapters may therefore be said to cover the field which the Wicksellians have investigated.

On the other hand, we have those authors who to some extent take their starting point and inspiration in J. M. Keynes's *How to Pay for the War* (together with some stray ideas in *The General Theory of Employment, Interest, and Money*).[1] In that little book Keynes put forward a rather sketchy analysis of inflation, which in certain re-

---

[1] J. M. Keynes, *How to Pay for the War*, MacMillan & Co., London, 1940, and J. M. Keynes, *The General Theory of Employment, Interest, and Money*, Harcourt Brace & Co., New York, N. Y., 1936, p. 301 et seq.

spects resembles the Wicksellian analysis, in so far as it considers excess demand for commodities as the driving force behind rises in commodity prices. But the picture of inflation is somewhat different, because the disequilibrium in the factor-markets comes in the background as a causal factor in the process.

This is even more noticeable in the authors who have developed Keynes's ideas from *How to Pay for the War*. With these authors it is only in the commodity-markets that excess demand appears as the driving force behind price increases; the factor-markets, which as a rule comprise only the labour-markets, are dealt with simply by assuming full employment, and nothing more. This is of course not equivalent to considering the wage-rates as constant, but it is equivalent to considering the rises in wage-rates which occur as only spontaneous. These authors, for instance, introduce a certain "coefficient of wage-adjustment", which tightly connects the development of money wages with the development of prices, in the way which occurs when money wages are regulated according to a cost-of-living index.[1] The fact that there is full employment then only signifies that a maximum for total production is thereby fixed (that is undoubtedly important), but it neglects the point that an excess demand for labour-services can exist, i.e. that there can be overfull employment.[2] Therefore, when these post-Keynesian authors say that inflation is equivalent to the existence of a monetary excess demand in the commodity-markets when full employment is assumed, it is to be borne in mind that we also speak of a monetary pressure of inflation in the situation where there is monetary equilibrium in the composite commodity-market, but monetary excess demand in the composite factor-market, so that the analysis here will go farther than the post-Keynesian analysis of inflation.

Of course, the post-Keynesian writers have this virtue, that they do take spontaneous rises in wage-rates into account for these are undoubtedly rather important. But the disregard of the possibility of excess demand in the factor-markets in their analysis of inflation is quite a serious deficiency compared with the Wicksellian analysis. In

---

[1] See, e.g. Tjalling Koopmans, "The Dynamics of Inflation", *The Review of Economic Statistics*, Vol. XXIV, May, 1942.

[2] This deficiency in post-Keynesian theory is also noticed by Bertil Ohlin, *The Problem of Employment Stabilization*, Columbia University Press, New York, N. Y., 1949, and A. C. Pigou, "Over-Employment", *Economica*, May, 1950.

a way, the asymmetry which has thus come into the Keynesian and post-Keynesian analysis is rather peculiar, since, while this analysis has laid more stress than any other on the possibility of unemployment, i.e. excess supply of labour-power, and its implications, it has almost entirely neglected the possibility of an economic system falling on the other side of equilibrium (full employment) in the labour-market, i.e. the possibility of there being direct shortage of labour-power at the prevailing wage-rates—or excess demand for labour-power. Put into perspective with the post-Keynesian analysis of inflation, the object of this study may therefore be said to be that of removing this asymmetry in the analysis.

There does exist an essential difference between the post-Wicksellian and post-Keynesian analysis on another point also, but since this difference will be the basis of the whole of Chap. III, we will not go into it here.

The great extent to which the method of excess demand analysis is useful and flexible is also borne out by the fact that it is possible to apply it to the so-called "moving dynamic equilibrium" analysis used by Lindahl and Hicks.[1] We now consider a special inflationary situation which has been the object of particular attention, namely that in which all economic subjects have fully correct expectations of future conditions. In a "moving dynamic equilibrium" process, where the time is divided up into periods, and where full adjustment is supposed to take place at the beginning of each period, this clearly signifies that a process of rise in prices may be obtained in which all expectations are always fulfilled and where it may be said that equilibrium continuously prevails, despite the continuously rising prices.[2] Even in such a process we can talk about excess demand, and think of the excess demand as the driving force in the process of rise in prices. Even if there is equilibrium in each period between supply and demand (i.e. excess demand is zero) at that price which has been arrived at for the given

---

[1] Erik Lindahl, *Penningpolitikens medel* (*The Means of Monetary Policy*), Malmö, 1930, (English translation, *Studies in the Theory of Money and Capital*, George Allen & Unwin, London, 1939, Part II, *The Rate of Interest and the Price Level*). And also J. R. Hicks, *Value and Capital*, and Tjalling Koopmans, "The Dynamics of Inflation".

[2] Lerner, "The Inflationary Process", therefore does not want to call such a process of price-increases inflation, contrary to Lindahl.

period, there is of course nothing to prevent us asking the question of how large the excess demand would have been in that period at the prices holding good in the previous period. Let us suppose, for instance, that the fixing of prices at the beginning of a period takes place according to trial and error, so that the price of the previous period is naturally used to start with. Then, if everyone expects the price in the period considered to be higher than in the one before, it must mean that an excess demand would occur if the previous period's price were maintained, since everyone will wish to buy and none to sell at the old price, and that is the same as saying that there is an excess demand which drives up prices in the new period above those in the old. If the fixing of prices does not take place according to such a trial and error procedure, the hypothetical situation that prices remain unchanged from the one period to the next can always be imagined. When we speak of excess demand as a definite fixed quantity of goods, it must always be at a definite given price; and it is just because we are at liberty to choose this price in an appropriate way that the excess demand analysis is as useful as it is in actual fact.

Although the analysis of both the post-Keynesians and (of course) the post-Wicksellians can be traced back to Wicksell, there are essential differences between their fields of application. This study is likewise Wicksellian in its analysis of inflation, but goes farther than the post-Wicksellians in that spontaneous price increases are taken into account, and farther than the post-Keynesians in that monetary excess demand in the factor-markets is also taken into account. Furthermore, repressed inflation, hitherto much neglected in purely theoretical analysis, is also considered.

9. *The concepts of "demand" and "supply"*

Previously we have spoken of excess demand without closer examination of the two concepts—demand and supply—which are the basis of the concept of excess demand. Since both demand and supply are "streams", defined per unit of time, excess demand at a certain instant must be understood to mean the intensity or speed of excess demand in that instant at the prices given. As soon as the analysis becomes discontinuous in the form of analysis over a period, as is the method of analysis used in Chaps. II to VI, the excess demand is calculated for a whole unit period at certain given prices; but this involves no difficulties.

It is much more important, however, that when a monetary pressure of inflation exists the concepts of supply and demand can be given various interpretations which are all reasonable and economically relevant.

In modern price theory, elaborated in terms of demand and supply, it is often loosely said that demand and supply are to be understood as "intended" or "*ex ante*" magnitudes. One way of interpreting the concepts of demand and supply is just to put them equal to "planned purchases" and "expected sales", respectively, in the *ex ante* sense of the Stockholm School. The value of the excess demand for a good thus becomes equal to the difference between planned purchases and expected sales of that good, and obviously it is assumed in this that both planned purchases and expected sales are expressed in definite fixed sums of money. There is a weakness here which is generally recognized, which is that economic subjects will usually rather work with certain alternatives, which are associated with different probabilities regarding their fulfilment. By weighting each alternative expectation with the probability which has been attached to it, a sort of average ("most probable") expectation can be arrived at, so that a definite fixed sum of money is obtained as expression for the expectation. So the above difficulty is not hard to overcome, but a whole series of difficulties which are to some extent of a similar nature crop up in an inflationary situation, and they cannot always be so easily overcome.

There is no difficulty in identifying planned purchases of commodities with the concept of demand, if it can be assumed that purchasing plans are always carried out. On the other hand, the relations which apply to the identification of the concepts of supply and expected sales are not so simple. Quite apart from the fact that it is always necessary to understand supply as meaning such expected possibilities of sales as the seller has thought he would like to make use of, the plans for production can go wrong, so that the seller is not in a position to make use of the possibilities of sales that he had previously hoped to utilize. The question then becomes, whether the supply for a period shall be understood to mean the expected sales with or without taking unrealized production plans into account. If there are no stocks, and the seller thinks he will be able to sell 1000 articles and therefore attempts to produce these goods, but, contrary to expectations, the production achieved is only 900 is the supply then to be taken as 1000 or 900 articles? The problem usually occurs in an inflationary situation because of unexpected alterations in production due to excess demand for factors and raw materials.

If the assumption that purchasing plans are always carried out is dropped, formidable difficulties arise over the relation between the concepts of planned purchases and demand. The planned purchases which enter into the *ex ante* balances of the economic subjects (on earning of income and use of it) are of course those planned purchases which the subject concerned himself thinks are "most probable" attainable. If the subject concerned is not certain that he can make purchases so big as would be worth-while or desirable for him, there is lack of correspondence between 1) planned purchases which are expected to be realizable (and therefore enter into his calculations (*ex ante* balances)), and 2) purchases which he attempts to carry out (and show themselves as demand in the market), and 3) those purchases which it would be reasonable for him to carry out if he did not need to take any limitations into account ("the optimum purchases").

Consider, as an example, an enterprise which wants to purchase 1000 units of labour-power, but can only rely on concluding contracts for 900. If it is quite fortuitous which attempts to purchase will succeed, and which will not succeed, and if the enterprise has some idea of the proportion of attempts at purchasing that usually fail, it may well be that the demand made by the enterprise, taken in the sense of binding offers of purchase, will exceed the planned purchases. The same holds good if the enterprise does not know what proportion of the offers of purchase may draw blank. If the labour-market is organized in such a way that offers of employment are sent to a labour-exchange, the enterprise will probably tell the exchange how much labour-power it is really willing to employ, but in spite of that the enterprise may very well reckon on getting a smaller number of applicants. The demand, as it manifests itself in orders to the labour-exchange, thus becomes larger than the planned purchases. Moreover, it is possible that a "sham magnification" of the demand may arise because everyone offers to purchase considerably larger quantities than they really need, in order to obtain the quantities which they are willing to purchase. In the waiting lists at the apartment agencies, the same person crops up many times, despite the fact that he does not wish to rent more than one flat.

In the case of supply we thus have to distinguish between:

firstly, supply in the sense of *expected sales*, in the way in which these occur in the *ex ante* balances of the economic subjects with their "most probable" values; and

secondly, supply in the sense of *the quantity of goods actually available*, i.e. production actually carried out, plus changes in stocks. In Chap. III we shall define more precisely what is meant by this. It will then be seen that this interpretation of the concept of supply must actually be split into two.

And with regard to demand, the distinction must be made between:

firstly, demand in the sense of *planned purchases*, i.e. those *ex ante* purchases which the economic subjects have considered "most probable" to be carried out; and

secondly, demand in the sense of *optimum purchases*, i.e. those purchases which it would be worth-while to make from the point of view of a "rational" calculation (of utility or costs) if the economic subject were free in this respect, within his financial resources and within that framework of *legal* restrictions which is assumed to be given (optimum purchases must exceed or equal planned purchases); and

thirdly, demand in the sense of *active attempts to purchase*, i.e. the purchases which the economic subject tries to carry out by making binding offers of purchase (giving orders); the active attempts to purchase will never be less than the planned purchases, and they can be greater than the optimum purchases.

These different interpretations of the concepts of supply and demand give rise to a whole series of concepts of excess demand. In Chap. II, some consequences of putting excess demand equal to the difference between planned purchases and expected sales will be investigated, while Chap. III is built on other interpretations of the concept of excess demand. The distinction between these different interpretations of demand and supply will be utilized in later chapters also (see especially Chap. VIII).

CHAPTER II

A "SWEDISH" APPROACH
TO SOME FUNDAMENTAL
RELATIONSHIPS

1. *Introductory remarks on investment and saving*

Having given in Chap. I a short account of the excess demand characteristic of inflation and of the concept of monetary pressure of inflation, we can continue with a presentation of some basic relationships in a situation where monetary pressure of inflation exists. One of the objects of the following two chapters is to illustrate the connection between the excess demand which characterizes inflation and the saving-investment relation. We are starting from the Stockholm School's (neo-Wicksellians') treatment of the saving-investment problem in this chapter, so, in accordance with the remarks made in Chap. I, Section 9, we must talk about planned purchases instead of demand and expected sales instead of supply. Thus an interpretation of the concepts of excess demand and excess supply is adopted which allows us to show, if we make certain assumptions, that the monetary excess demand in the composite commodity-market and the composite factor-market taken together is equal to the difference between planned investment and planned saving, which itself is equal to the sum of the values of the excess supply of claims and money. This is the reason that the saving-investment relation is often used as an indication of whether inflation exists or not. The relation indicated here, between planned investment and planned saving on the one hand, and on the other, demand, i.e. planned purchases, and supply, i.e. expected sales, of everything other than claims and cash, together with the consequences of this relationship, are dealt with by Erik Lindahl.[1] This chapter's analysis is based on his treatment of the question.

---

[1] Erik Lindahl, *Studies in the Theory of Money and Capital*, London, George Allen and Unwin Ltd., 1939, "Algebraic Discussion of the Relation between some Funda-

26

2. *The disequilibrium method*

The method in Lindahl's analysis, a method later used in part by others, e.g. A. G. Hart[1], begins by setting up equations applying both *ex ante* and *ex post* and dealing with changes of cash-holdings and with the earning and use of income. A combination of the different equations, together with assumptions of equality between certain magnitudes *ex ante* and *ex post*, furnishes us *with possible incongruences between plans and expectations* of different economic subjects, consequently with those points where there is disequilibrium, and, further, a survey of the different ways in which expectations can be disappointed for individuals or groups of individuals. As soon as disagreement occurs between the plans and expectations of different economic subjects with respect to the same economic phenomenon, disagreement must arise between prospective and retrospective values. If all buyers of bananas plan to buy altogether X tons of bananas at a given price, whereas all the sellers expect to sell Y tons at the same price, the result *ex post* must be different from either the plans of the buyers or the expectations of the sellers, or from both. If we know which party is able to carry out its plans (expectations), we can say who is to be disappointed and in what way.

Even if we do not progress a great deal beyond the purely definitional way of reasoning[2] using this method of procedure, it is still very useful as an exposition of those points in which surprises and disappointments may appear, and as an account of the possible quantitative range which these surprises and disappointments can simultaneously have. The approach may be said to be indispensable as a beginning for every period analysis.

---

mental Concepts", p. 74—135. The relation mentioned has also been pointed out by J. R. Hicks, *Value and Capital*, Notes to Chap. XIV, A, p. 181 et seq., and by Tord Palander, "Om 'Stockholmsskolans' begrepp och metoder" ("On the Concepts and Methods of the 'Stockholm School'"), *Ekonomisk Tidskrift*, Stockholm, 1941, p. 123—129, especially p. 124, note 2. See also Erich Schneider, "Opsparing og investering i et lukket samfund" ("Saving and Investment in a Closed Economy"), *Nationaløkonomisk Tidsskrift*, Copenhagen, 1942.

[1] A. G. Hart, *Money, Debt, and Economic Activity*, Prentice-Hall Inc., New York, 1948, Appendix B.

[2] The assumption that certain plans are always carried out can be tested empirically, however. Accordingly Lindahl's discussion is not purely "analytical", cf. p. 30, note 1.

It may also be pointed out that it is in principle the same method which is used at a certain stage of drawing up national budgets. Here, the analysis starts with the drawing up of statistics of plans (estimation of the sizes of all plans concerning production, consumption, etc., which are in existence in the country for the period). This gives a survey of the possibilities of "residues" occurring, and also makes it possible to foretell where it is best to interfere, in order to make plans consistent, and in agreement with specified political aims.[1] As a starting point for this sort of forecasting the method has achieved "world-citizenship".

Apart from the use of the concept of the "period", the fundamental assumption on which the method is based is, that all prices are regarded as given within the period, so that the prices are taken as known at the beginning of the period, whereupon every individual (firm) draws up his plans in whatever way is best for him. Since the prices are given for the period, disagreement can only occur between prospective and retrospective magnitudes in respect of the turn-over of quantities of goods. Unexpected changes of prices do not enter into the matter[2], and correction of prices because of excess demand or excess supply cannot occur during the period. That is not to say, of course, that supply and demand do not influence the prices. The price quotations of the entrepreneurs at the beginning of a period will be influenced by their expectations as to what will happen during the period, and these expectations will be influenced by what happened in previous periods so that the occurrence of an excess demand in the previous period will usually imply an inclination towards marking-up of prices at the beginning of the current period.

We shall only make a few remarks about the concept of the *period*. The method of period analysis is that the results *ex post* for a period are determined without ambiguity from all the plans and expectations drawn up by the economic subjects, and the interactions of these, and further, prices, plans, and expectations for the following period are determined from the results of the previous period (periods). It is clear that the period must be chosen sufficiently short for no plans to be

[1] See e.g. Ingvar Ohlsson, "Nationalbudgetbegreppet" ("The Concept of National Budgets"), Chap. VI in *Meddelanden från Konjunkturinstitutet*, Serie B: 10, *Ekonomiska utredningar, våren 1949*, Stockholm, 1949.

[2] But see Chap. VI, Section 5.

28

changed during the period. New plans are drawn up only at the change-over from one period to the next. This fixing of the maximum length of the period in the way Lindahl has done it is now generally accepted, and depends upon the very method of period-analysis.

On account of the characteristics of the method it has been called "the disequilibrium method", in contradistinction to the "equilibrium methods" in which it is assumed that prices are determined in such a way that there is equilibrium (partial or total, according to the particular equilibrium method used) between supply and demand during each period.[1]

All these methods can be used in the analysis of open inflation, but there are various reasons for preferring the disequilibrium method, and we use it in all the analyses which follows.

When the inflation is repressed, prices are fixed by the public authorities, in some way or other, either by maximum prices, normal prices, or simply by price-ceilings and wage-ceilings. When prices are fixed at such a level that no one feels inclined to offer lower prices than those permitted, the disequilibrium method is clearly the one to use. Therefore, if we wish our analysis of inflation to be applicable to both open and repressed inflation, the disequilibrium method will be indispensable.

It is stressed in modern dynamical theory that it is necessary to regard the adjustment of prices to an equilibrium position as a process taking time, and this is taken into account even in statical theory.[2] So, if we take into account that the equilibrium methods assume that price adjustment in a market is always instantaneous, it is seen that we have here yet another reason for adopting the disequilibrium method.

Owing to these considerations, we shall continue in the following chapters (unless otherwise stated) with the assumption that all prices are announced—either publicly or privately—at the beginning of each period, and are recognized by everyone and remain unaltered throughout the period.

---

[1] Lindahl, *Studies* . . ., p. 60—69.

[2] Paul A. Samuelson, *Foundations of Economic Analysis*, Harvard Economic Studies, Vol. LXXX, Harvard University Press, Cambridge, Mass., 1947, Ch. IX.

3. *Lindahl's assumptions*

With the disequilibrium method as a framework, Lindahl's analysis continues by assuming that all purchase plans which exist at the beginning of the period are completely realized, so that purchases *ex ante* and *ex post*, are equal. This applies both to purchases of commodities and to purchases of factors.[1] When this assumption is made, the turn-over of quantities of goods (*ex post*) is unambiguously fixed. It is a typical assumption of a not insignificant part of the Stockholm School that purchase plans are always 'fulfilled without exception[2], but as we have already mentioned in Chap. I, Section 9, it turns out to be a wholly or partly untenable assumption when applied to the analysis of inflation—in any case so long as prices are fixed throughout the period.

It is perhaps most obvious that all purchase plans cannot be carried out if there is monetary pressure of inflation when we consider the factor-markets. Let us have as factor labour-power. The value of the excess demand for labour-power ≥ 0, i.e. there is demand for more labour-power than can in general be supplied, in accordance with what has already been said in Chap. I. If demand is identified with planned purchases and supply with expected sales, and we assume that no unexpected sales of labour-power can take place, simply because all

---

[1] Lindahl, *Studies* . . ., p. 92.

[2] Cf. Palander, "Om 'Stockholmsskolans' begrepp och metoder", p. 126. Strangely enough, the assumption that the purchase plans are always realized seems to have been taken by some authors as very nearly the only *possible* assumption regarding the determination of the quantities dealt with, see Palander, before mentioned, and Hans Brems, *Reklame, Købelyst og Købeevne* (*Advertizing, Purchasing Propensity, and Purchasing Power*), Einar Harchs Forlag, Copenhagen, 1950, p. 107: "As is implicitly assumed by the whole of the Stockholm School and as is explicitly said by Alvin Hansen, William Fellner, and Erik Lindahl, plans are always realized. This is simply a methodological necessity for our model, for—as [Alvin] Hansen says —plans that are not carried out can have no significance." This assumption came to be regarded as almost sacrosanct, probably because economics dealt with buyers' markets during the thirties, and it was in relation to such markets that the theory of the Stockholm School was worked out in the main. J. M. Keynes's *General Theory* is sometimes called "depression economics", but the term might more justifiably be applied to parts of the theory of the Stockholm School. As is shown in the text, Keynes's assumption about unemployed production factors may be regarded as equivalent to the assumption of the Stockholm School that purchase plans for factors are always realized.

labour-power is employed and expects to be employed, then it is evident that part of the purchase plans for labour-power cannot be realized, disregarding the special case where the excess demand is zero. Of course, it might be suggested that there are unexpected sales of labour-power in overtime work. But in the first place there is a limit of 24 hours work per day for each worker, and secondly, it is natural to suppose that the possibilities for overtime are either fully utilized beforehand, so that the workers themselves reckon all overtime into their sales expectations, or that the workers simply refuse to work "unexpectedly", a phenomenon rather usual under repressed inflation.

Accordingly, we cannot work with the assumption that all purchase plans in the factor-market are carried out. For that assumption implies that there are always, in all circumstances, unemployed factors of production sufficient to satisfy the demand. In the general case we may reckon that some of the purchase plans for factors will not be carried out.

A rather similar argument can be put forward with respect to the purchase plans for commodities. According to the theory of the Stockholm School, we should always expect the difference between the purchase plans and sales expectations in the commodity-markets to be made good from existing stocks, if the purchase plans are greater than sales expectation. Here also it is true that it is impossible to buy more than exists, and therefore certain purchase plans must necessarily break down, if the existing (or rather: planned) stocks are less than the difference between planned purchases and expected sales. So whether or not it can be assumed that all purchase plans for commodities will be executed in a given inflationary situation depends on the size of the stocks of commodities. Things other than the size of the stocks of commodities are of significance for the execution of purchase plans, however. Excess capacity in the production of services may play much the same rôle as stocks of commodities. Furthermore, even if the purchase plans do not exceed the sales expectations, the sellers may find that they have a smaller quantity of goods at their disposal than they expected, e.g. because of unexpected decreases in productivity, or on account of the planned production programme not being realizable because of over-estimation by the entrepreneurs of the quantity of production factors obtainable.[1] Furthermore, there is reason

---

[1] In defence of the generality of his assumption, Lindahl says: "Since this assumption (. . . that purchasing plans are realized . . .), however, merely signifies that

to suggest that the assumption that the sellers of commodities are willing to make up the difference between planned purchases and expected sales from stocks is not always realistic either. If the sellers have stocks which for some reason or other they want to sell at a later period, it is quite likely that they will refuse to sell more than a certain quantity in the period. concerned, so that the purchasing plans cannot be realized. During inflation that is quite a common practice, especially on the part of retail traders, who may reserve commodities privately for specially chosen customers, who are not allowed, or are not able, to clear the stocks in one period.

What follows completes the criticism which has been put forward in this section of the general assumption made by the Stockholm School that purchasing plans are always realized:

It is not always clear what is to be understood when a prospective magnitude is called "planned" or "expected". There is nothing to prevent the adjectives "planned" and "expected". being defined in such a way that, for instance, the magnitude which is called "planned purchases" must be realized, so that planned purchases = purchases realized *by definition*. This is what occurs when, for example, Hans Brems says [1]: "That a magnitude appertaining to a subject is to be taken as 'expected' means that its realization has *not* been conditioned solely by the will of that subject at any time before the realization. And that a magnitude appertaining to a subject is to be taken as "planned" means that its realization has been conditioned at some time or other before that realization only by the will of the subject concerned." Although it does not follow of absolute necessity from this defini-

the period considered must be taken sufficiently short, it does not remove us from reality" (*Studies* . . ., p. 127—128). The idea behind this argument may be that, the shorter the period is made, the larger all *stocks* will be in relation to the *streams* of the period, and however much the planned purchases exceed the expected sales, it is always possible to shorten the period so much that the difference (which becomes less, of course, as the length of the period diminishes) can be made up from the existing stocks.

The argument presupposes, however, that there are stocks of the commodities in question. That *need not* be the case when commodities are concerned (since stocks can be zero), and it *cannot* be the case when factor-services are concerned, as these cannot be stored. Referring to the idea that the difference between purchasing plans for factors and sales expectations for factors can be made good by overtime from the workers, it is obvious that the possibility of working overtime diminishes with the length of the period in much the same way as the difference between purchasing plans and sales expectations.

[1] Hans Brems, "Om Stockholmskolens begreber og metoder". ("On the Concepts and Methods of the Stockholm School"), *Ekonomisk Tidskrift*, Stockholm, 1944, p. 41, note 1.

tion that a planned magnitude *must* be realized, yet it is clear that Brems conceives the relation to be such that this is so; if a prospective magnitude is not realized it is simply not "planned". In this case it is of course altogether superfluous to assume that planned purchases are always realized, and it is self-contradictory to maintain that planned purchases cannot always be realized.

That does not deprive this section of any of its justification. The criticism may be merely adjusted to say that it is a mistake always to call *ex ante* purchases "planned purchases". Compare with the following quotation from Brems: "In consequence of our definitions of "planned" and "expected", *ex ante* purchases are always a planned quantity of purchases and sales always an expected quantity of sales." [1] It is this statement which is now wrong.

So far as can be seen, Lindahl conceives of "plan" in another way, as an inventory of the activities which an economic subject intends to pursue in the future. "Plans are thus the explicit expression of the economic motives of man, as they become evident in his economic actions." "The actions of the individual prescribed in the selected alternative represent the 'plan' in the strict sense." [2] In Palander's writings [3] it is also clear that the expressions "planned" and "expected" merely mean "*ex ante*" or "prospective", and that in his use of the expression "planned purchases" there is no implication that *ex ante* purchases will necessarily be realized.

Both Lindahl and Palander use the expressions "planned" and "expected" merely to imply that the quantities in question enter into the subjects' *ex ante* calculations (equations), namely, their calculations on earning of income, use of income, and cash. This is also the sense in which the expressions "planned" and "expected" are used here.

4. *General assumptions for the analysis which follows*

When we give up the assumption that purchasing plans are always carried out, the question then arises as to what simplified assumptions can be introduced for the comparisons between existing plans and expectations and between prospective and retrospective magnitudes. It follows from the discussion about the untenableness of the assumption that purchasing plans are always realized, that there is reason to distinguish between models in which there are stocks of commodities and excess capacity in the production of services sufficient for all purchasing plans for commodities and services to be always realizable, and models where there are no stocks of commodities and capacity in the production of services is fully utilized.

From a logical point of view the case where there are no stocks turns

---

[1] Hans Brems, "Om Stockholmskolens begreber og metoder".

[2] Lindahl, *Studies* . . ., p. 37 and 40.

[3] Palander, "Om 'Stockholmsskolans' begrepp och metoder", p. 123—28.

out to be a more general case than where sufficient stocks exist because a smaller number of premises is involved. Therefore, we shall concentrate upon this case in what follows, and it will be understood that the only assumption about equality between prospective and retrospective magnitudes which we can now reasonably put forward, is, that *all sales expectations for factors are fulfilled*. It is to be noticed that we only reckon labour-services as "factors", so that all goods[1] which are not money, claims, or labour-services, are to be reckoned in the commodity-markets.

We can use the somewhat unfamiliar assumption that certain sales expectations are always fulfilled, because the wage-rates are given for the period, and there is full or overfull employment (excess demand for factors) such that the individual worker always sells that quantity of labour he wishes to sell and expects to sell.[2] As previously mentioned, instead of speaking about sales expectations, it is equally possible to speak about sales *plans* from the workers' side, plans (expectations) which, in the circumstances prevailing, it is altogether within the power of the workers to carry out to whatever extent they wish. The intermediate case, where there is full employment, but the possibilities of working overtime are not fully utilized, is not considered.

It may appear that, in the situation where no stocks of commodities are available, we could quite well add the assumption that the sales expectations of the sellers of commodities are also always fulfilled, for, when there are no finished commodities in stock, the entrepreneurs cannot, of course, expect to sell more than they plan to produce. With excess demand in existence, it should always be possible for them to carry out their sales expectations to the extent desired, and to be aware of this. However, this supposition cannot be generally applied, for, production plans may become unrealizable to the same extent that plans for the purchase of factors (and possibly also the entrepreneurs' purchasing plans for commodities) cannot be realized in full. Actual production and sales are thus in the general case less than planned production and expected sales. This follows from the assump-

---

[1] Everything that has a price is a "good". Factor-services and other services are accordingly goods.

[2] This, of course, only holds good as an approximation since we have defined "full or overfull employment" to mean that $\Sigma X_i \cdot P_i \geqq 0$ (cf. equation (I: 3)), and consequently some partial unemployment may exist.

tion about excess demand for labour-power, and is a very important circumstance of the process of inflation.

Lindahl's results[1] can now be modified in the light of these changed assumptions, so that they become relevant to inflationary situations. It is necessary to make a general division of all purchases and sales, into purchases and sales of commodities and purchases and sales of factors[2], and the significance of state and foreign trade must be made more explicit than it is in Lindahl's treatment.

On choosing the various magnitudes as in the models considered, we are faced with the choice of making the system as general as possible, or as simple as possible. The generalization of the system should lead to the inclusion of all those magnitudes which ordinarily occur in a national budget or national account. On the other hand, if we wish to make the model as easily comprehensible as possible, we should include in it as few magnitudes as possible. Here, we will take those magnitudes which are usually most significant as to quantity in a national budget for a modern community. Quite a lot of magnitudes are excluded, which are of no great importance in an analysis of Lindahl's sort, simply because the different *ex ante* estimations of these quantities must agree almost of necessity, and they would consequently fall out of the analysis even if they were included in the beginning. This applies to all the transfer payments of the state (social services, made according to fixed rates, payments of interest, etc.), and likewise to all private payments of interest fixed by contracts. The most important of these excluded magnitudes for which there will probably be *ex ante* incongruence is the payment of dividends to shareholders, where the entrepreneurs' and shareholders' conceptions of the earning ability of the undertaking may be different. Quantitatively, however, that is a relatively insignificant magnitude.

The desire for the greatest possible lucidity has the further effect that what follows is built up according to the method of decreasing

---

[1] See in particular Lindahl's *Studies* . . ., p. 125—131.

[2] This division is not to be found in Lindahl's treatment. But Hicks and Palander make the division. The significance of this special, but very natural, division of purchases and sales was first pointed out by I. Grünbaum, "Inkongruente forventninger og begrebet monetær ligevægt" ("Incongruent Expectations and the Concept of Monetary Equilibrium"), *Nationaløkonomisk Tidsskrift*, Copenhagen, 1945.

abstraction, so that we begin with a simplified model for an economy
without state (i.e. without public finances) and without foreign trade.
This model, presented in Section 6 (and further elaborated in Chap. III,
Section 5), is the basis of the whole of the presentation of repressed
inflation in Chaps. IV, V, and VI. It is assumed here that the economy
consists of capitalists, who own real capital themselves and are consequently entrepreneurs (the business activities of the state may be included
here), together with workers. So financial capital and its part in giving
rise to incongruences between plans and expectations is neglected. This
of course implies a limitation in the system set up, but this limitation
is hardly serious. In Lindahl's system, which may be referred to,
financial capital and the transactions arising from it are included. It
is of course more serious that the state and foreign trade are omitted
from our system. Therefore, the model is extended in Section 7 to
include public finances, and in Section 8 to include foreign trade. The
assumptions which the inclusion of the state and foreign trade give
rise to are dealt with in the appropriate sections.

It should be mentioned that the models set up in this chapter are
all "incomplete" in that they have a considerable number of "degrees
of freedom".

5. *Notation*

The following symbols are used:—

A = sales (at market-price).
B = purchases for productive purposes (at market-price).
C = purchases for purposes of consumption (at market-price).
E = income.
I = investment.
S = saving.
^iT = indirect taxes. These are to be thought of as collected from the
producers in the form of a levy on commodities (and services).
^dT = direct taxes on personal income.

These symbols are used entirely for transactions within the country,
even in Section 8 where foreign countries are taken into account.
When foreign countries are taken into account the following symbols
must be added:—

A^* = export = sales of commodites to foreign countries.
B^* = import = purchases of commodities from foreign countries.

The symbols are used with the following additional subscripts and superscripts:—

0 and 1   as subscripts to the right, indicating the time aspect of the estimate, *ex ante* and *ex post* respectively;

g and l as superscripts to the left, indicating the nature of the transactions, commodity (finished *g*oods) and factor (*l*abour) respectively;

c, w, and s as superscripts to the right, indicating the group which intends to make or has made the transaction concerned, or to which the economic magnitude concerned is otherwise related, *c*apitalists, *w*orkers and *s*tate respectively.

Since the notation given above, which corresponds more or less to that used by Lindahl and Frisch, becomes a little complicated, each single symbol is explained in Appendix II, headed List of Symbols Used.

6. *Simplified model of a closed economy*

In this section we shall describe a *simplified model of a closed economy*, where public finances and foreign trade are neglected. We begin by formulating two equations for the *earning of income*. The expected income of the capitalists is determined by the following:

$$E_0^c = {}^g A_0^c - {}^g B_0^c - {}^l B_0^c + I_0^c, \tag{II: 1}$$

which means that the expected income of the capitalists (E_0^c) is equal to the difference between the expected sales of goods (${}^g A_0^c$) and the planned purchases for productive purposes, consisting of the purchases of commodities (${}^g B_0^c$) and purchases of labour-services (${}^l B_0^c$), to which is added the planned investment (I_0^c).

A corresponding, but simpler, equation holds good for the expected incomes of the workers (E_0^w):

$$E_0^w = {}^l A_0^w. \tag{II: 2}$$

The expected income of the workers is thus equal to their expected sales of labour-services (${}^l A_0^w$), as the possible purchases by the workers for productive purposes are neglected. Such purchases are usually in-significant amounts, which are only of importance in very special situations. The possibility of the workers' investing in themselves, in the form of education, training, etc., is also neglected.

If we turn to the *use of income*, and if we consider the capitalists and workers together (and neglect taxes and the like) we arrive at:

$$E_0^{c+w} = C_0^{c+w} + S_0^{c+w}, \qquad (\text{II}: 3)$$

which means that the combined expected incomes of capitalists and workers (E_0^{c+w}) is either planned for consumption (C_0^{c+w}) or saving (S_0^{c+w}).

If equations (II:1) to (II:3) are now written as follows and added together, we obtain equation (II:4),

$$I_0^c = E_0^c - {}^gA_0^c + {}^gB_0^c + {}^lB_0^c \qquad (\text{II}: 1)$$

$$0 = E_0^w - {}^lA_0^w \qquad (\text{II}: 2)$$

$$-S_0^{c+w} = -E_0^{c+w} + C_0^{c+w} \qquad (\text{II}: 3)$$

$$\overline{I_0^c - S_0^{c+w} = {}^gB_0^c + C_0^{c+w} - {}^gA_0^c + {}^lB_0^c - {}^lA_0^w,} \qquad (\text{II}: 4)$$

which signifies, on omitting the now superfluous superscripts:

$$\underbrace{I_0 - S_0}_{\substack{\text{planned} \\ \text{investments} \\ \text{—planned} \\ \text{saving}}} = \underbrace{{}^gB_0 + C_0 - {}^gA_0}_{\substack{\text{ex ante} \\ \text{commodity-gap}}} + \underbrace{{}^lB_0 - {}^lA_0}_{\substack{\text{ex ante} \\ \text{factor-gap}}}. \qquad (\text{II}: 5)$$

Thus we find that the difference between planned investment and planned saving corresponds to the difference between planned purchases of commodities (${}^gB_0 + C_0$) and expected sales of commodities (${}^gA_0$)—this difference is to be called the *ex ante commodity-gap*—*plus* the difference between the planned purchases of factors (${}^lB_0$) and the planned sales of factors (${}^lA_0$)—this difference will be called the *ex ante factor-gap*.

We call to mind the characteristic of inflation mentioned in Chap. I —monetary excess demand in the composite markets of factors and commodities—and what is assumed in this chapter, that the sign of equality may be placed between demand and planned purchases, and also between supply and expected sales. Consequently, when a monetary pressure of inflation exists (see equations (I: 1), (I: 2), and (I: 3)), neither the *ex ante* commodity-gap nor the *ex ante* factor-gap can be negative, and at least one of them must be greater than zero. It follows immediately from equation (II: 5) that planned investments must be larger than planned savings $(I_0 > S_0)$ when there is a monetary pressure of inflation. On the other hand, the condition $I_0 > S_0$ is clearly not sufficient for a monetary pressure of inflation to exist.

Equation (II: 5)—the "fundamental equation" of the Stockholm School—obviously holds good irrespective of whether stocks of goods exists or not; it is a purely definitional relationship.

We shall now proceed to the comparison of *ex ante* and *ex post* magnitudes. According to the remarks in Section 4, this comparison will be carried out under the assumption that all sales expectations for factors are fulfilled, i.e.

$$^lA_0^w = {}^lA_1^w = {}^lB_1^c. \qquad (II: 6)$$

Equation (II: 6) says that the workers' expectations for sales of labour-services $(^lA_0^w)$ are always fulfilled, and furthermore says that direct consumption of labour-services is neglected, as only the capitalists (i.e. the entrepreneurs) are regarded as purchasers of labour-services.

On replacing $^lA_0$ in (II: 5) by $^lB_1$, cf. (II: 6), and adding to (II: 5) the identity $0 = {}^gA_1 - {}^gB_1 - C_1$, expressing the evident fact that sales *ex post* must necessarily be the same as purchases *ex post*, we have

$$\underbrace{I_0 - S_0}_{\substack{\text{planned}\\\text{investment}\\\text{— planned}\\\text{saving}}} = \underbrace{{}^gA_1 - {}^gA_0}_{\substack{\text{unexpected}\\\text{sales of}\\\text{commodities}}} + \underbrace{{}^gB_0 + C_0 - {}^gB_1 - C_1}_{\substack{\text{unrealizable purchases}\\\text{of commodities}}} + \underbrace{{}^lB_0 - {}^lB_1}_{\substack{\text{unrealizable}\\\text{purchases}\\\text{of factors}}}. \qquad (II: 7)$$

The difference between planned investment and planned saving is therefore equal to the unexpected sales of commodities *plus* unrealizable purchases of commodities and factors (labour-services).

In order to understand this equation, it should be noticed that what is called "unexpected sales of commodities" will in general not be a positive magnitude, i.e. in general $^gA_1 < {}^gA_0$. Where no stocks of commodities exist, the expected sales of commodities can at most be equal to the quantity of commodities which it is planned to produce in the period, while the quantity of commodities actually disposed of is equal to the production actually achieved. But, since $('B_0 - 'B_1)$ is positive (in the boundary case equal to zero) in accordance with the assumptions, production plans are to a certain extent unrealizable, and $^9A_1$ must therefore be $< {}^9A_0$, so that actual sales are less than planned sales; we disregard the possibility of excess capacity in the production of services, it will be remembered. $^9A_1$ can exceed $^9A_0$ only in the case where the firms' planned increases of stocks of their own products ($^9A_0 =$ planned production *minus* the planned increases of stocks of the products, taken at the current market-price) are greater than the production not carried out. In contrast to what is customary, here we cannot consider the disappointed expectations of sales as in themselves somewhat deflationary. For, that there were not so many sales as the capitalists expected is not to be attributed to an exaggeration of the expectations of the selling possibilities, but on the contrary, is to be attributed to the failure of the capitalists to obtain that quantity of commodities which they had planned to have available. So, in all cases here it is the plans for the purchases of factors and the plans for purchases of commodities for productive purposes, both of which miscarried, that are decisive for the result of the period for the capitalists, and for their further activities.

Also we have

$$E_1^c = {}^9A_1^c - {}^9B_1^c - {}^lB_1^c + I_1^c. \tag{II: 8}$$

If from (II: 8) we subtract (II: 1), we obtain, on rearranging and adding $C_0 - C_1$ to both sides of the equation arrived at on rearrangement,

$$\underbrace{{}^9A_1 - {}^9A_0 + {}^9B_0 - {}^9B_1 + {}^lB_0 - {}^lB_1 + C_0 - C_1}_{= I_0 - S_0} = \underbrace{E_1^c - E_0^c}_{\substack{\text{unex-}\\\text{pected}\\\text{income for}\\\text{capitalists}}} + \underbrace{C_0 - C_1}_{\substack{\text{unrealiz-}\\\text{able plans}\\\text{for pur-}\\\text{chases of}\\\text{commodities}\\\text{for con-}\\\text{sumption}}} + \underbrace{I_0 - I_1}_{\substack{\text{unrealiz-}\\\text{able in-}\\\text{vestments}}}. \tag{II: 9}$$

The left-hand side of (II: 9) is equal to the difference between planned investment and planned saving, in accordance with equation

(II: 7). If we consider the *ex ante* relationships as the cause of the results *ex post* it follows that, when investment is greater than saving (planned), or what comes to the same thing, planned purchases of commodities and factors exceed the expected sales of them, this leads to unexpected (decrease in) sales of commodities and to unrealizable purchases of commodities and factors, the combined value of which is equal to the sum of the unexpected income for the capitalists[1], unrealizable purchasing plans for consumer-goods, and unintended alteration in the amount of investment. We shall discuss these items more closely.

It may be pointed out by way of introduction that, in the considerations which follow, it makes a very big difference whether the situation is one of open or of repressed inflation, because a situation of repressed inflation is simpler in certain respects connected with the expectations of the future.

To begin with, since $C_0 - C_1$ may be taken to be positive, we can say that, if $I_0 > I_1$, the unexpected income for the capitalists can be either positive or negative, in that it is only $E_1^c - E_0^c + C_0 - C_1 + I_0 - I_1$

---

[1] It is easily seen that there cannot be unexpected income for the workers. For, we have $E_0^w = {}^lA_0^w$ and $E_1^w = {}^lA_1^w$, and, from assumption (II: 6), $E_1^w = E_0^w$. For the workers then, expected income is the same as realized income.

It should be mentioned, however, that the neglect of purchases by the workers of commodities for productive purposes implies the neglect of the possibility, when plans for the purchase of commodities are miscarrying everywhere, that the income actually earned by the workers may diverge from their expected income. If a term ${}^gB^w$ for the workers' purchases of commodities for productive purposes is introduced, it is easily seen that $E_1^w - E_0^w = {}^gB_0^w - {}^gB_1^w$. If the right-hand side of this equation is positive, there is a gain of income, but that is obviously unreasonable. What the equation says is: that if not all of the workers' plans to purchase commodities for productive purposes, i.e. such purchases of goods as are necessary that they can carry out their work, are realized, then there should be a gain of income for the workers! As in the case of commodity production, unrealizable purchasing plans here may also lead to unexpected decrease of supply, so that assumption (II: 6) does not hold in these circumstances. If the supply of labour-power does not diminish as a consequence of the workers' purchases of commodities for productive purposes not being carried out, this fact must be attributed to the consumption of durable goods owned by the workers, which we have disregarded. In most cases ${}^gB^w$ can be neglected as quantitatively insignificant, but it must be admitted that this term has its effect in situations of serious shortage, for instance, when there are "bottle-necks" entering into the workers' purchases (e.g. clothing for work, means of transport).

which needs to be greater than zero; so there can be either gain of income or loss of income. It is only if $C_0 - C_1 + I_0 - I_1 < 0$ that the unexpected income is always positive (an income gain).

However, it should be noticed that no definitions of income, investment and saving have been given as yet. This is due to the fact that we have followed Lindahl's method of procedure, and have confined ourselves to defining the concepts correlatively, so that equation (II:1), according to which $E_0^c - I_0^c = {}^gA_0^c - {}^gB_0^c - {}^lB_0^c$, can be regarded as a correlative definition of (the capitalists') income·*minus* investment; and in the same way equation (II:3), according to which $E_0^{c+w} - S_0^{c+w} = C_0^{c+w}$, can be regarded as a definition of income *minus* saving. If we give a concrete definition of one of the concepts, income (capitalists'), investment or saving, the other two concepts are thereby automatically defined. Further discussion of the magnitudes $(E_1^c - E_0^c)$ and $(I_0 - I_1)$ is therefore pointless until unambiguous and corresponding definitions of the concepts income and investment have been chosen.

With regard to investment, it may first be mentioned that $(I_0 - I_1)$ physically involves that part of the investments which had been planned (including planned increases of stocks) but could not be carried out because of shortage of labour-power. As long as no wider assumptions are introduced, it is impossible to say anything about the proportion of investment planned but not carried out when there is quite arbitrary allocation of labour-power among those who want it. However, it is often permissible to assume, with repressed inflation, that the control by the public authorities also implies limitation of the volume of "fixed" investments (control of investment) combined with the imposition of direction of labour and allocation of commodities so that the planned "fixed" investments are just carried out. If this is the case, $(I_0 - I_1)$ physically comprises just the planned but unrealizable increases in stocks, and all unrealizable production plans come into the consumption industry. Control of investment can also occur in connection with open inflation, although it is more unusual; the remark just made about $(I_0 - I_1)$ also applies in this case.

Now we can take as a basis for the investigation of $(E_1^c - E_0^c)$ and $(I_0 - I_1)$ the concept of subjective income, and the corresponding concept for investment. Income is then regarded as interest on the subjective value of capital[1], so that we are now concerned with the comparison of subjective estimations of the income for the period, at the beginning of the period and at its end. It is clear that the question which overshadows everything else here is that of the development cf expectations from the beginning to the end of the period (i.e. to the beginning of the next period); and that the contradistinction of repressed and open inflation becomes of great significance in this connection, in so far as we may often reckon with a systematic difference between the development of expectations in open and repressed inflation.

The simplest case occurs with "completely" repressed inflation, where control of prices and wage-rates is so strict, so effectively carried out and so stable from the political point of view, that no one reckons with increases in either wage-rates or prices during a relevant period of time, regardless of what may happen during the period. Everyone supposes without uncertainty that the prices for the period will continue in the future. What now befalls the capitalists during the period is that the plans for purchase of factors during the period miscarried (and the production plans along with them) to a greater or less extent (only in the boundary-case of monetary pressure of inflation, where $^gB_0 + C_0 > {}^gA_0$ does this not apply).[2] If this results in the capitalists coming to the conclusion that they cannot expect to achieve production at the desired level in the future either, and they therefore set their hopes for future production (and sales of commodities accordingly) lower, it is obvious that the income for the period calculated *ex ante* must exceed the income calculated *ex post*. But the entrepreneurs (capitalists) may be so optimistic that they all think that it was only in this one period their plans for purchase of

---

[1] See Erik Lindahl, "The Concept of Income", *Economic Essays in Honour of Gustav Cassel*, London, 1933, together with *Studies* . . ., p. 96—111.

[2] A similar line of reasoning in the explanation of the upper turning-point of the business cycle is to be met with in the writings of those who advocate a monetary over-investment theory for the business cycle. According to these authors it is the investment-plans which are unrealizable, cf., for instance, F. A. Hayek, *Prices and Production*, George Routledge & Sons, Ltd., London, 1934 (2nd Ed.). In the case mentioned in the text the production plans can go wrong everywhere. But the production plans will go wrong only in the industries producing commodities for consumption if there is control of investment and allocation of raw-materials (and labour-power).

factors and production went wrong, but that in the following periods they will be succesful in buying the factor-services they want and later, possibly, will be able to get those commodities produced and sold which they were unable to have produced in the period concerned. Then the income loss resulting from the break-down of production plans will be less. But there will be a certain loss in any case, because the production not carried out in this period can only be made good at a later time, if at all.

On the other hand it is also possible that gains of income may arise. If increases in stocks were planned, these plans must to a greater or less extent break down, and this may imply a certain gain of income, since this unexpected fall in the planned increase in stocks takes place at the same price as the capitalists concerned could expect to obtain for their commodities at a later time. Only in the boundary case where $^gB_0 + C_0 = ^gA_0$ and where no increases in stocks are planned, is there no such gain.

Thus we have one case which results in loss of income, and one which results in gain of income. Nothing can be said *a priori* about the scales of magnitudes here; that depends, among other things, on the size of the unexpected break-down in the planned increase of stocks, i.e. of the *ex ante* commodity-gap, and on the extent to which the plans for purchase of factors are not realizable, i.e. on the size of the *ex ante* factor-gap. What is most important is that, in these circumstances (expectations that existing prices and wage-rates will hold good in the future), we can get either income gain or income loss for the capitalists. This is consistent with what was previously stated, that, when $I_0 > I_1$, equation (II:9) allows of the occurrence of both gain and loss of income.

Where prices and wage-rates are not expected to remain unchanged, in an inflationary situation prices will usually be expected to increase so that, at the end of the period higher prices are expected in the future than were expected at the beginning of the period. A new point for consideration arises here in the tendency towards gains of income, which depends on the changed estimation of the future. The possibility that the result of the period will be a loss of income consequently decreases as the change of expectations increases. During very advanced open inflation, when the expectations have become to a great extent fluid, a gain of income for the period is the over-whelming probability.

On the other hand we could consider the situation where the expectations at the end of the period are that prices will fall. In this case loss of income for the period is likely (it is to be noticed that the development of expectations from expectations of rising prices at the beginning of the period to expectations of falling prices at the end is not in itself a contradiction of the existence of monetary pressure of inflation during the period, and neither does it of itself necessarily prevent the next period showing a monetary pressure of inflation).[1]

If we start from a more conventional, book-keeping concept of income instead of the concept of subjective income, another complication immediately appears.

The calculation of income depends on the way in which the internal book-keeping of the firms is carried out, i.e. in what way the accounts between the departments of the firms are made out. If the goods go from the production department to the sales department (stocks) at the full market-price, the result for the period must be, without doubt, a loss. (For the sake of simplicity we are considering only the case of repressed inflation and fixed prices and wage-rates, so that marking up of the value of equipment and the like, which could be reckoned as income, is not taken into account.) For, as the income in this case is calculated exclusively on the current production, a possible miscarriage of production plans owing to shortage of labour-power is of decisive importance. It is not possible, however, to state anything about the absolute magnitude of the loss on the basis of the budget equations used here. In order to do that a structure equation would be required, which would give information about the form of the cost curves (cf. the geometric treatment in Chaps. IV to VI). The same applies if the accounting price between the production department and the sales department is less than the market price and if the firms' planned increases of stocks of their commodities do not exceed the unrealizable production. Only in the special case where the firms' planned increases of stocks of their commodities exceeds the

---

[1] See the League of Nations publication, *The Course and Control of Inflation, A Review of Monetary Experience in Europe after World War I*, League of Nations, 1946, Chaps. I and II, where there are interesting considerations of the development of expectations during the great post-war inflations of the twenties.

unrealizable production and where the accounting price between the production department and the sales department is less than the market-price, can an income gain for the period be thought of.

Whatever concept of income is used, it is seen that during inflation there is a possibility of a damping element arising from the continual disappointment of the capitalists' expectations of income. Unexpected profits (gains) are therefore not a necessary characteristic of inflation, as is often maintained.

This phenomenon may be regarded as gradually damping the income expectations of the capitalists, their plans for the purchase of commodities for consumption, and investment purchase plans, and at the same time lowering the expectations for purchases of factors; so that not only the demand for commodities (the planned purchases of commodities), but also the demand for factors (the planned purchases of factors) tends to fall. Furthermore, the possible lowering of the subjective capital-values may also have the effect of diminishing the inclination to invest. Consequently, we have come upon a possible stabilising element in inflation, which is most likely to appear in a controlled, repressed inflationary situation.

In the previous part of this section we have assumed that no stocks of commodities (and no excess capacity in the production of services which are here reckoned as commodities) exist. The above equations also apply when stocks do exist but are insufficient for all purchasing plans for commodities to be fulfilled. The equations are also easily adapted to the case where *there are sufficient stocks of commodities* (and excess capacity in the production of services) for all purchasing plans for commodities to be fulfilled. In this case we can add to the assumption that all sales expectations for labour-services are fulfilled (II: 6) the following further assumptions, that all purchasing plans for commodities are always carried out:

$$ {}^g B_0^c = {}^g B_1^c \qquad\qquad\qquad (\text{II: } 10) $$

and

$$ C_0^{c+w} = C_1^{c+w}. \qquad\qquad\qquad (\text{II: } 11) $$

Equation (II: 7) then immediately reduces to

$$ I_0 - S_0 = {}^g A_1 - {}^g A_0 + {}^l B_0 - {}^l B_1 \qquad\qquad (\text{II: } 12) $$

and equation (II: 9) to

$$I_0 - S_0 = E_1^c - E_0^c + I_0 - I_1. \qquad (II:13)$$

The interpretation of equations (II: 12) and (II: 13) is in some respects different from the interpretation of equations (II: 7) and (II: 9), but involves no special problems. So, we shall only remark that the above-mentioned possibility of a loss of income within the period also arises here, but that income gain is more likely than in the case where no stocks of commodities exist. This is because an unexpected decrease of stocks will in itself involve an income gain, and also because unexpected sales of services will add (unexpectedly) to the net income of the capitalists practically the whole sales value of the unexpected increase in sales.

7. Model of an economy with public finances but without foreign trade

When we leave the simplified model of a closed economy and consider a model where *the state also has revenue and expenditures* and carries out transactions, all of which have their effects on supply of and demand for commodities and factors, equations (II: 1) to (II: 3) may be rewritten as follows.

The equation for the earning of income becomes, for the capitalists,

$$E_0^c = {}^gA_0^c - {}^gB_0^c - {}^lB_0^c - {}^iT_0^c + I_0^c. \qquad (II:14)$$

(II: 14) is different from (II: 1) in that the expected liability of the capitalists to pay indirect taxes to the state (${}^iT_0^c$) is taken as a "cost", A and B being reckoned at market-price, i.e. including indirect taxes. We could, if we wished, interpret ${}^iT^c$ as taxes minus subsidies.

The equation for the workers' earning of income remains unaltered at

$$E_0^w = {}^lA_0^w. \qquad (II:2)$$

Equation (II: 3) for the use of income is changed to

$$E_0^{c+w} = C_0^{c+w} + {}^dT_0^{c+w} + S_0^{c+w} \qquad (II:15)$$

because we now have the further important possibility that income taxes may have to be taken into account.

In the case of the state, we choose to use the following combined earning-and-use equation, which can be taken as a definition of the state's budget surplus, which may be put equal to the state's savings.

$$S_0^s = {}^dT_0^s + {}^iT_0^s - {}^gB_0^s - {}^lB_0^s + I_0^s. \qquad \text{(II:16)}$$

The state's budget surplus, or planned saving, occurs as the difference between expected revenue from direct and indirect taxes (${}^dT_0^s$ and ${}^iT_0^s$) and the planned purchases of commodities and labour-services (${}^gB_0^s$ and ${}^lB_0^s$) *plus* the state's planned investments. This is the usual way of defining the budget surplus in practice, when the budget is split up into a current budget and a capital budget as is the case in the Scandinavian countries. There are other ways of defining the budget surplus, however, but it does not matter which one we choose in this connection. So it is reasonable to take a definition which is in accord with Scandinavian budget practice.

In equation (II:16) we neglect the state's revenue from its trading activities together with transfer payments such as social relief, pensions, payments of interest and the like. However, the revenue from trading activities can, if so desired, be included in ${}^iT_0^s$ and transfer payments in ${}^lB_0^s$, in which case it must be remembered that ${}^lA_0^w$ includes the expectations of income of those in receipt of relief and others. It is also necessary then to introduce into (II:14) a special term which denotes the capitalists' expectations of income from the state (especially payments of interest). However, we shall disregard all that, and the reason for doing so is, as was earlier stated, that since essential disagreements between the *ex ante* estimates can hardly be considered for these payments, they do in any case eventually drop out of the analysis.

By suitable combination of equations (II:14), (II:2), (II:15), and (II:16), we arrive at

$$\underbrace{I_0 - S_0}_{\substack{\text{total} \\ \text{planned} \\ \text{invest-} \\ \text{ment—} \\ \text{total} \\ \text{planned} \\ \text{saving}}} = \underbrace{{}^gB_0 + C_0 - {}^gA_0}_{\substack{\textit{ex ante} \\ \text{commodity-gap}}} + \underbrace{{}^lB_0 - {}^lA_0}_{\substack{\textit{ex ante} \\ \text{factor-gap}}} + \underbrace{{}^iT_0^c + {}^dT_0^{c+w} - {}^iT_0^s - {}^dT_0^s}_{\substack{\text{the disparity of expectations} \\ \text{with regard to taxes}}}. \qquad \text{(II:17)}$$

48

This equation agrees with the original equation (II:5) except that on the right-hand side we have included the difference between the taxpayers' idea of the taxes to which they are liable during the period and the state's opinion on the matter.

It should now be noticed that, whereas we previously came to the conclusion that $I_0 - S_0 > 0$ was a necessary but not sufficient condition for the existence of a monetary pressure of inflation, it is nevertheless clear here, where due consideration is made of the disparity in tax expectations, that $I_0 - S_0$ does not at all need to be greater than zero in order that there may be a monetary pressure of inflation. Since, if the state's estimate of the payments of taxes for the period exceeds the private estimate to such an extent that

$$^iT_0^s + {}^dT_0^s - {}^iT_0^c - {}^dT_0^{c+w} > {}^gB_0 + C_0 - {}^gA_0 + {}^lB_0 - {}^lA_0 \qquad (II:18)$$

then $I_0 - S_0 < 0$, even if the right-hand side of (II:18) is positive. Therefore, the extent to which the saving-investment relation may still be used as an indication of a monetary pressure of inflation depends on what disparity of expectations with regard to taxes is *typical* for an inflationary situation. We shall make some remarks on this intricate question, but first we will write out the equations analogous to (II:7) and (II:9). The case without sufficient stocks of commmodities is still to be regarded as the general one, so we can only use the assumption (II:6) in the comparison between prospective and retrospective magnitudes.

$$(II:19)$$

$$I_0 - S_0 = \underbrace{{}^gA_1 - {}^gA_0}_{\substack{\text{unexpected} \\ \text{sales of} \\ \text{commodities}}} + \underbrace{{}^gB_0 + C_0 - {}^gB_1 - C_1}_{\substack{\text{unrealizable purchases} \\ \text{of commodities}}} + \underbrace{{}^lB_0 - {}^lB_1}_{\substack{\text{unrealiz-} \\ \text{able} \\ \text{purchases} \\ \text{of factors}}} + \underbrace{{}^iT_0^c + {}^dT_0^{c+w} - {}^iT_0^s - {}^dT_0^s}_{\substack{\text{disparity in respect of} \\ \text{taxes}}}.$$

Equation (II:19) is the counterpart of equation (II:7), and instead of equation (II:9) we have

$$I_0 - S_0 = \underbrace{E_1^c - E_0^c}_{\substack{\text{unex-} \\ \text{pected in-} \\ \text{come of} \\ \text{the capi-} \\ \text{talists}}} + \underbrace{S_1^s - S_0^s}_{\substack{\text{unex-} \\ \text{pected in-} \\ \text{crease in} \\ \text{the state's} \\ \text{budget} \\ \text{surplus}}} + \underbrace{I_0 - I_1}_{\substack{\text{unrealiz-} \\ \text{able in-} \\ \text{vestments}}} + \underbrace{{}^dT_0^{c+w} - {}^dT_1^{c+w}}_{\substack{\text{unexpected} \\ \text{liability to} \\ \text{payment of} \\ \text{direct taxes}}} + \underbrace{C_0 - C_1}_{\substack{\text{unrealiz-} \\ \text{able pur-} \\ \text{chases of} \\ \text{commodities} \\ \text{for con-} \\ \text{sumption}}}. \qquad (II:20)$$

With the exception of the magnitude $S_1^s - S_0^s$, which is discussed briefly below, these equations require no comments.

Now we have the question of disparities of expectations concerning taxes, and what is important is partly the connection between ${}^dT_0^{c+w}$ and ${}^dT_0^s$, i.e. between the taxpayers' and state's *ex ante* estimates of the liability to payment of income-taxes during the period, and between these and ${}^dT_1^{c+w} = {}^dT_1^s$, i.e. the actual liability to direct tax payments during the period; and partly the connection between ${}^iT_0^c$ and ${}^iT_0^s$, i.e. between the entrepreneurs' and state's *ex ante* estimates of the liability to payment of indirect taxes during the period, and between these and ${}^iT_1^c = {}^iT_1^s$, i.e. the actual liability to indirect tax payments during the period.

It would be very convenient if we could put forward with some confidence the assumptions ${}^dT_0^{c+w} = {}^dT_0^s = {}^dT_1^{c+w} = {}^dT_1^s$ and ${}^iT_0^c = {}^iT_0^s = {}^iT_1^c = {}^iT_1^s$, for that would greatly simplify the whole analysis.

First let it be remarked that it is quite intentionally that we speak of the *liability* to payment of taxes. It is this which is relevant, when we exclude all credit transactions, as we do here. For, if a person plans to pay a smaller amount in direct taxes than he knows (or only expects) he is liable to pay during the period, and instead plans to consume the deficit, this means that he plans to take out a credit with the state and with it to finance an increase of his consumption. In reality his planned saving should be decreased by the same amount, and that is what we must do in such a case, credit transactions having no place in the model here. It is probably on this point that the exclusion of credit transactions from the models is of greatest importance. In an open inflation, where the rise in prices is steep, the taxpayers will often speculate on the falling value of money and therefore put off the payment of taxes due as long as it is at all possible. In this way the planned and the settled payments of taxes may be far below the payments expected by the state and those actually due. This will be the cause of large unexpected budget deficits on a cash basis.[1] However, this is not taken into account in what follows, so that we do assume that the taxpayers' planned payments of taxes are equal to their *ex ante* estimates of liability for the period.

---

[1] *The Course and Control of Inflation*, League of Nations, Chap. 3.

The choice of the period is of great importance. In this chapter, cf. Section 2, we deal with an unit period that is short enough for all plans to be unchanged during the period. But, of course, that does not prevent the planning period of certain economic subjects from being a multiple of the unit period, and that will supposedly be the case where the state is concerned. The unit period can hardly be longer than a week, for the payment of wages to the workers (and their employment contracts) are usually reckoned on a weekly basis, and the workers' planning period can therefore be taken as one week. But the state's planning period is usually the financial year, since a budget is drawn up only once a year. It is, however, not at all an invariable rule that the planning period for the state is the financial year, since emergency budgets and alterations to the original budget may be set before parliament at any time during the course of the year. It often happens that a special committee (in Denmark, for instance, "finanslovsudvalget") can sanction beforehand expenditures on expected votes of supply in parliament, and in so far as this is possible the planning period can become quite short. As regards taxes however, and it is in them that we are specially interested, in most countries changes in tax requirements require the approval of parliament. So the planning period for the income side of the current budget becomes quite long, and usually coincides with the financial year in the case of income-tax. Anyway, it is quite certain that the state's planning period as regards revenues is longer than the unit period of the model and includes several of them.

Under effectively repressed inflation the matter is relatively simple. Since prices and wage-rates are known without uncertainty for a long period forward, the disparities of expectations in respect of taxes must belong to the "second order of smallness" of the magnitudes in the problem. The only systematic divergence between expected taxes and taxes actually due seems to arise from the tendency of the capitalists to overestimate the possibilities of production, which causes ${}^{t}T_0^c$ to exceed ${}^{t}T_1^c$, and from the income losses or income gains of the capitalists which make ${}^{d}T_0^{c+w}$ differ from ${}^{d}T_1^{c+w}$.

Under open inflation the relationships are somewhat more complicated and the possibilities for significant divergences between expected and realized taxes are much greater than under repressed inflation, especially where direct taxes are concerned. Here, the system of taxation is of great importance. There is, for instance, what may be called the "assessment system" of taxation. The assessment system, which was formerly in operation in Sweden and is still in operation in other Scandinavian countries, is the system in which the state imposes payments of certain sums of money according to people's declarations of their incomes for an earlier period, with the help of fixed scales of taxes made out for the financial year (tax-year). Each taxpayer is liable for payment of certain sums of money at certain dates fixed beforehand. Since the statement of tax due is made out at the beginning of the financial year as a rule, the state's parameter of action for the assessment-system may be said to be this sum of money decided upon by means of the tax-scales. This also means that the state should be able to calculate to a farthing at the beginning of the financial year the amount of the direct taxes due for the financial year and for each single unit period. In the same way the taxpayers should know with certainty at the beginning of the financial year how much they are to pay and when they are to pay it. So, in principle at least, the state's and the taxpayer's estimates of the direct taxes due for a particular unit period and for the whole financial year should coincide with the actual liability.

The relationships are quite different in a "pay-as-you-earn system", depending on the fact that tax-scales are not only formally but really the state's parameters of action. Under the assessment system, the tax notification must be based on the declared income for an earlier period, so that the tax actually due is already known at the beginning of the financial year. But under the pay-as-you-earn system the tax payments due for the year depend on the income (*ex post*) during the actual financial year, which must imply that it is impossible to know the actual amount of tax due until after the end of the financial year. After the end of the financial year a reassessment is made, which is necessary, partly because the taxpayers in certain categories of income are free to decide how much tax they want to pay as "pay-as-you-earn", and partly because the calculation of tax during the course of the year may take place on an incorrect basis (e.g. where the same family has income from different sources). The tax actually due for the financial year must therefore include not only the voluntary or compulsory preliminary payments during the year, but also the final reassessment for the previous year. It is clear that it may be difficult to say to which unit period within the past financial year the tax-adjustments are to be referred.

Under open inflation and with the pay-as-you-earn system, the taxpayers will be likely to under-estimate the tax actually due for a given unit-period, because there are likely to be income gains, and because the tax actually due is dependent also on the *ex post* incomes in the remaining periods of the financial year, and rising incomes will bring the taxpayers on to successively higher levels of tax-rates. However, we cannot disregard the fact that the expectations of both the taxpayers and the state may be so inflated that both parties exaggerate the taxes due for the period, but this will be the exception rather than the rule. The League of Nations publication previously quoted indicates that the usual tendency is for the state to underestimate the rises in prices and incomes.

The result of this very sketchy discussion of the disparities of expectations regarding taxes may be expressed as: The disparities may supposedly be neglected for a good approximation in the case of repressed inflation, and therefore the difference between planned investment and planned saving may be taken as an expression of the sum of the values of the excess demands (in the *ex ante* sense) in commodity and factor markets. But it is highly doubtful whether such a procedure is permissible in the case of open inflation. Only when the inflation may be taken to be repressed should equation (II: 17) be reduced to the simpler one, (II: 5).—

For the estimation of the magnitude $S_1^s - S_0^s$, i.e. the unexpected change in the budget surplus, not only the possible mistakes on the part of the state in calculating the taxes due for the period are of significance, but also possible unrealizable plans for the purchase of commodities and labour-services, and state investments which may not be carried out as a result. For, we have

$$S_1^s - S_0^s = \underbrace{{}^dT_1^s - {}^dT_0^s + {}^iT_1^s - {}^iT_0^s}_{\substack{\text{unexpected change in} \\ \text{the taxes due}}} + \underbrace{{}^lB_0^s - {}^lB_1^s + {}^gB_0^s - {}^gB_1^s}_{\substack{\text{unrealizable purchases} \\ \text{of factors and} \\ \text{commodities}}} - \underbrace{(I_0^s - I_1^s)}_{\substack{\text{unrealiz-} \\ \text{able in-} \\ \text{vestments}}}. \quad \text{(II: 21)}$$

We shall begin with the case of repressed inflation, and will deal with the difference between the accounting (*ex post*) surplus and budget (*ex ante*) surplus for a given arbitrarily chosen unit period,

$S_1^s - S_0^s$, and say something about this same difference taken over the whole financial year, (i.e. $\Sigma\,(S_1^s - S_0^s)$ summed over all the unit periods of the financial year). The unexpected change in taxes due for a unit period or for the whole financial year is likely to be insignificant for the state when the inflation is repressed and when the assessment system is used for income-tax. So the decisive thing is the amount of the unrealizable purchases of commodities and factors and the possible unrealizable state investments resulting therefrom. Nothing exact can be said about the size of the unrealizable purchases if allocation is quite arbitrary. However, if there is rationing and compulsory direction of labour-power, the state will probably try to attend first to its own needs. Also, there may be a tendency for labour-power to look for a place under the state before turning to private enterprise; a reason of considerable importance for this is that a significant part of the labour-power which the state wishes to employ has more secure positions under the state, with long notice periods from both sides. The state's unrealizable purchases of factors are therefore to a great extent confined to the labour-power more casually engaged, but here it is of significance that the more casual labour is often used for those activities concerned with investments which figure in the capital budget; the salaries of civil servants are found for the most part in the current budget. Therefore, unrealizable purchases of factors will largely result in unrealizable investment plans, and since unrealizable purchases of factors and unrealizable investment plans enter into (II:21) under opposite signs, their net effect on $S_1^s - S_0^s$ will even itself out to some extent. Both for the unit period and for the financial year as a whole, there seems thus to be no typical systematic tendency, provided, of course, that prices and wage-rates remain unchanged throughout the financial year. $S_1^s - S_0^s$ can be positive or negative, but must be of comparatively small size in any case.

During open inflation, increases of prices and wages become of the greatest significance, not only for the changes in taxes due, but also for the expenditure of the state on purchases of goods and labour-power. This is clear when the state's plans at the beginning of the financial year, as put forward in the budget, are that the state shall spend such-and-such a sum of money during the financial year and that expenditure must not exceed this sum. In this case, unexpected increases of prices and wages imply a corresponding drop in the state's purchases, taken quantitatively. But what will often happen is that the state will try to carry out purchases of certain quantities, and the sums of money which appear in the budget are the values of these quantities estimated at the price-level which the state expects to hold good at the time (in the unit period) when it intends to make the purchases concerned. If prices and wage-rates rise above this level, the state's expenditure increases automatically and unexpectedly in the same proportion. Even if we assume in the analysis of a particular period of the financial year that prices are given and known during open inflation—this assumption is at the basis of all the analysis of this chapter—there is still nothing to prevent them exceeding the state's expectations at the beginning of the financial year of what they should be for this or that unit period. Of course, we could say —something which is also implicit in the method of procedure used here—that if the state pays out more money during the financial year than was planned at the beginning, then the state must have altered its plans during the meantime. This interpretation is also permissible where the parliament has a committee which can give preliminary grants during the course of the financial year, when it is necessary to exceed the budget estimates in order to fulfill the quantitative plans. But this interpretation does to some extent veil an important problem of financial policy: the difference between the original budget and the final account of the financial year.

So, if we consider $S_1^s - S_0^s$ for a unit period, when the interpretation mentioned is taken and the assessment system for income tax is in force, we come to more or less the same result as we had for repressed inflation, but with a tendency for $S_1^s - S_0^s$ to be positive; when pay-as-you-earn is in force, $S_1^s - S_0^s > 0$ may definitely be expected, cf. previous discussion of disparities regarding taxes. Applied to the financial year, this would imply that an unexpected increase in the budget surplus normally occurs during open inflation. This hardly agrees with the experiences of the great open inflations, and this disagreement is dependent upon just that interpretation which has been used with respect to the purchasing plans of the state. If the plans at the beginning of the financial year are compared with the results of the final account, the unexpected increases in expenditure are of the greatest importance. In the case of the assessment system of taxing income they must lead to an unexpected decrease in the budget surplus; but the result is not so certain with the pay-as-you-earn system.

When sufficient stocks of commodities exist we can add to the assumption (II: 6) not only the assumptions (II: 10) and (II: 11), but also the assumption

$$^{\sigma}B_0^s = {}^{\sigma}B_1^s, \tag{II: 22}$$

i.e. that the state's purchasing plans for commodities are carried out. The reduction of equations (II: 19), (II: 20), and (II: 21), which follows from these assumptions, is evident.

8. *Model of an economy without public finances but with foreign trade*

The models in Sections 6 and 7 do not take into consideration the economic relations with other countries, i.e. *foreign trade,* and apply only to closed communities, possibly including public finances. The object of this, the last section of the chapter, is to consider briefly the modifications of the former models which occur when the existence of trade with other countries is taken into account in the equations. In order to simplify the presentation we disregard public finances. The presentation in Section 7 and that in this section may, however, be combined without difficulty. We consider only the relations of private enterprises with foreign countries, and credit transactions are still not explicitly included in the equations.

First of all, we assume that only commodities are traded internationally, while factor-services can only be bought within the country by the country's entrepreneurs. Also, we assume that only the capitalists—entrepreneurs—deal internationally, which means that the consumers (including the capitalists in their rôles as consumers) only buy commodities from entrepreneurs within their own country.

The new consideration which must enter into the equations is therefore that the capitalists' expectations of sales must be split up into expectations of sales of commodities abroad and expectations of sales of commodities at home, and that the capitalists' purchasing plans with respect to commodities for productive purposes must be split up into plans for purchases at home and plans for purchases from abroad. All other concepts remain unchanged, and we therefore add to the symbols already used the extra symbols $^{\sigma}A_0^*$, which is the capitalists' expected sales of commodities abroad, and $^{\sigma}B_0^*$, which is the capitalists' planned purchases of commodities from abroad. Analogously, we also use $^oA_1^*$, which is the actual (*ex post*) sales of commodities abroad, and $^oB_1^*$, which is the actual purchases of commodities from abroad. It is to be noticed that, since all importation takes place through entrepreneurs, including the importation of commodities for consumption, all commodity purchases from abroad are reckoned as commodities purchased for productive purposes. All other symbols are used unchanged, because, (cf. Section 5), as in the previous sections, these refer exclusively to transactions at home.

The equation which gives the capitalists' income now becomes, in place of (II: 1), the following:

$$E_0^c = {}^oA_0^c + {}^oA_0^* - {}^oB_0^c - {}^oB_0^* - {}^lB_0^c + I_0^c. \qquad (II:23)$$

The equation for the earning of income by the workers remains unaltered:

$$E_0^w = {}^lA_0^w, \qquad (II:2)$$

and the same applies to the equations for the use of income:

$$E_0^{c+w} = C_0^{c+w} + S_0^{c+w}. \qquad (II:3)$$

Upon rewriting and adding, and after omission of superfluous superscripts, we arrive at equation (II: 24):

$$I_0 - S_0 = {}^oB_0^c + C_0 + {}^oB_0^* - {}^oA_0^c - {}^oA_0^* + {}^lB_0^c - {}^lA_0^w. \qquad (II:24)$$

We now wish to compare all the plans (made out at home or abroad) for purchases of commodities from entrepreneurs at home with all the expectations of these entrepreneurs for sales of commodities (whether at home or abroad), and all the plans for purchases of factor-services with all the expectations of sales of factor-services. However, in equation (II: 24) there is no term which denotes foreign plans for purchases of commodities from entrepreneurs at home. As an expression for foreign plans for purchases of commodities we shall write $^oA_1^*$, i.e. actual (*ex post*) export. In doing this we have made the assumption that foreign plans for purchases of commodities are always carried out; an assumption which cannot be expected to hold good in general when no stocks of commodities exist in the country. Then we have:

$$I_0 - S_0 = {}^oB_0^c + C_0 + {}^oA_1^* - ({}^oA_0^c + {}^oA_0^*) + {}^lB_0^c - {}^lA_0^w + {}^oB_0^* - {}^oA_1^*. \quad (II:25)$$

$$\underbrace{\phantom{{}^oB_0^c + C_0 + {}^oA_1^*}}_{\substack{\text{planned purchases}\\\text{of commodities}\\\text{from entrepreneurs}\\\text{at home}}} \underbrace{\phantom{({}^oA_0^c + {}^oA_0^*)}}_{\substack{\text{sales of}\\\text{commodities}\\\text{expected by}\\\text{entrepreneurs}\\\text{at home}}} \underbrace{\phantom{{}^lB_0^c - {}^lA_0^w}}_{\substack{\text{ex ante}\\\text{factor-}\\\text{gap}}} \underbrace{\phantom{{}^oB_0^* - {}^oA_1^*}}_{\substack{\text{ex ante}\\\text{import}\\\text{surplus}}}$$

ex ante commodity-gap

Thus, in equation (II:25), we arrive at a result similar to that previously found, (II:5), that the difference between planned investment and saving is equal to the *ex ante* commodity-gap plus the *ex ante* factor-gap, but with the addition here of a magnitude which is called the "*ex ante* import surplus". This consists of the difference between the purchases planned at home of commodities from abroad and the actual export, i.e. the foreign planned purchases of commodities from the country.

It should be noticed that the expression "*ex ante* import surplus" is not a very good one in this connection, since we might also thus describe a magnitude which is the difference between the planned purchases of goods from abroad and the expected sales of goods abroad. This latter will as a rule be the "*ex ante* import surplus" which may be used in trying to forecast the development of the balance of payments; but it is not what is relevant to the analysis of the saving-investment relation.[1]

Because we understand by monetary equilibrium that the *ex ante* commodity-gap is equal to zero and the *ex ante* factor-gap is equal to zero, it is seen that such an equilibrium only implies that planned investment is equal to planned saving under the exceptional condition

[1] See Lindahl, *Studies* ..., p. 127. As is pointed out there, it follows from the conditions of equilibrium which have been set up that there must in general be partial disequilibrium in order that total equilibrium may exist (in the sense of equality between the total quantities). An exception occurs when the foreign planned purchases of commodities from the country is equal to the expected sales of commodities abroad, a condition which it is perhaps permissible to use when full control of foreign trade is assumed. This lack of agreement between the conditions of equality between total magnitudes and between partial magnitudes is not, however, something peculiar to foreign trade activities, but crops up in general when conditions for total equilibrium are formulated which are like those employed here. For, they are only necessary conditions, and not sufficient, for perfect (both total and partial) equilibrium to prevail.

that actual exports (i.e. foreign planned purchases of commodities) are equal to the planned purchases of commodities from abroad. If there is control of foreign trade, the concepts "foreign planned purchases of commodities" and "planned purchases of commodities from abroad" must of course be understood to mean the plans as limited by the control of exports and the control of imports respectively. In dealing with the thirties, and more so with such foreign trade policies, as were applied after the second World War where very extensive control of foreign trade and inflation coexisted and where the object of the control was often to effect a balance in the current accounts of the balance of payments, the assumption $^gB_0^* = {}^gA_1^*$ may be justified. In this case too, the equality between planned investment and saving may be used as a condition of equilibrium (with the reservations previously stated). If, on the other hand, we cannot assume that $^gB_0^* = {}^gA_1^*$, then equilibrium in both commodity and factor markets requires that planned investment exceeds planned saving by the same amount that the planned purchases of commodities from abroad exceed the actual export (foreign planned purchases of commodities).

When such conditions prevail that the entrepreneurs at home can carry out plans for purchases of commodities abroad, i.e. that

$$^gB_0^* = {}^gB_1^* \qquad\qquad (II:26)$$

then equation (II: 25) may be rewritten as

$$(II:27)$$

$$I_0 - S_0 = \underbrace{{}^gA_1 + {}^gA_1^* - ({}^gA_0 + {}^gA_0^*)}_{\substack{\text{unexpected sales} \\ \text{of commodities}}} + \underbrace{{}^gB_0 + C_0 - {}^gB_1 - C_1}_{\substack{\text{unrealizable pur-} \\ \text{chasing plans for} \\ \text{commodities}}} + \underbrace{{}^lB_0 - {}^lB_1}_{\substack{\text{unrealizable} \\ \text{factor-} \\ \text{purchases}}} + \underbrace{{}^gB_1^* - {}^gA_1^*}_{\substack{\text{deficit in} \\ \text{the balance} \\ \text{of trade}}}.$$

The difference between planned investment and planned saving results in unexpected sales of commodities, unrealizable purchases of commodities and factors and deficit in the balance of trade (balance of trade in the wide sense).

It is not possible to analyse some of the more important phenomena of inflation concerned with foreign trade and the balance of payments in a one-period analysis such as is used in this chapter; in particular, the phenomenon that an excess demand for commodities in the inflationary economy tends to find an outlet abroad, so that a heavy unfavourable balance of payments arises. For, a tendency such as this will be concentrated to a great extent at the change-overs from period to period, in such a way that the purchasing plans from period to period shift more and more towards purchases from abroad instead of at home. We shall not go further into this large and important topic here, since the present study is not concerned with the problems of foreign trade. We have only been interested in the establishment of the most elementary connections between the saving-investment rela- tion and foreign trade. In conclusion we will just remark that the adaptation of the equations to the case where sufficient stocks of commodities exist within the country is performed in a way similar to that used in Sections 6 and 7.

CHAPTER III

ANALYSIS OF THE INFLATIONARY GAP

1. *Brief historical survey*

In the discussion in the previous chapter of certain relations, wholly or partly definitional in character, and holding good in a situation where a monetary pressure of inflation exists, we made use of that interpretation of the concept of monetary pressure of inflation which is a consequence of putting demand = planned purchases, and supply = expected sales. In this way, excess demand became equivalent to excess of planned purchases over expected sales, and the existence of a monetary pressure of inflation became equivalent to the case of the *ex ante* commodity-gap and/or *ex ante* factor-gap being positive, and neither being negative. The analysis was concentrated on the relation between the excess demand in the commodity and factor markets, which is characteristic of monetary pressure of inflation, and the saving-investment relation, where the line of thought of the Stockholm School was used, with certain deviations arising from the inflation problem itself.

During and after the second World War it has been considered to a great extent preferable to discuss inflation with the help of the idea of the so-called *inflationary gap* or *excess of purchasing-power*, which, however, has been applied only to the markets for commodities (and services) or parts of them. As has already been suggested in Chap. I, Section 9, there are, in the case when the realisation of purchasing plans cannot be taken for granted, other economically relevant inter-pretations of the concepts of supply and demand than the expected sales and planned purchases of the Stockholm School. If another of these different interpretations of either demand or supply, or both, is considered preferable (and we shall later consider reasons for this pref-erence), the analysis is, of course, correspondingly changed. The concept of monetary pressure of inflation must likewise come to cover a different set of situations, and it is just here that the analysis of the inflationary gap is to be distinguished from the analysis of the previous chapter. As we shall see, it is in the interpretation of the concept of demand as well as of the concept of supply, that the idea of the inflationary gap is principally distinguished from the *ex ante* gaps, which the analysis according to the methods of the Stockholm School leads to.

The concept of the inflationary gap, as it is used in both the theoretical analysis and in the attempts to calculate statistically the pressure of inflation, may be said to have had its origin in the pamphlet by J. M. Keynes, *How to Pay for the War,* which has been previously mentioned, in so far as Keynes not only put forward the inflationary gap there as the decisive driving force in the mechanism of inflation, but also found a quantitative expression for its size in a particular hypothetical situation.[1] The actual expression "inflationary gap" was first launched by the Chancellor of the Exchequer in his presentation of the Budget in the House of Commons in 1941. The idea of computing such an inflationary gap as a guide in economic policies was taken up afterwards, partly in the U. S. A., both officially and by a series of authors[2], and partly in Sweden, by Erik Lundberg of the *Konjunkturinstitut* (Institute of Business-Cycle Research).[3] The

---

[1] J. M. Keynes, *How to Pay for the War,* Chapt. IX, "Voluntary Saving and the Mechanism of Inflation".

[2] There is reference to and closer consideration of British and American investigations in Chap. XI of *Inflation and the American Economy,* by S. E. Harris, McGraw-Hill Book Co., Inc., New York and London, 1945. Special reference can be made to A. G. Hart, "What it takes to Block Inflation", *The Review of Economic Statistics,* Vol. XXIV, 1942; Walter S. Salant, "The Inflationary Gap", and Milton Friedman, "Discussion of the Inflationary Gap", *American Economic Review,* 1942; M. Friedman, C. Shoup and Ruth P. Mack, *Taxing against Inflation,* Columbia University Press, New York, 1942, together with a series of articles in the *American Economic Review,* 1943 and 1944.

[3] A presentation of the manner in which the post-Keynesians introduce the inflationary gap into the ordinary theory of income formation with the help of the well-known 45°-diagram is to be found in, for example, Lawrence R. Klein, *The Keynesian Revolution,* The MacMillan Co., New York, 1947, p. 154—64. Since this type of inflation theory, like the ordinary Keynesian equilibrium theory, does not undertake any explicit analysis of the demand and supply relations in the labour-market (cf. Chaps. VII and VIII), we shall not go further into it.

[3] *Inkomstutveckling och köpkraftsöverskott under krigsåren (The Development of Income and Excess of Purchasing-Power during the War Years),* (Erik Lundberg et al.), *Meddelanden från Konjunkturinstitutet,* Ser. B: 2, Stockholm, 1943. Also *Meddelanden från Konjunkturinstitutet,* Ser. B: 9 and B: 10, together with all the succeeding

basic methods in all these calculations of the inflationary gap are the same; but the American investigations have been quite sporadic, while the Swedish have continued for almost ten years, and the Swedish calculations seem to be more thorough and better thought out (which naturally goes with the longer experience). So we shall take here in its essentials the Konjunkturinstitut's construction on the concept of the inflationary gap as starting-point for the discussion and for the comparison with the *ex ante* gaps of the previous chapter. Yet there will be occasion to utilize certain points of view from the American investigations. That is the topic of Sections 2 and 3. In Section 4 there is a short comparison of the magnitudes of the inflationary gaps and the *ex ante* gaps, and in Section 5 the algebraic discussion of Chap. II is continued, in that an application of the concept of the inflationary gap is made to the saving-investment analysis in order to investigate the applicability of the saving-investment relation as an indicator of monetary pressure of inflation. Lastly, in Section 6, a problem is touched upon which arises in the statistical calculation of the inflationary gap, namely the lumping together of several unit periods and computation of an inflationary gap for several such periods (usually calendar or finance years) taken as one.

2. *Definitions of the inflationary gaps*

In Chap. I, Section 9, it was pointed out that, although the concepts of supply and demand become rather vague when it can no longer be assumed that all purchasing plans can be realized, yet three distinct interpretations can be made concerning the concept of demand, and two concerning the concept of supply, all of which are relevant for the analysis.

By combining these different demand and supply concepts, a whole series of different excess demand concepts could be obtained, which could be put into the basic definition of monetary pressure of inflation. Not all such combinations are of interest, however. Thus, it would hardly be worthwhile to combine demand = planned purchases with supply concepts other than supply = expected sales, and *vice versa*.

---

surveys of the economic situation from Spring 1944 inclusively (Ser. A: 11—17). A summary of the calculations for a single year (1951) is given in Appendix I. See also, *Statsverkspropositionen*, 1951 and earlier years.

So in this chapter we confine ourselves to defining excess demand either by

active attempts to purchase — available quantity of goods = excess demand, or by

optimum purchases — available quantity of goods = excess demand.

It is apparent that the inflationary gap, as it is used by the Konjunkturinstitut or in the various American investigations, must be understood in one of these ways. Also, it will be seen that it cannot be said *a priori* which is best or most correct, since that may quite well depend on the problem encountered. Therefore, we will begin with listing the problems to which we want the calculation of the inflationary gap to give a solution.

There are now two problems, quite distinct from one another, which are of special interest. Firstly, we may ask by how much demand must be decreased (or supply increased) in order that the market considered may be said to have achieved equilibrium. Secondly, what will happen, i.e. how will prices develop, if nothing is done to bring the market into equilibrium? It is clear that the calculation of the inflationary gap can give an answer to the first of these questions. That it can also give an answer to the second depends on the fact that we often—and presumably with some justification, cf. also Chaps. VII to IX—reckon with having in the size of the excess demand an indication of the tendency of prices to increase.

It is now clear that the same concept of excess demand cannot in general be used for the calculation of the inflationary gap for both these problems. When the problem is the achievement of equilibrium, it is evident that we must take for the supply the available quantity of goods (with the provision that "normal" stocks shall be attained), i.e. actual production at full employment *minus* such alteration of stocks as is necessary in order that "normal" stocks will be attained, and for the demand the optimum purchases, i.e. that quantity of goods which the purchasers regard as optimum with respect to their financial resources at that time. If we consider all the commodity-markets in one, we arrive at a definition of the monetary excess demand in the composite commodity-market which is stated thus:

the inflationary gap in the commodity-markets =
optimum purchases of commodities — value of the available quantity of commodities,

and in the same way, for the monetary excess demand in the composite factor-market (the concept of the inflationary gap being extended to factor-markets):

the inflationary gap in the factor-markets =
optimum purchases of factors — value of the available quantity of factors.

The interpretation of the concept of monetary pressure of inflation is altered in accordance with this, of course.

It is most easily seen that it is these magnitudes which are of interest in this problem—achievement of equilibrium—if the situation is considered where there is rationing, which contracts the quantity of goods in demand to precisely the quantity of goods available, and where purchasers are so law-abiding that they do not try to buy more than just the amount of the ration. Here the active attempts to purchase are clearly = the quantity of goods available for sale (= planned purchases), but if we wish to achieve equilibrium in the sense that rationing can be abolished without the active attempts to purchase exceeding the available quantity of goods, then the quantity of goods available must clearly be increased (or the optimum purchases decreased) just sufficiently for the optimum purchasing requirements to be met. In that case the purchasers will not have occasion to try to purchase (or plan to purchase) quantities other than the optimum quantities.

If we leave this simple example, and look at the matter more generally, we see that, when the optimum purchases can be just carried out, all three interpretations of the concept of demand coincide, so that planned purchases = active attempts to purchase = optimum purchases. For, it is necessary to distinguish the different concepts in the particular case when the optimum purchases cannot be carried out. That a situation in which optimum purchases can just be made good from the available quantity of goods is an equilibrium situation can be seen by considering, for instance, an increased supply (i.e. increased available quantity of goods) which must now lead to unfulfilled expectations of sales. If, on the other hand, equilibrium had only been attained in the sense that the quantity of goods available for sale is equal to planned purchases, but planned purchases are less than optimum purchases because the purchasers think they are unable to realize the latter, then an increase of supply does not lead to disappointed sales expectations.

For, if the active attempts to purchase are greater than the planned purchases (as is of course likely), then the purchasers automatically take up the increased supply of goods by unexpected purchases, until the supply of goods has become equal to the optimum purchases. The situation discussed here cannot be regarded as a regular equilibrium (perhaps as a "neutral" equilibrium in the Marshallian sense).

Of course, the result of such a calculation of the inflationary gap, with emphasis on the attainment of equilibrium, will depend on what is understood by equilibrium. For, some might quite well speak of a state of equilibrium when this state is obtained only by the institution of rationing in one or more fields or by other quantitative restrictions of demand. It should be observed that it is, of course, possible to give the concepts of "equilibrium" and "optimum" such meanings that optimum purchases and active attempts to purchase become identical; in order to arrive at this result, it is sufficient to identify optimum behaviour and actual behaviour. However, this is hardly practical. We take the optimum behaviour to be a potential behaviour.

If we concentrate, on the other hand, on the question of the increases in prices which are to be expected if measures are not taken against them, it cannot be the optimum purchases which are of relevance, since these are hypothetical in a sense, or rather, potential. Here it must be the active attempts to purchase (binding offers of purchase) which are relevant, so that we arrive at the interpretations:

the inflationary gap in the commodity-markets =
active attempts to purchase — value of the available quantity of commodities,
and
the inflationary gap in the factor-markets =
active attempts to purchase — value of the available quantity of factors.

It is reasonable to use the active attempts to purchase here, and not the planned purchases or the optimum purchases, since the only thing of which the sellers are aware is the active attempts to purchase, both the planned purchases and the magnitude of optimum purchases being known only to the individual purchaser. Yet the sellers may be quite sure that not all the offers to purchase given as binding can be taken seriously in actual fact (cf. the "sham magnification" of demand mentioned earlier, Chap. I, Section 9) or that the potential (optimum) demand exceeds the active attempts to purchase (the flow of orders). But in spite of that, it must always be the demand, which takes as its expression the offers to purchase, that serves as the main basis for the decisions of the sellers about changes in prices. Retailers have in general no other indication of their sales possibilities, and it is well known that the stock of orders and the changes in it, are to a great extent decisive for the policy of large firms.

That it may be the available quantity of goods and not the expected sales, or, disregarding alterations in stocks, the production which is really carried out and not the planned production, which is relevant to the tendency of prices to increase, can be seen from the considerations which follow, where we first consider a commodity-market with perfect competition. Let us suppose that the price has been fixed to begin with by the conclusion of contracts, so that the market is just cleared in the sense that the sellers have concluded contracts for the sale of the whole of their planned production, while the purchasers have concluded contracts which just correspond to their wants (at the price which has been decided upon). Then the sellers discover that they are not in a position to fulfil the contracts out of their own actual production, when deliveries according to contract are required to be made good, and they must consequently make covering purchases of that quantity of goods which corresponds to the unrealizable production plans, in order to fulfil the contracts. At the price fixed in the beginning, therefore, there is an unsatisfied demand, and so there are no grounds for calling it an equilibrium price: prices will tend to rise.

If we leave this picture of an ideal market, and continue by considering the prices to be noted at the beginning of the period and fixed throughout the period in accordance with the disequilibrium method, the question becomes one of the effect of an excess demand in one period on the fixing of prices in the next period. Here we may assume, in order to have a basis for comparison, that the current planned production and the current demand (planned and expected) are unchanged from period to period. The decisive feature becomes that the higher the degree to which the production plans cannot be carried out (i.e. the more the available quantity of goods decreases), the greater the extent to which a queue of unfulfilled orders piles up with the sellers; and that must certainly be an inducement to the sellers to increase prices, other things being equal.

Thus, it seems clear that in setting up indicators for the tendency of prices to increase, break-downs in productions plans must be taken into account. This consideration need not be altered if changes of stocks are taken into account. In that case, of course, no queues of unfulfilled orders arise. But unexpected sales from stocks will appear; and they will be greater the greater the extent of the unrealizable production plans. If the sellers want to maintain a certain desirable level of stocks, then the deficiences in production may of themselves have the effect of raising prices here too.

3. *The "excess of purchasing-power" of the Swedish Konjunkturinstitut*

In the light of these remarks, we can now consider more closely the calculation of the inflationary gap in the commodity-markets, as carried out by the Konjunkturinstitut, and we shall speak of "the inflationary gap in the commodity-markets" everywhere, where the Konjunkturinstitut uses the unqualified terms "inflationary gap" or "excess of purchasing-power." This is because we also want to work with the analogous concept for the factor-markets: "the inflationary gap in the factor-markets", which, strangely enough has not been the subject of similar thorough investigations.

The matter is simplest in connection with *supply*. Here the Konjunkturinstitut (and likewise British and American investigators) use just the actually available quantity of goods, and as starting-point for the calculation of that, the production actually carried out, and not the planned production. It should be stated here, that the Konjunkturinstitut is aware of the significance of the distinction between planned production and production actually carried out:

"Excess demand is to be taken as the difference between planned demand and planned supply ... The private production plans are not to be taken into account, for statistical reasons among others, ... All the enterprises could of course plan to increase production by taking labour-power from one another. A high national product could in that way be obtained, *ex ante*. It is here that a 'clearence' (in the statistical sense; B. H.) enters into the matter ... It is the probable supply of production factors which is transformed to end-products and entered as gross national product in the balance of goods and services. 'Full employment' is thus a fundamental working hypothesis. It can also be said, more strictly, that the planned supply of labour-power is taken into consideration, and this serves to determine the limit of actual production in the calculation of the excess demand ... On the other hand, calculations of a balance of labour-power could with advantage make use of information about the planned demand for labour made out by enterprises."[1]

This is in complete agreement with the considerations in Section 2.

If we turn now to the question of taking stocks into account, there is also fairly good agreement. In Section 2 the result arrived at was that irrespective of whether one or the other aspect of the problem is taken as starting-point, to the actual production should be added the difference between actual stocks at the beginning of the period and "normal" stocks (where it is the equilibrium point of view which is the basis of the calculation), or "desirable", planned, stocks (in the case where it is the disequilibrium point of view which is the basis of the calculation). If the actual stocks are less than the "normal", or, it may be, the "desirable", then this difference is to be deducted from the production actually carried out, before arriving at the supply in the sense of quantity of goods available for sale.

The Konjunkturinstitut generally takes such an attitude to stocks.[2] But, Keynes, in *How to Pay for the War*, (and with Keynes, many American investigators too) seems inclined to take the existence of stocks as something which of itself always diminishes the inflationary gap in the commodity-markets, because the existing stocks can be added to the actual production to arrive at the quantity of commodities actually available for sale. Perhaps it holds from an "austerity" point of view that stocks are something which *can* be sold to satisfy purchasing wants, and perhaps this treatment of stocks is reasonable also from the point of view that an excess demand affects prices more slowly when it can find an outlet in unintended decreases of stocks, than when that is not possible.

In the case of the *demand* the calculations of the Konjunkturinstitut can also be traced back to considerations like those put forward in Section 2. The starting-point—as far as can be seen—is what we

---

[1] Ingvar Ohlsson, "Nationalbudgetbegreppet", p. 121 et seq.

[2] For example, *Översikt över konjunkturläget 1946—49* (*Survey of the Economic Situation 1946—49*), Ser. B: 9, p. 14, and Ingvar Ohlsson "Nationalbudgetbegreppet", p. 126—7.

have called the optimum purchases[1], and next a "clearance" is made so that the demand may be found which really shows itself as active demand: "The plans concerning demand are thus introduced into the calculation of the excess demand in that form in which they may be considered to exercise *active* demand in the open market."[2] It is not quite obvious what is meant by "active demand" here. It seems, however, that what the Konjunkturinstitut is suggesting is what we have called "active attempts to purchase", but the Konjunkturinstitut at the same time seems to take the concept of equilibrium in such a sense that optimum purchases and active attempts to purchase become identical (cf. Section 2). As an example, we can mention the treatment of the effect of control of investments, in which, in order to arrive at the demand for investment-goods, all such profitable investments (*ex ante*) are cleared away as are not permitted by the investment control; and similarly for the treatment of the effect of all other rationing and the like.

A special point of interest is the manner in which the demand for consumer-goods is calculated. In practice this is done by estimating the incomes which the consumers have—or expect to have—in the period considered, and then multiplying these incomes with a certain average consumption-ratio in order to arrive at the demand. Obviously we can talk about different consumption-ratio's here. We could speak of an "optimum consumption-ratio" using "optimum" in the same sense as elsewhere. Here it is natural to use a consumption-ratio which may be regarded as "normal" according to previous experience (if it can be supposed that the pattern of the consumers' preferences has been constant since then). Or, a consumption-ratio could be used which leads to the active attempts to purchase consumer-goods. Such an "active" consumption-ratio, under the influence of rationing, difficulties in carrying out optimum purchases, etc., might well become quite different from the optimum ("normal") consumption-ratio. Unfortunately the Konjunkturinstitut is rather vague on this significant point, but it looks as if (in principle) an "active" consumption-ratio is used, which is to be expected when it is the "active" demand which

---

[1] Ingvar Ohlsson, "Nationalbudgetbegreppet", talks about "planned" demand, but the meaning of this seems to be more or less the same as that of "optimum purchases" in the text.

[2] Ingvar Ohlsson, "Nationalbudgetbegreppet", p. 122—3.

is being investigated. On the other hand, some American investigations seem to use a "normal" consumption-ratio—possibly for lack of a better.

So we come to the conclusion that, so far as the definition of the inflationary gap in the commodity-markets is concerned, the investigations mentioned—especially that of the Konjunkturinstitut—start out to find an expression for the upward pressure on the prices of goods, and in so doing seem to come to the definition of the inflationary gap in the commodity-markets as

the inflationary gap in the commodity markets = the active attempts to purchase commodities — the value of the available quantity of commodities.

On the other hand there is so far no very great interest on the part of the investigators in the other method of consideration—the equilibrium consideration (but see Section 6). Here, the inflationary gap in the commodity-markets must be defined as the difference between such purchases of commodities as would be optimum for the purchasers, and the available quantity of commodities (actual production corrected for the difference between "normal" stocks and the actual stocks at the beginning of the period). The use of a "normal" consumption-ratio in calculating the purchases of consumer-goods may possibly be regarded as an attempt to arrive at the optimum purchases.

Furthermore it should be mentioned that, because we have distinguished commodity and factor markets in the way explained in Chap. II, Section 4, and therefore consider the inflationary gap in the commodity-markets to be calculated just on all *commodities*, the treatment is thus somewhat different from that in the aforementioned investigations. But these differences are not essentially matters of principle. The American calculations have usually concentrated on computing the excess demand for smaller or larger parts of the commodity-markets. For instance, they have, like Keynes, worked with the excess demand for all those commodities which are available for private individuals and private enterprises; or only with the excess demand for consumer-goods which are available for private individuals, or the excess demand for all commodities, apart from raw-materials and intermediate products. As a rule there is no question of principle involved in this difference of treatment, because those investigators who concentrate on parts of the commodity-markets usually assume that the other quantities of commodities which are produced are at the disposal of purchasers, who in all circumstances get what they want and pay what it costs. For instance, this applies to the state, if its purchasing plans are fixed as to physical quantity, and it applies to investments when there is control of investments combined with allocation.

If we consider the Swedish calculations, we can see two points on which there is a difference between the definition of excess demand as we have given it (the inflationary gap in the commodity-markets), and the calculated excess demand (excess of purchasing-power or inflationary gap according to the terminology of the Konjunkturinstitut). In the first place, the Konjunkturinstitut computes an excess demand for commodities *and* services, which means that a part of what we have called the factor-markets enters in a formal way into the calculation of the inflationary gap in the commodity-markets, because the production of civil service is reckoned in the production of services, and the state's planned payments of salaries is reckoned in the demand for services. However, since these two magnitudes are always equal (both the value of and the demand for the production of the civil service is the total of salaries that are paid to the civil service), it makes no difference to the calculation of the inflationary gap in the commodity-markets if these services are taken into account or not. Secondly, the Konjunkturinstitut reckons a smaller gross than we have done, since it exclude supply of and demand for raw-materials and intermediate products between firms at home. This may quite well be taken as a difference of principle[1], because there is nothing at all to suggest on *a priori* grounds that supply of and demand for these commodities are automatically equal, disregarding the case when there is rationing of raw-materials.

If we now turn to the inflationary gap in the factor-markets, the statistical investigations are not much of a guide, since they are almost entirely focussed on the commodity-markets, as has been mentioned. Of course, there are sometimes so-called balances of labour-power in the national budgets which are now so common, and these, suitably treated, should yield some information about the excess demand in that essential part of the factor-markets, the labour-market. In the reports

[1] See Erik Lundberg, "Inflationsanalys och ekonomisk teori" ("Inflation-Analysis and Economic Theory"), *Ekonomisk Tidskrift*, Stockholm, 1948, p. 148.

6

of the Konjunkturinstitut there are also certain considerations of the extent of the excess demand in the labour-market, and of the difficulties in finding the "active" demand for labour-services[1], which difficulties are of much the same character as those that occur in the commodity-markets (cf. Section 2.). But this has not found expression in any systematic calculation of the gap in the factor-markets. However, it is clear that if we look for an expression of the tendency of (factor) prices to increase—as we did for the commodity-markets—it is reasonable to define the inflationary gap in the factor-markets as the difference between active attempts to purchase factors and the quantity of factors actually available.

4. *Ex ante gaps and inflationary gaps compared*

If we now compare the *ex ante* gaps (commodity and factor) which are used in Chap. II and the inflationary gaps (in the commodity and factor markets) discussed here in Chap. III it is seen that the inflationary gap in the commodity-markets must in general be larger than the *ex ante* commodity-gap. For, we have that

the *ex ante* commodity-gap = planned purchases of commodities — expected sales of commodities,

and

the inflationary gap in the commodity-markets = active attempts to purchase commodities — value of the available quantity of commodities,

and further, the active attempts to purchase commodities are in general greater than the planned purchases' of commodities, and the available quantity of commodities smaller than expected sales. Therefore the *ex ante* commodity-gap must be less than the inflationary gap in the commodity-markets. The same result will be obtained if the inflationary gap in the commodity-markets is defined from equilibrium considerations, as the difference between optimum purchases and the value of commodities available for sale.

Similarly, the inflationary gap in the factor-markets is in general larger than the *ex ante* factor-gap, for we have that,

---

[1] See, *Konjunkturläget Hösten 1949* (*The Economic Situation Autumn 1949*), *Meddelanden från Konjunkturinstitutet*, Ser. A: 17, Stockholm 1950, p. 109 et seq.

the *ex ante* factor-gap = planned purchases of factors — expected sales of factors,
and

the inflationary gap in the factor-markets = the active attempts to purchase factors — value of the available quantity of factors.

In general active attempts to purchase factors exceed planned purchases of factors, while, with full employment, it can be taken that the expected sales of factors = the available quantity of factors (cf. Chap. II, Section 4); so, in general, the inflationary gap in the factor-markets is larger than the *ex ante* factor-gap. This will also apply when the inflationary gap in the factor-markets, in accordance with the equilibrium point of view, is defined as the difference between optimum purchases of factors and the quantity of factors available for sale.

However, as we will, in what follows, almost entirely disregard the differences between planned, active and optimum purchases, so that the *ex ante* factor-gap and the inflationary gap in the factor-markets obviously become identical, we shall only talk about the *factor-gap*. Consequently, when this expression is used and nothing to the contrary is explicitly stated, it implies the assumption that active attempts to purchase factors = planned purchases of factors = optimum purchases of factors.

5. *Algebraic presentation*

Now we shall continue with the algebraic discussion begun in Chap. II, and try to build the concept of the inflationary gap into the investment-saving analysis, in order to see what particular significance this change in the interpretation of the concept of excess demand has for the investment-saving relationship as an indicator of a monetary pressure of inflation.

As in Chap. II, Section 6, foreign trade and public finances are neglected, and the case without stocks of commodities is taken to be the general case. Also, we start the algebraic presentation by taking planned purchases = active attempts to purchase = optimum purchases, in both the commodity and factor markets. So, what is really dealt with algebraically is the effect on the analysis of the investment-saving relationship of substituting the available quantity of commodities for the expected sales of commodities.

The total planned demand for commodities at the prices holding good at the beginning of the period is equal to

$$\text{planned purchases of commodities} = {}^{g}B_0 + C_0. \qquad \text{(III:1)}$$

Suppose we now make the merely formal alteration of the definition of the inflationary gap in the commodity-markets, that the planned increases in stocks are to be included as an added item in the planned purchases of commodities (consequently in the demand), instead of as a subtracted item in the supply. Then, with this purely formal alteration, the quantity of goods actually available becomes = actual production for the period, and we have that this is equal to the actual sales of commodities during the period, so that

$$\text{the actual production} = {}^{g}A_1 = {}^{g}B_1 + C_1, \qquad \text{(III:2)}$$

which leads to

the inflationary gap in the commodity-markets =

$$= {}^{g}B_0 + C_0 - {}^{g}B_1 - C_1. \qquad \text{(III:3)}$$

We can now obtain two distinct expressions for the relationship between the inflationary gap in the commodity-markets and $I_0 - S_0$. On putting (III:3) directly into (II:7) we get

$$I_0 - S_0 = \underbrace{{}^{g}B_0 + C_0 - {}^{g}B_1 - C_1}_{\substack{\text{the inflationary gap in} \\ \text{the commodity-markets}}} + \underbrace{{}^{l}B_0 - {}^{l}B_1}_{\substack{\text{the factor-} \\ \text{gap}}} + {}^{g}A_1 - {}^{g}A_0. \qquad \text{(III:4)}$$

This equation, which expresses the connection between $I_0 - S_0$ and the sum of the monetary excess demand in the composite commodity and factor markets according to the inflationary gap interpretation, contrasts with the fundamental equation in the Swedish approach, (II:5), which states that

$$I_0 - S_0 = ex\ ante \text{ commodity-gap} + \text{the factor-gap.} \qquad \text{(II:5)}$$

Equation (III:4) is clearly not of the same simple nature as (II:5). Moreover, if we add

$$I_0 - S_0 = E_1^c - E_0^c + C_0 - C_1 + I_0 - I_0 \qquad \text{(II:9)}$$

and

C = the inflationary gap in the commodity-markets —

$$^gB_0 - C_0 + {}^gB_1 + C_1, \quad \text{(III:3)}$$

we arrive at the following expression:

$I_0 - S_0$ = the inflationary gap in the commodity-markets +

$$+ E_1^c - E_0^c + I_0 - I_1 + {}^gB_1 - {}^gB_0. \quad \text{(III:5)}$$

It should be noticed that we do not find any necessary equality between $I_0 - S_0$ and the inflationary gap in the commodity-markets *plus* that in the factor-markets, nor between $I_0 - S_0$ and the inflationary gap in the commodity-markets by itself.

The relation between the three gaps is obtained by subtracting equation (II:5) from equation (III:5), whereupon we have

the inflationary gap in the commodity-markets =

$$= \underbrace{{}^gB_0 + C_0 - {}^gA_0}_{\substack{\textit{ex ante} \text{ com-} \\ \text{modity-gap}}} + \underbrace{{}^lB_0 - {}^lB_1}_{\substack{\text{factor-} \\ \text{gap}}} - (E_1^c - E_0^c) - ({}^gB_1 - {}^gB_0) - (I_0 - I_1). \quad \text{(III:6)}$$

The case where sufficient stocks of commodities exists for all purchase-plans for commodities to be fulfilled presents no special problems.

So, if the particular problem to be dealt with makes it advisable to replace expected sales by the quantity of goods actually available, it follows at once that the difference between planned investment and planned saving (in the *ex ante* sense) ceases to be of immediate independent interest in the problem of inflation.

Even if the *ex ante* interpretation of the concepts of supply and demand were accepted as relevant for the analysis, there would be, as was pointed out in Chap. II, several circumstances which would limit the value of $I_0 - S_0$ as an indicator for the existence of a monetary pressure of inflation. Thus, $I_0 - S_0$ only says something about the *sum* of the monetary excess demand in the composite commodity and factor market together, so that positive $I_0 - S_0$ could go together with negative monetary excess demand in one of the groups of markets, in which case a monetary pressure of inflation does not exist, according to the definition. So $I_0 > S_0$ is in any case only a necessary (but not sufficient) condition for the existence of a monetary pressure of inflation. When, in interpreting the concept of excess demand, we replace supply of commodities = expected sales of commodities by supply of commodities = actually available quantity of commodities, i.e. a quantity which is not in general included in individual plans, the simple relationship between $I_0 - S_0$ and the monetary excess demand disappears, because:

In the first place, $I_0 - S_0$ tells us nothing about the size of the inflationary gap in the commodity-markets or of the factor-gap. If we consider equation (III: 4) we see that $I_0 - S_0$ may be either greater than or less than the sum of the inflationary gap in the commodity-markets and the factor-gap. Neither is $I_0 - S_0$ equal to one of the two gaps by itself, since $I_0 - S_0$ may be either greater than or less than the factor-gap—which is seen from (III: 4) to depend on whether $|{}^gA_1 - {}^gA_0| \gtrless |{}^gB_0 + C_0 - {}^gB_1 - C_1|$, and, likewise, either greater than or less than the inflationary gap in the commodity-markets.

Secondly, as a consequence of the first point, the sign of $I_0 - S_0$ can never be taken as an indication of the state of affairs on the commodity and factor markets taken together. That is, $I_0 - S_0$ cannot even be taken as a *necessary* condition for the existence of a monetary pressure of inflation, for it is possible for $I_0 - S_0$ to be negative— planned saving exceeding planned investment—at the same time as there exists a positive inflationary gap in the commodity-markets and a positive factor-gap. If we consider equation (III: 4), of which the last term $({}^gA_1 - {}^gA_0)$ will usually be negative (it may be remembered that equation (III: 4) applies to the case without stocks of commodities), it is seen that $I_0 - S_0 < 0$, if $({}^gA_1 - {}^gA_0) < 0$ together with

$$|\underbrace{{}^gB_0 + C_0 - {}^gB_1 - C_1}_{\substack{\text{inflationary gap in the}\\\text{commodity-markets}}} + \underbrace{{}^iB_0 - {}^iB_1}_{\substack{\text{factor-}\\\text{gap}}}| < |{}^gA_1 - {}^gA_0|. \qquad \text{(III: 7)}$$

As will be seen in Chap. IV, the functional relationships which can reasonably be set up in a complete model are of such a character that these conditions may very well be fulfilled.

All this was a consequence of putting supply = the actually available quantity of goods in the concept of excess demand. But in the algebraic presentation of this section, we have up to now maintained the identification of demand, planned purchases, active attempts to purchase and optimum purchases. The justification of this identification during an inflationary process may, however, be the object of severe criticism, for, according to our previous examination of the topic, the demand which appears on the market in the form of binding offers to purchase (the active attempts to purchase) does not necessarily equal the planned purchases which enter into the individual equations of earning and use of income. Neither is it equal to the optimum purchases, and it is only when the sign of equality may be used here that there exists any immediate connection between demand and the investment-saving relationship (*ex ante*).

This is easily seen, for example, if we suppose that a consumer wishes to buy in a certain period a vacuum-cleaner, and consequently orders one to be delivered as soon as possible from some firm. The firm's list of orders increases by one if delivery cannot be made immediately, and the firm of course records this as an increase in the demand for the current period. At the same time, the consumer may reckon (as is very likely) that he will not have his vacuum-cleaner delivered in the period, whereupon he plans (in the *ex ante* sense) to save his money until a later period. So, in this example, we have simultaneous increase in demand and corresponding *ex ante* saving (or, possibly, an unchanged demand together with increased *ex ante* saving).

If we go all the way and interpret excess demand as active attempts to purchase (or as optimum purchases) *minus* the quantity of goods actually available, the simple correspondence between planned investment *minus* planned saving and the monetary excess demand in the composite commodity-market and the composite factor-market disappears completely.

We must conclude that the interpretation of the concepts of demand and supply according to the inflationary gap point of view deprives the investment-saving relation (in the *ex ante* sense) of its significance as an indicator of the state of the commodity and factor markets, especially as an indicator of whether a monetary pressure of inflation exists. But this conclusion does not deprive the investment-saving relation (in the *ex ante* sense) of all significance. Planned investment and planned saving are still of significance for the dealings of the economic subjects on the credit-markets, which are of course always of importance as far as the analysis of the inflationary process is concerned, because it cannot be denied that the development of the rates of interest influences the course of the inflation. It is only because this study is concentrated on the relations in the commodity and factor markets and the interplay of them that the investment-saving relationship must become unimportant.

Finally, it should be noticed that there is obviously nothing to prevent the defining of investment and saving in such a way that the difference between investment and saving does become identical with the inflationary gap in the commodity-markets (for example). That is the method of procedure followed by the post-Keynesians[1], but nothing is thereby gained—quite the contrary. For the difference between investment and saving defined in that way is without significance in the credit-markets.

6. *The year as the period for calculation*

Hitherto we have confined our attention almost exclusively to a single unit-period; and the excess demand and gaps considered have all been defined for a single unit period. Such a unit period is, of course, quite short and indefinite. Because of this, and because much of the information necessary in the calculation of the excess demand is given for a longer period, also because it is wholly impossible to make these calculations at the beginning of each unit period if this could be fixed, and lastly because the political decisions, for which the calculation of the inflationary gap serves as a basis, are taken at less frequent intervals, the calculation of the gaps has usually been confined to periods of a calendar or financial year. A calendar year comprises many unit periods (we assume that it begins at the beginning of a unit period), during which a development takes place, where, among other things, a steady shift of prices occurs. So the important problem crops up of how the gaps may be calculated for a whole series of unit periods taken together, and what significance may be attached to such multi-period gaps.

This problem has not been the subject of much discussion, but we can at once state that there is no universal solution because the way in which the gaps are calculated over several unit periods taken together and the significance of the gaps must depend on the problem which it is wished to solve.

When we are occupied with defining excess demand and inflationary gaps in a unit period, the definition has to depend on whether we wish to know how large an excess demand we must reckon with if it

---

[1] Lawrence R. Klein, *The Keynesian Revolution*, for instance.

is desired to create an equilibrium such that the buyers can carry out just those purchases which is regarded as optimum; or whether we wish to know how large an excess demand will appear in the markets (as active attempts to purchase), assuming that no attempt is made to bring about equilibrium.

Similar considerations apply when we want to calculate the inflationary gaps for several unit periods taken together. Here also it is decisive for the calculations and for the significance of the gaps calculated, whether we wish to know how large an excess demand must be reckoned with for the year as a whole if it is wished to bring about equilibrium in each single one of the year's unit periods (the "equilibrium aspect"), or whether we wish to know how large an excess demand will appear in the markets for the whole year, if no attempt is made to bring about equilibrium (the "disequilibrium aspect"). This distinction is of decisive importance, as we will see, in two different ways.

Let us first consider this multi-period aggregation problem from the equilibrium aspect, since the discussion which has been carried on deals with the problem from this point of view.[1] To begin with, it is clear that the excess demand which must be looked for in each single unit period within the year for summation into the excess demand for the whole year, is the excess demand in the sense of optimum purchases *minus* available quantity of goods. Furthermore, the excess demand, or the gaps, for each unit period are obviously to be calculated on the assumption that there actually was equilibrium in the previous unit period(s) within the year, because it may usually be taken that the excess demand in each unit period depends, among other things, on the development in the preceding periods. There is also the problem of the price at which this multi-period excess demand shall be calculated; the answer is, of course, that the calculation should be made at those prices at which it is desired to establish equilibrium (i.e. excess demand eliminated), which will usually, but not necessarily, be the prices prevailing at the end of the previous year (i.e. those in the last period of the previous year), or the prices prevailing at the beginning of the current year (i.e. in the first period of the current year).

---

[1] Ralph Turvey, "A Further Note on the Inflationary Gap", (in English), *Ekonomisk Tidskrift*, Stockholm, 1949.

The authorities who administer the equilibrium policy may now arrange to remove just as much (optimum) excess demand in the coming year as is given by the gaps for the whole year calculated in the way indicated above. But it may well happen that the distribution in time of the measures for diminishing the excess demand becomes inappropriate, because the excess demand may be different for different periods within the year, on account of plans which cover several periods, and because of time-lags. Ralph Turvey has been into this problem[1], and thinks that, in order to achieve appropriate distribution according to time of the measures for removing the excess demand, the excess demand for the year must be calculated, not by summation of the excess demand in all the unit periods of the year, but as a yearly rate on the basis of the excess demand in the first period of the year considered. That may be correct, but it can be seen at once that since such a yearly rate of excess demand must now be calculated at the beginning of each one of the year's unit periods, it is therefore actually identical with maintaining that a lumping together of all the unit periods of the year is impossible.

When we say that the gap in a definite unit period is to be calculated on the assumption that there was equilibrium in the previous periods, this must be understood to imply, if we divide the markets up into certain groups for each of which its own gap is to be calculated, that it is also assumed that simultaneous equilibrium is brought about in all the market-groups in the period considered. For, the gap for a particular group, e.g. the commodity-markets, is of course dependent in size on whether or not the factor-gap is eliminated, and in what way that is achieved (cf. Chap. V, and Chap. VII, Section 5, and also Chap. IX).

If on the other hand, we apply the "disequilibrium aspect" and take an interest in what rises in prices will appear if nothing is done to prevent them, the calculation of the excess demand for the year becomes another matter. In the first place, the excess demand which must be considered in each unit period must be the excess demand in the sense of active attempts to purchase *minus* the available quantity of goods, and secondly the excess demand for each unit period must be calculated on the assumption that there was not equilibrium in the

---

[1] Ralph Turvey, "A Further Note on the Inflationary Gap".

previous period. Without setting up any numerical model as illustration, it is easy to see that if 1) the monetary excess demand for each of the unit periods of the year is reckoned in this way, 2) the excess demand for each unit period is deflated by means of a price index to the prices prevailing at the end of the previous year (or the beginning of the current year), 3) the excess demands reckoned at the same price-level are added together for all the unit periods, 4) the available quantity of goods is similarly calculated at the same price-level, and lastly 5) it is supposed, for instance, that there is a relation between the excess demand and the quantity of goods available, which in some known way determines the magnitude of the tendency of prices to increase (see, for instance, Chap. IX, Sections 1—3), then 6) the relation between the excess demand calculated in this way for the whole year and the quantity of goods available for the whole year, ought to tell us how much the price-level for the year will, *on an average*, exceed the price-level at the end of the previous year (or the beginning of the current year), if nothing is done to check rise in prices.

Both these methods have a good deal of meaning, and both answer most essential problems. But it is easily seen that, strictly speaking, neither of them really does away with the difficulties which are the actual reasons for preferring to calculate per year instead of per unit period. If we consider the first method ("equilibrium aspect"), then we see that it does lead to a continual recalculation of the gaps for a year (yearly rate), but these yearly gaps are obtained simply by multiplying the gap for each new unit period with the number of periods in the year, so that the actual basis of the calculation is the gaps for the unit periods. The same applies to the other method ("disequilibrium aspect"), since that obviously assumes that it is possible to forecast the development through all the unit periods of the year, including the development of prices. When, therefore, the yearly figure is used to say how much the average price-level for the year will exceed the price-level at the beginning of the year, this really expresses less than was used to arrive at the result!

Both these methods suffer the practical disadvantage, that they involve going *from* the gaps in the unit periods *to* the gap for the year, whereas the practical possibilities of calculation require the direct calculation of the yearly gap, without proceeding by way of the gaps for the unit periods.

The method of procedure used by the Konjunkturinstitut is not quite clear in this respect. On the one hand, the Konjunkturinstitut seems to think of the excess of purchasing-power as a yearly rate of excess of purchasing-power existing at a certain instant. So, the excess of purchasing-power gives no direct answer to questions like these: By how much must the government diminish demand during the financial year in order that equilibrium may be attained, or, by how much will prices increase on an average during the year. It can at most tell us something about the tendency for prices to rise at the instant considered, or, about the rate of decrease in demand (increase in supply) necessary to bring about equilibrium, since these two questions seems to be taken by the Konjunkturinstitut to be identical (cf. Section 3). But, on the other hand, in the attempts to measure the yearly rate of excess of purchasing-power such increases of income as are known to be going to occur during the year to come (at the prices given) through wage-negotiations, wage-slidings, etc., are taken into account, and this makes it less obvious that the excess of purchasing-power of the Konjunkturinstitut is really to be understood as a yearly rate at a certain instant.

In the calculations for 1951, described in Appendix I, it is obvious that it is intended to calculate the excess of purchasing-power for the year, and it is also obvious that the particular aspect behind the calculation is the equilibrium aspect. It should be remembered, however, that this calculation was not performed by the Konjunkturinstitut but by the government's National Budget Committee.

CHAPTER IV

A SIMPLIFIED MODEL OF REPRESSED INFLATION

Demand for commodities
is not demand for labour
J. St. Mill

A. Perfect Competition in the Commodity-Markets

1. *General assumptions for the models of repressed inflation*

The previous chapters were to a great extent definitional in character, if not quite completely so. Since no structural relationships entered into the models used, the conclusions which could be drawn there were very limited, however. The following geometric presentation has two objects in view; partly to provide an illustration to the previous discussion, and partly to carry that discussion further, since, by the establishment of some curves, structural relationships are introduced which were lacking in the previous algebraic presentation. Thus it becomes possible to draw several additional conclusions.

The assumptions which we now introduce for the sake of simplification are the following:

a) It is supposed that there are general ceilings for prices and wage-rates. At a certain stage all the prevailing commodity prices and wage-rates have been declared to be maximum prices and wage-rates. It follows that it is *repressed inflation* which we are considering. Changes in prices and wage-rates take place only when the state permits or prescribes them; changes in prices and wage-rates are assumed to happen only by an alteration of all prices or all wage-rates in the same proportion, i.e. all relative prices are taken to be unchanged and all relative wage-rates are taken to be unchanged when changes of prices or wage-rates are permitted (prescribed). A special case arises if the sellers do not wish to keep prices as high as the maxima permitted. In this case also we assume that the relative prices are constant. A natural extension of the assumptions made here is that everyone expects the prevailing prices (wages) to be maintained in the future. This assumption is also made here.

b) Foreign countries and payments to and by the state are disregarded, but the state enters into certain considerations as *deus ex machina*.

c) It is assumed that there is control of investment and allocation to investments, so that planned and permitted ("fixed") investments are carried out. The control of investments is taken to be a control of the demand for investment commodities, not a control which restricts the production of investment commodities — but more about this later.

d) The correlative defining of the concepts of income, and investment, and saving, is given unambiguous content by the use of a bookkeeping concept of income, in which the income for each single period is made out from the production for the period and the corresponding costs calculated in the conventional manner. A firm is thus taken to be trying to make its income for each individual period a maximum without taking into account the effects on the income of later periods. This allows us to work with simple cost curves of the usual type. It should be noticed that earning of income is reckoned entirely on production and not on sales. The commodities go from the firm's production department to the stocks (sales department) at full market-prices, and variable costs of stock-keeping and delivery from stocks are not taken into account. Indirect taxes are neglected (cf. b)). We shall work with gross income and not net income.

e) It is assumed that the production of the whole community can be lumped together and regarded as the production of one big enterprise, which produces one average-commodity at a definite average-price, and which has a definite cost structure. The period is still that of the Stockholm School, and is assumed to be just as long as the production period, so that input in a period results in output within the same period. Since we are considering the whole country as one big enterprise, we may take it that the variable costs consist only of wages. Correspondingly, it is also assumed that no wage-costs enter into the fixed costs. Furthermore, it is assumed that there is a common "aggregate" curve for the enterprises' (the big communal enterprise's) expected sales at alternative prices. This curve is called the *expected sales curve* in what follows.

According to the assumption stated in a) that all (relative) prices and wages are given, it follows that the expected cost curves and the expected sales curve can also be constructed from a horizontal summation of the costs and sales relations of all the individual enterprises—where the price of commodities becomes an average of all actual commodity prices, and where the quantities are weighted with their respective prices. A quantity index will be the abscissa. So long as the division of production into various commodities is unchanged, but only so long, no index problem arises. Some remarks on the consequences of the non-fulfilment of this last condition will be made later.

It is further assumed that there is a common curve for the commodity-buyers' total planned demand for commodities (purchases of commodities) at alternative prices. This curve will be called *the planned demand curve* and so must not be confused with the expected sales curve, since it would be a very strange coincidence if these two were the same. We shall later return to the properties of the planned demand curve. It is seen that a curve is involved which gives the relation between prices and the total effective demand for commodities.— The "fixed" investments only occur in the purchasing and stocking of commodities, and are made by particular persons. The entrepreneurs always plan to hold unchanging stocks; this latter assumption will now and again be relaxed, however.

f) When we talk about the expected sales curve and the planned demand curve, etc., as we did in e) for instance, we neglect certain difficulties in fixing the content of the concepts of supply and demand. These difficulties, as we saw in Chap. I, Section 9 and in Chap. III, arise when a monetary pressure of inflation exists. When nothing to the contrary is said, we shall in what follows take planned purchases = active attempts to purchase = optimum purchases, while the supply is taken to be the quantity of goods available. This means that supply = production actually carried out, the assumption in e) concerning stocks being taken into account. So it is approximately the "equilibrium aspect" of the problem of the inflationary gap which is dealt with in this chapter. We take the inflationary gap in the commodity-markets as being the optimum purchases of commodities minus the value of the production actually carried out, and the factor-gap as the optimum purchases of factors minus the value of the quantity of factor-services actually available. There are no difficulties in all this; but what is arbitrary is that planned purchases and active attempts

to purchase are put equal to optimum purchases. However, this is
done partly in order to be able to include the investment-saving relation in a simple way in the geometrical figures, and partly because it
is the optimum purchases, after all, which serve as the starting-point
for the fixing by the economic subjects of their planned purchases and
their active attempts to purchase. Even if these last two magnitudes
diverge from the optimum purchases, it should be possible to reckon
that they will normally change in the same direction as the optimum
purchases, so that it is possible to use the optimum purchases as an
expression for both the planned purchases and the active attempts to
purchase. However, we shall occasionally remark on the significance
of a disparity between optimum purchases and planned purchases and
active attempts to purchase. The above is not contradicted by the
fact that, as stated in c), we reckon with the existence of control of
investment which determines the extent of the "fixed" investments,
since what is taken as optimum purchases must be determined as
previously stated, with due regard to the quantitative restrictions
supposed to be given in the problem.—

With these general assumptions, it becomes necessary to distinguish
between two cases in this chapter. These are the case where there is
perfect competition in the commodity-markets, and the case where
there is monopoly in all the commodity-markets. This division is made
because we wish to have an opportunity to consider the significance
of the structure of the commodity-markets for anti-inflation policy.
This problem has not been dealt with to any great extent in the
literature of monetary theory nor in writings on inflation. The following
treatment, where only the cases of perfect competition and "all-round"
monopolism are taken into account, must naturally be considered as
very primitive in view of the rich scope of market situations between
monopoly and perfect competition, which have been discussed of late
and usually occur side by side in the same community. But what
follows in this and the following two chapters may be taken as a
modest introduction to the treatment of the implications of the market-
forms for monetary policy.

2. *The expected sales curve*

First we shall say a little about the entrepreneurs' expected demand for commodities, i.e. the entrepreneurs' *expected sales curve*.

If there is *perfect competition* in the commodity-markets, the summation of the horizontal expected sales curves of all the single firms will obviously give a horizontal expected sales curve for all the firms taken together. This common (aggregate) expected sales curve is shown in Fig. 1 as the horizontal line through A_1 at the given price p_0. This line is also called the *price-line*. That the entrepreneurs individually expect to be able to sell whatever quantities they are able to make

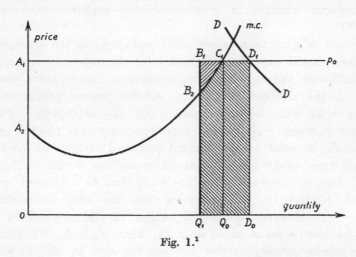

Fig. 1.[1]

available does not mean, of course, that they will expect to sell unlimited quantities of commodities during a given period. The actual sales expectations depend on how much they can put on the market. If forward-markets are neglected, it is impossible to sell more than is actually available for sale or more than may perhaps be reckoned as becoming available in the period. The actual expectation of sales of commodities is now dealt with under the heading of the supply of commodities.

3. *The planned supply of commodities*

If we understand by the planned supply of commodities the expected sales of commodities, it is seen at once that the expected sales of com-

---

[1] For the sake of clarity, all dimensions in this and the following figures are greatly distorted.

7

modities cannot be larger than the planned production of commodities, since it is in general assumed that the entrepreneurs always wish (plan) to hold their stocks unaltered from period to period. This assumption is adopted until something is said to the contrary.

Since there is a given wage-rate, say, w_0, (which is measured in $ per man per period), we can take it that the expected cost curves and the actual cost curves coincide with $m.c.$ as marginal cost curve. So unexpected changes in productivity are neglected (however, cf. Chap. VI).

Obviously it must seem worth-while (optimum) to the entrepreneurs that they should extend production until the expected marginal cost curve intersects the expected marginal revenue curve, which coincides here with the expected sales curve, and the planned production then becomes $= Q_0$ with a sales value $= Q_0 \cdot p_0 = A_1 O Q_0 C_1$. Planned payments of wages $= A_2 O Q_0 C_1$, corresponding to the planned production, which is equal to the planned (expected) volume of sales. The expected gross profit for the planned production is thus $= A_1 A_2 C_1$.

The planned payments of wages correspond to a planned employment of $A_2 O Q_0 C_1 / w_0 = L_0$ workers, since the wage per worker per period $= w_0$. However, the actual number of workers who offer themselves for hire is taken to be only L_1, where $L_0 > L_1$. The (ex post) wage-payments actually carried out are therefore $w_0 \cdot L_1$, so we may obviously find on the abscissa somewhere to the left of Q_0 a point Q_1, which is so chosen that $A_2 O Q_1 B_2 / w_0 = L_1$. Q_1 is then the production actually carried out. The ex post sales of commodities will therefore equal $A_1 O Q_1 B_1$ plus possible decreases in stocks, where there are stocks and the entrepreneurs are willing to let the stocks be depleted despite the planned constancy of stocks.

It follows that a reservation must be made in the assumption stated above that the expected and actual cost curves coincide. By the "actual", "ex post", curve we mean an aggregate of points which may alternatively be realized ex post. There is of course only one point which becomes actual in the given situation. This actual ex post point (when unexpected changes in productivity are neglected) must certainly be somewhere on $m.c.$, but it cannot lie to the right of B_2. The actual cost curve can therefore be said to be $A_2 B_2 B_1$, so that the marginal cost curve (from the ex post point of view), can be said to be vertical when B_2 is reached. This is quite a usual way of expressing the attainment of full employment.[1] But, as will appear from what follows, it would be equivalent to doing away with the whole problem of lack of labour-power, if the *ex ante* curves were taken to have this form. As a consequence, to the right of Q_1 a distinction between the actual and expected cost curves should be made. The expected cost curve will be vertical at B_2 only on the special assumption that the capacities (in the absolute sense) of all firms are fully taken up by the employment of the existing quantity of labour-power. But there seems no reason to believe that this would be the case in the situation prevailing in the Scandinavian countries, for example.[2] In countries heavily hit by war and in under-developed areas, the relationship might be considered to be just the opposite, that all production capacity would be fully utilized before all workers found employment, so that the expected marginal cost curve would then be perpendicular before full employment was achieved.[3] In the Scandinavian countries a serious shortage of raw-materials could have a similar effect. However, the problems which arise in these circumstances will not be considered here.

4. *Expected and realized income*

The actual gross profit is $A_1 A_2 B_2 B_1$, which is less than the expected profit, which was $A_1 A_2 C_1$, by an amount corresponding to the shaded three-corned area, $B_1 B_2 C_1$. The entrepreneurs thus have an unexpected loss of income *ex post*, which is equal to the expected profit on that part of the planned production which was not carried out owing to shortage of labour-power.

The situation for the workers is that they themselves know how much they supply, and what wages they receive. So, for the workers, we can assume (cf. Chap. II, Section 4) that the expected (*ex ante*) income = actual (*ex post*) income = $A_2 O Q_1 B_2$. It is seen that we have

---

[1] M. Kalecki, "What is Inflation", *Studies in War Economics*, The Oxford Institute of Statistics, Basil Blackwell, Oxford, 1947.

[2] cf. Alvin H. Hansen's discussion of American relationships, "Cost Functions and Full Employment", *The American Economic Review*, Vol. XXXVII, 1947.

[3] See E. S. Simpson, "Inflation, Deflation, and Employment in Italy", *The Review of Economic Studies*, 1949—50, Vol. XVII (3), p. 219 et seq.

Total gross income *ex ante* $= A_1 O Q_1 B_1 + B_1 B_2 C_1$;

total gross income *ex post* =

= total value of production *ex post* $= A_1 O Q_1 B_1$.

The difference between expected and realized gross income, or, if it is preferred, between expected gross income and the actual production of commodities, is consequently equal to the expected profit on the unrealizable production plans. This unexpected loss of income falls altogether on the entrepreneurs.

It should be noticed that, if we compare Fig. 1 with the notation used in the previous chapters, we have

$$^g A_0^c = A_1 O Q_0 C_1,$$

$$^g A_1^c = A_1 O Q_1 B_1 \; plus \; \text{possible decreases in stocks},$$

$$^l B_0^c = A_2 O Q_0 C_1,$$

$$^l B_1^c = \,^l A_0^w = \,^l A_1^w = A_2 O Q_1 B_2,$$

$$E_0^c = A_1 A_2 C_1,$$

$$E_1^c = A_1 A_2 B_2 B_1.$$

It follows that, if we suppose wages to be held fixed and the price to be allowed to rise (the price-line through A_1 is moved upwards), the planned production will increase as long as the marginal cost curve (*ex ante*) is not vertical. On the other hand the actually realizable production remains unchanged and equals Q_1, assuming, of course, that the supply of labour-power is not affected by the drop in real-wages. But this implies that expected gross income will increase faster than the actual value of production when wage-rates are constant and prices rising (even if everyone expects that the prevailing prices will not change). The workers' expected incomes are equal to $A_2 O Q_1 B_2$ and unaffected by rise in prices, but the entrepreneurs' expected incomes will be represented by the area between the *m.c.*-curve, the ordinate axis and the price-line, and this area ($A_1 A_2 C_1$) obviously increases with prices. The value of the actual production of commodities increases with the rectangle bounded by the axes, the vertical line through Q_1 and the price-line, whereas the total expected income increases with the same rectangle *plus* the three-cornered area bounded by the *m.c.*-curve, the price-line and the vertical line through Q_1, and this three-cornered area increases with price. Consequently the expected total gross income increases faster than the total value of production of commodities which can be carried out. This applies even more so to the expected gross profit (and yet more to the expected net profit). The contrary is true with fixed wages and falling prices. This will be used later on.[1]

We may also express this relation mathematically, which may be useful for the later treatment of the planned demand curve, among other things.

The marginal cost curve can be represented by

$$m.c. = F(Q),\qquad\qquad\text{(IV: 1)}$$

where Q is the planned quantity of production, or, since (as an optimum condition for the firm)

$$m.c. = p,\qquad\qquad\text{(IV: 2)}$$

where p is the price:

$$p = F(Q).\qquad\qquad\text{(IV: 3)}$$

Since we now wish to deal with p as independent variable, and assuming (IV: 3) to be monotone increasing, i.e.

$$\frac{dp}{dQ} = F'(Q) > 0,\qquad\qquad\text{(IV: 4)}$$

we get the following inversion of (IV: 3),

$$Q = f(p),\qquad\qquad\text{(IV: 5)}$$

where

$$\frac{dQ}{dp} = f'(p) > 0.\qquad\qquad\text{(IV: 6)}$$

The $m.c.$-curve meets the p-axis in $p = a$, $(O\,A_2 = a > 0)$. For the expected gross profit — E_0^c — we have

$$E_0^c = \int_a^p f(\tau)\,d\tau,\qquad\qquad\text{(IV: 7)}$$

from which, on differentiating with respect to p,

$$\frac{dE_0^c}{dp} = f(p).\qquad\qquad\text{(IV: 8)}$$

The actual value of the total production, V, is given by

---

[1] The text is written in such a way that the mathematical parts of this chapter, printed in compact form, may be passed over.

$$V = Q_1 \cdot p, \qquad \text{(IV: 9)}$$

and, differentiating,

$$\frac{dV}{dp} = Q_1 = f(p_1), \qquad \text{(IV: 10)}$$

where p_1 is the price at which the planned production is equal to the actually realizable production.

Since $p > p_1$ and $f(p)$ is monotone increasing[1], the expected gross profit, and the total expected income with it, must rise more sharply with increasing p than the value of the actual production, for the total expected workers' income is constant and $= Q_1 \cdot p_1 - \int\limits_a^{p_1} f(p) \, dp.$

What we have thus shown is that, assuming increasing marginal costs for productions greater than Q_1, the value of expected total income rises more sharply than the value of the production carried out, when prices and the planned production rise.

5. *The planned demand curve*

The reasoning progresses thus far without taking into account the demand for commodities which is planned by the purchasers of commodities, at the price p_0, if only the planned demand curve intersects the price-line through A_1 to the right of B_1, and the entrepreneurs expect to be able to sell at least that quantity (Q_0) which it pays them to produce at the given price; this latter, will always be the case when there is perfect competition.

If it is now assumed that the *planned demand curve*, i.e. the purchases of commodities planned by the buyers of commodities at alternative prices is as in Fig. 1, where it is DD, the quantity in demand at the given price p_0 is D_0 and its value $A_1 O D_0 D_1$. As long as the price remains constant it is only one point of this curve, D_1, which is of interest, and the rest of the curve is superfluous. Since the curve itself is later used in the discussion, however, and since it shows how the point D_1 is determined, we shall go further into the derivation of the curve.

---

[1] It should be noticed, that the assumption that the expected marginal costs are increasing everywhere, is not fundamental to our arguments. This assumption is introduced only to simplify the mathematics of the case. For the following results to be arrived at it suffices that expected marginal costs are increasing for productions greater than (or equal to) Q_1. And this is, I think, a reasonable assumption.

An ordinary demand curve tells us what quantities of commodities will be bought at various possible prices—other things being equal. The demand curve which is used here should likewise tell us what are the total demands for commodities at alternative prices, and so give us the effective demand for commodities as a function of price. However, the difficulty is that "other things" are not equal when there is change of price, because when wage-rates are fixed, the distribution of income changes with price, and that implies a displacement of the ordinary demand curve. So we must construct the demand curve in such a way that at each price we determine the corresponding total expected income and its division among the two groups, workers and capitalists. If we know the consumption-ratio for each group (perhaps as a function of the expected nominal income, real income, previous real income, or the like), we get the planned demand for consumer-goods corresponding to the given price. If we then add the demand for investment commodities (perhaps as a function of the price), we get the total effective demand for commodities corresponding to the given price. If we do this for each single price, we arrive at the complete planned demand curve, point by point.

Let us express this with the help of the functional relationship used previously (IV: 5).

For the sake of simplicity we now assume that the planned purchases of consumer-goods is such a function of expected income that the average consumption-ratio is constant.[1] This implies that it does not matter if we regard the outlays in connec-

---

[1] This assumption, that the planned consumption is a function of expected income is essential for a couple of points in the following reasoning. Therefore there is some cause for noticing that the assumption is disputable and that it is possible to consider the planned consumption as determined in other ways, e.g. as a function of the previous periods' actual income, or, for those who are very prosperous or very poor, determined without any connection whatever with either expected income or actual income in the previous periods. It need hardly be added that the assumption in the text is neither strengthened nor weakened by investigations of the type which it is customary to use for the determination of the consumption function, because these always deal with relations between *ex post* magnitudes. The connection between share prices and consumption which is sometimes pointed out can perhaps be credited to the assumption in the text. The interview method could, however, be used to test our hypothesis.

A hypothesis of a similar, but much more extreme, relationship between changes in expected income and planned saving is put forward by George Katona, "Effect of Income Changes on the Rate of Saving", *The Review of Economics and Statistics*, Vol. XXXI, May 1949.

tion with consumption purchases as functions of nominal or real income. The capitalists' consumption-ratio is called c^c and the workers' c^w, c^w being $> c^c$. In the case of investment commodities we may distinguish several situations;—where control holds the total value of investments constant; where control holds the quantity of investments Q_I constant; and where the quantity of investments is rising with prices.[1] The question of the dependence of investments on prices is of special importance when the slope of the demand curve at a given price is being discussed.

D_0 is the total planned quantity of commodities in demand, and I_0, as before, the total value of planned investments.

We have

$$D_0 \cdot p = E_0^c \cdot c^c + E_0^w \cdot c^w + I_0, \qquad (IV: 11)$$

or

$$D_0 = \frac{c^c}{p} \int_a^p f(\tau)\, d\tau + \frac{c^w}{p} \left(Q_1 \cdot p_1 - \int_a^{p_1} f(p)\, dp \right) + \frac{I_0}{p}. \qquad (IV: 12)$$

Here we have the total planned quantitative demand expressed in terms of p and the known magnitudes c^c, c^w, Q_1, p_1, a and I_0, together with the function $f(p)$. If we wish to find the quantity in demand at the price p_0, we merely put $p = p_0$ in (IV: 12). We thereby find the point D_1 in Fig. 1.

Next we come to the question of the slope of the planned demand curve at a given price. It can be shown that the curve can have either a positive or a negative slope. This can be seen with the help of the relation which has just been pointed out, that the capitalists' expected gross income, and the total expected income along with it, rises more steeply than the value of production carried out when wage-rates are fixed and prices rising. The change of income-distribution must be to the advantage of the capitalists, whose consumption-ratio is low (corporate saving taken into account here), and to the disadvantage of the workers, whose consumption-ratio is higher, and the consumption-ratio for the whole community must thereby fall. Yet the total expected income of the community rises more steeply than the value of production, and the result may obvious be either a rise or a fall in the quantity of consumer-goods which are in demand. Also we have the effect of the dependence of the demand for investment commodities on prices.

Taking everything into consideration in this way, it is seen that the

---

[1] Bertil Ohlin, in *The Problem of Employment Stabilization*, Chap. 1., points out, that intended investments may increase with the shortage of labour power. This is, however, equivalent to the assumption that investments increase with prices, because the factor-gap is an increasing function of prices.

planned demand curve can have either a positive or negative slope at a given point (at a given price).

A more exact idea of the possibilities for the shape of the curve may be obtained from equation (IV: 12), which determines the total planned demand as a function of price. We must distinguish between different alternatives in considering the fixing of the magnitude of investments.

(1)   The total quantity of investment is constant at Q_I.
The demand equation becomes

$$D_0 = \frac{c^c}{p} \cdot \int\limits_a^p f(\tau)\, d\tau + \frac{c^w}{p} \left(Q_1 \cdot p_1 - \int\limits_a^{p_1} f(p)\, dp \right) + Q_I. \qquad \text{(IV: 13)}$$

The slope of the curve is given by

$$\frac{d D_0}{d p} = \frac{c^c \cdot \left(p \cdot f(p) - \int\limits_a^p f(\tau)\, d\tau \right) - c^w \cdot \left(Q_1 \cdot p_1 - \int\limits_a^{p_1} f(p)\, dp \right)}{p^2}, \qquad \text{(IV: 14)}$$

(IV: 13) being continuous and differentiable in the interval $p_1 \leqq p < \infty$.

Since the denominator of the right hand side of (IV: 14) is always greater than zero, we have

$$\frac{d D_0}{d p} \gtreqless 0 \qquad \text{(IV: 15)}$$

according as

$$c^c \cdot \left(p \cdot f(p) - \int\limits_a^p f(\tau)\, d\tau \right) - c^w \cdot \left(Q_1 \cdot p_1 - \int\limits_a^{p_1} f(p)\, dp \right) \gtreqless 0, \qquad \text{(IV: 16)}$$

or as

$$c^c \gtreqless c^w \cdot \frac{Q_1 \cdot p_1 - \int\limits_a^{p_1} f(p)\, dp}{Q \cdot p - \int\limits_a^p f(\tau)\, d\tau}. \qquad \text{(IV: 17)}$$

Equation (IV: 17) expresses that $d D_0/d p \gtreqless 0$, according to whether the capitalists' consumption-ratio is greater than, equal to, or less than the workers' consumption-ratio multiplied by the ratio of actual to planned payments of wages.

As an extreme case we can, firstly, take that for which $p = p_1$, i.e. where the planned production is equal to the realizable production. Here the ratio of actual payments of wages to planned payments of wages becomes = 1, and

$$c^c < c^w, \qquad\qquad\qquad \text{(IV: 18)}$$

according to the assumptions.

We are only interested in the shape of the planned total demand curve for prices greater than or equal to p_1, so the total demand curve in this case begins to rise to the left like an ordinary demand curve.

When the price rises ($> p_1$), the actual payments of wages will be constant, whereas the planned payments of wages will change with p. If we call the planned payments of wages $^lB_0^c$, as we did before, we get the equation

$$\frac{d\,^lB_0^c}{d\,p} = f'(p) \cdot p + f(p) - f(p) = f'(p) \cdot p. \qquad\qquad \text{(IV: 19)}$$

Since $p > 0$ and $f'(p)$ also > 0, in accordance with the assumptions, $d\,^lB_0^c/d\,p > 0$, and the planned payments of wages increase steadily with p. Sooner or later, as p increases, we thus come to (because actual payments of wages $= {}^lB_1^c$) a price at which

$$c^c = c^w \cdot \frac{^lB_1^c}{^lB_0^c}, \qquad\qquad\qquad \text{(IV: 20)}$$

and for higher prices

$$c^c > c^w \cdot \frac{^lB_1^c}{^lB_0^c}. \qquad\qquad\qquad \text{(IV: 21)}$$

Thus, for increasing p, the curve for the total planned demand for commodities must sooner or later become vertical and afterwards turn back again and rise to the right.

If it is agreed that the marginal cost curve (*ex ante*) must finally become vertical, i.e. $f'(p)$ approaches 0 for sufficiently large values of p, it must be taken into consideration that the planned payments of wages, $Q \cdot p - \int\limits_a^p f(\tau)\,d\,\tau$, may approach a definite limiting value. We get the following three cases:

i) $^lB_0^c$ approaches a definite limiting value which is

$$< \frac{c^w}{c^c} \cdot {}^lB_1^c. \qquad\qquad\qquad \text{(IV: 22)}$$

If this is the case, $d\,D_0/d\,p$ will always be < 0, and the planned demand curve consequently everywhere rises to the left.

ii) $^lB_0^c$ approaches a definite limiting value which is

$$= \frac{c^w}{c^c} \cdot {}^lB_1^c. \qquad\qquad\qquad \text{(IV: 23)}$$

In this case, $d\,D_0/d\,p$ approaches 0 and the demand curve becomes vertical.

iii) $^{l}B_0^{c}$ approaches a definite limiting value

$$> \frac{c^{w}}{c^{c}} \cdot {}^{l}B_1^{c}, \qquad \text{(IV:24)}$$

or is divergent. In this case $d D_0/d p$ always becomes > 0, sooner or later, and the planned demand curve consequently turns back again and rises to the right.

(2) The total value of the investments is constant $= I_0$.

The equation for the planned demand curve becomes (cf. (IV: 12))

$$D_0 = \frac{c^{c}}{p} \cdot \int\limits_{a}^{p} f(\tau)\, d\tau + \frac{c^{w}}{p} \left(Q_1 \cdot p_1 - \int\limits_{a}^{p_1} f(p)\, d p \right) + \frac{I_0}{p}, \qquad \text{(IV: 25)}$$

and

$$\frac{d D_0}{d p} = \frac{c^{c} \cdot (p \cdot f(p) - \int\limits_{a}^{p} f(\tau)\, d\tau) - c^{w} \cdot (Q_1 \cdot p_1 - \int\limits_{a}^{p_1} f(p)\, d p) - I_0}{p^2}. \qquad \text{(IV: 26)}$$

In the same way as in case (1), there are conditions for $d D_0/d p$ to be $\gtreqless 0$, and it may be seen that this case offers just the same possibilities for the shape of the planned demand curve as did case (1).

(3) Alternatively, we may suppose that the total quantity of investments increases with p. This is not very probable when there is control of investment, which is likely to limit the quantity of investment quite stringently when prices rise. The situation may, however, occur, either when an increase in the quantity of investment is purposely allowed, in the belief that the price increases which are permitted at the same time will bring the system nearer equilibrium and therefore make room, so to speak, for more investments; or because the control of investment has as a "principle" for its limiting of investments that only a certain percentage of the applications for investment permits are refused.

It is easily seen that, if only the quantity of desired (permitted) investments increases sufficiently sharply with the price, the planned demand curve may be considered as rising to the right along the whole of its length.

(4) Lastly it should be stated that justifiable objections may be made against the assumption we have put forward about the consumption-ratio's c^{c} and c^{w}. In the first place these were taken to be constant. However it is probably more reasonable to assume that the consumption-ratio at a certain nominal income increases with increasing price, or that the consumption-ratio (the average one) falls with rising nominal income at a given price. But it is not difficult to see that this does not provide other possibilities for the shape of the planned demand curve, and neither, on the other hand, does it invalidate any of the possibilities already considered.

Secondly, we have taken $c^c < c^w$. However, it is by no means unthinkable that both c^c and c^w will be greater than 1 during repressed inflation, or even under open inflation for that matter. And if both c^c and c^w are greater than 1, we could also quite well imagine that $c^c > c^w$, simply because the capitalists are better able to finance a consumption in excess of their current income. If $c^c > c^w$, it is at once apparent, from (IV: 17), that $d D_0 / d p$ must always be > 0, i.e. the planned demand curve must rise to the right along the whole of its length.

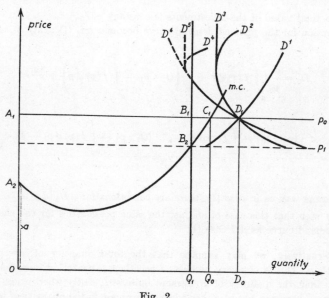

Fig. 2.

The possibilities for the shape of the planned demand curve, which were visualized in (1), (2), (3), and (4), may be illustrated by the following Fig. 2, where the significance of the letters used is the same as in Fig. 1.

If the quantity in demand at the price p_0 is equal to D_0, we must take as a consequence of what has been said that the passing of the planned demand curve through the point D_1 is one of the six typical cases $D^1, \ldots, D^6$.

D^1 illustrates the possibility considered in (3) and (4), where the planned demand curve rises to the right along the whole of its length.

D^2 illustrates the possibility mentioned in both (1) and (2), that the lower part of the planned demand curve rises to the left, but the curve turns back again as the price rises.

D^3 illustrates the possibility mentioned in ii) that the planned demand curve rises increasingly sharply to the left and becomes vertical.

D^4 is the same shape of curve as D^2, except that the demand quantity at which the curve turns back is less than Q_1. Since our general assumptions break down when $D_0 < Q_1$ (there is then no monetary pressure of inflation in the sense defined in Chap. I), we are interested only in the part of the curve to the right of Q_1, that is, a lower branch, where we begin from the lowest price (p_1) and consider the effect of increasing price and an upper branch, where we begin from the highest price and consider the effect of decreasing price.

D^5 corresponds to D^3 in the same way as D^4 corresponds to D^2.

D^6 illustrates the possibility mentioned in i) that the planned demand curve rises to the left along the whole of its length.

6. *The geometrical illustration of the gaps*

Now that the planned demand curve and its shape has been dealt with, we can go on to say that, as the curve is drawn in Fig. 1, the planned demand (planned purchases of commodities) will be the magnitude D_0 at the price p_0, and consequently

$$^gB_0^c + C_0^{c+w} = A_1\,O\,D_0\,D_1,$$

because $^gB_0^c$ here only consists of the demand for investment commodities and we have disregarded possible demand for commodities on the part of the state.

We now have (Fig. 1):

$$\underbrace{A_1\,O\,D_0\,D_1}_{\substack{\text{value of planned de-}\\\text{mand for commodities}}} - \underbrace{A_1\,O\,Q_0\,C_1}_{\substack{\text{value of planned supply}\\\text{of commodities (expec-}\\\text{ted sales)}}} = \underbrace{C_1\,Q_0\,D_0\,D_1}_{\substack{ex\ ante\ \text{commodity-}\\\text{gap}}}, \quad \text{(IV: 27)}$$

together with

$$\underbrace{A_2\,O\,Q_0\,C_1}_{\substack{\text{value of planned de-}\\\text{mand for labour}}} - \underbrace{A_2\,O\,Q_1\,B_2}_{\substack{\text{value of planned supply}\\\text{of labour}}} = \underbrace{B_2\,Q_1\,Q_0\,C_1}_{\text{factor-gap}}, \quad \text{(IV: 28)}$$

and

$$\underbrace{A_1\,O\,D_0\,D_1}_{\substack{\text{value of planned de-}\\\text{mand for commodities}}} - \underbrace{A_1\,O\,Q_1\,B_1}_{\substack{\text{value of actual produc-}\\\text{tion (available quanti-}\\\text{ty of commodities)}}} = \underbrace{B_1\,Q_1\,D_0\,D_1}_{\substack{\text{inflationary gap in the}\\\text{commodity-markets}}}. \quad \text{(IV: 29)}$$

The assumptions set out in Section 1 above should now be borne in mind. They imply that the relevant model here is the one without public finances and without foreign trade, which was used in the algebraic approach in Chap. II, Section 6 and in Chap. III, Section 5; and that $I_0 - I_1$ is equal to zero when stocks of finished commodities do not exist (or where the stocks are preserved unchanged without regard to the possibility of sales), and is equal to the unexpected decrease in stocks where these exist. Then, the general relation between the three gaps given in Chap. III, Section 5, (equation (III: 6)), is reduced to the expression:

the inflationary gap in the commodity-markets = the *ex ante* commodity-gap + the factor-gap—unexpected increase of income for capitalists. (III: 6)

In Fig. 1 this corresponds to

$$B_1 Q_1 D_0 D_1 = C_1 Q_0 D_0 D_1 + B_2 Q_1 Q_0 C_1 + B_1 B_2 C_1 \qquad \text{(IV: 30)}$$

which is seen at once to be valid.

In general we had

$$I_0 - S_0 = \text{the } ex \ ante \text{ commodity-gap} + \text{the factor-gap.} \qquad \text{(II: 5)}$$

This, in terms of Fig. 1 is

$$I_0 - S_0 = B_2 Q_1 D_0 D_1 C_1, \qquad \text{(IV: 31)}$$

i.e. the difference between planned investment and planned saving is equal to the five-cornered area shaded N.W.-S.E.

As is reasonable to expect, all the other equations from Chap. II, Section 6, and Chap. III, Section 5, which deals with the difference between I_0 and S_0 have corresponding results in terms of Fig. 1, if the assumptions of this chapter are taken into account.

As was pointed out in the algebraic discussion (Chap. III, Section 5), if we take into account the functional relationships which may be set up, there is nothing to prevent $I_0 - S_0$ being < 0 at the same time as both the inflationary gap in the commodity-markets and the factor-gap are positive. This may be illustrated by the following Fig. 3.

The factor-gap[1] is seen to be equal to $B_2 Q_1 Q_0 C_1$, here as in Fig. 1,

---

[1] See Chap. V, A, Section 1.

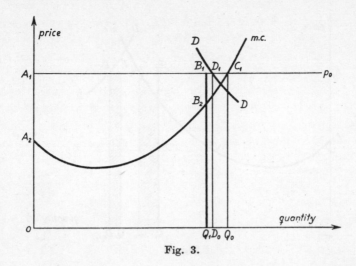

Fig. 3.

whereas the inflationary gap in the commodity-market $= B_1 Q_1 D_0 D_1$; both are consequently positive. However, since the planned demand curve cuts the price-line to the left of C_1, the *ex ante* commodity-gap is now negative and numerically equal to $D_1 D_0 Q_0 C_1$, and we have

$$I_0 - S_0 = -D_1 D_0 Q_0 C_1 + B_2 Q_1 Q_0 C_1.$$

It may be seen from the figure that $D_1 D_0 Q_0 C_1$ can be larger than $B_2 Q_1 Q_0 C_1$, so that $I_0 - S_0$ can be less than zero, even if both the inflationary gap in the commodity-markets and the factor-gap are positive.

In order to illustrate further the difference between planned investment and saving, we shall show what happens when we drop the assumption hitherto used that the entrepreneurs plan to preserve their existing stocks unaltered.

Let us suppose, in Fig. 4, that the entrepreneurs, instead of planning to preserve their existing stocks, plan a decrease in stocks equal in quantity to $Q_0 Q_F$, i.e. it is planned to lower stocks by an amount represented in value by $C_1 Q_0 Q_F F_1$. From this it follows, (cf. what was stated above), that the difference between planned investment and planned saving is given by

$$I_0 - S_0 = B_2 Q_1 Q_0 C_1 + F_1 Q_F D_0 D_1, \tag{IV: 32}$$

i.e. the shaded area.

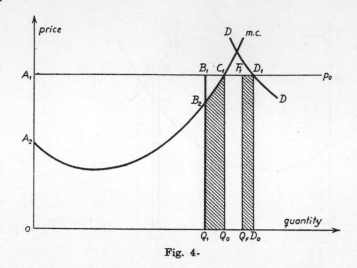

Fig. 4.

This means that the difference between planned investment and saving is to be distinguished even more from the inflationary gap $B_1 Q_1 D_0 D_1$ than it was in Fig. 1 with the assumptions holding good there. Yet other assumptions about planned stocks could be made. We have only attempted here to show the way in which this question may be handled by means of figures.

In the previous part of this chapter we have assumed that planned purchases = active attempts to purchase = optimum purchases. Now we shall consider the significance of dropping the assumption that planned purchases = optimum purchases, so far as the labour-market is concerned. But we continue to assume that planned purchases = active attempts to purchase in the labour-market, and that planned purchases = active attempts to purchase = optimum purchases in the commodity-markets. When the quantity of labour-services actually available in a period is less than the quantity of labour-services which would be optimum for the entrepreneurs to put into production, it is conceivable that the entrepreneurs give up their objective of obtaining the optimum amount of labour-services, and therefore plan an employment (and production) which is less than the optimum. We may also take it that there is agreement between the entrepreneurs not to take labour-power from one another[1], which implies that each entrepreneur

---

[1] For instance, such agreements were concluded after the second World War between the employers in the metal industries in Denmark.

only plans to employ just that number of workers which he succeeds in engaging from the supply in the market. Even in such circumstances the planned employment (= planned purchases = active attempts to purchase) may exceed the actual supply of labour-services, because the workers engaged by each enterprise may unexpectedly (for the enterprise) work shorter hours per period than the normal hours for the period; this is the effect of the well-known "absenteeism", which

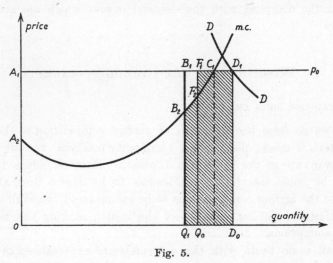

Fig. 5.

has had no little importance for the volume of production in all countries which have experienced repressed inflation. This is illustrated in Fig. 5.

In this figure we have that the *ex ante* commodity-gap = $F_1 Q_0 D_0 D_1$, while the factor-gap = $B_2 Q_1 Q_0 F_2$; so that $I_0 - S_0 = B_2 Q_1 D_0 D_1 F_1 F_2$, which is the shaded area. The unexpected loss of income for the capitalists = $B_1 B_2 F_2 F_1$.

As is apparent, this does not essentially alter anything in the formal presentation, but it should be remembered that the demand curve, which gives the planned purchases (= the active attempts to purchase = the optimum purchases), is in general not unaffected by the change in assumptions. Now it must be calculated on the basis of an expected profit (at the price p_0), which is = $A_1 A_2 F_2 F_1$ instead of $A_1 A_2 C_1$.

We may drop further assumptions about planned purchases = active attempts to purchase = optimum purchases, and consider only the active attempts to purchase, or the optimum purchases without having them equal to the planned purchases. This does not involve any difficulties in the algebraic or geometric presentation. The main thing is that the consumption-ratio used in the calculation of the planned demand curve shall be the one which is relevant for the particular point of view. However, it is clear that it is not possible to express in a simple manner the difference between planned investment and planned saving in the diagrams with the demand curves which are arrived at in this way.

B. Monopolism in the commodity-markets

7. *The expected sales curve*

When we go from the situation of perfect competition to the one in which there is monopolism in all commodity-markets, various complications crop up in the geometric approach. However, since there do seem to be some interesting conclusions to be drawn from this case in spite of the further complications to be encountered, we shall examine it and illustrate the construction of the model, making the necessary further assumptions.

We shall again begin with the entrepreneurs' expectations of the demand for commodities, i.e. what we have called the *expected sales curve*.

By definition, the difference between the case of perfect competition and the case of monopolism in all the commodity-markets is that, whereas, with perfect competition, each single enterprise's expected sales curve is horizontal, when there is monopolism each single enterprise's expected sales curve falls to the right. As a consequence, upon summation to an expected sales curve for all enterprises together, the total common expected sales curve falls to the right when there is all-round monopolism. There are two things to be noticed here.

In the first place, it is at once obvious that we are obliged to assume that there is not perfect competition in any one commodity-market, for, if there were just one market with perfect competition (however insignificant), upon summation the common expected sales curve would always be horizontal, for every price.

Secondly, it should be noticed that a customary expected sales curve for an enterprise under monopolism will often be affected by simultaneous changes in the prices of commodities produced by other enterprises. We have confined ourselves to the case in which all relative prices remain fixed the whole time, so the individual expected sales curves which are summed must be those expected sales curves which the enterprises formulate on the assumption that all other commodity prices change in proportion to the enterprise's own prices. Where this is of importance for the sales curves of the entrepreneurs, it must, of course, tend to make the individual sales curves, and with them the total curve, steeper than would otherwise be the case.

If maximum prices are introduced, the part of each single enterprises "original" expected sales curve lying abové the maximum price is cut off and replaced by a horizontal line at the given maximum price. So we find that the "aggregate", "controlled", expected sales curve becomes horizontal when the "original" expected sales curves have all reached their respective maximum price levels.

It must also be remembered as in the case of perfect competition, that this expected sales curve only expresses how much the entrepreneurs reckon, at most, to be able to sell at a given price in the given period, but does not always say what are the true sales expectations of the entrepreneurs. These depend on how much of the commodity the entrepreneurs have to put on the market, or, at any rate, reckon to make available or want to make available for sale during the period. For the determination of the expected sales we must therefore refer to the following treatment of the planned supply of commodities.

Fig. 6 includes the common expected sales curve $F^1 F$, which, however, is changed to $A_1 F_1 F$ on introduction of maximum price p_0. The original expected sales curve of course exists even when there is maximum price, but the upper part just becomes irrelevant when a maximum price is introduced. Q_1 is still the greatest possible production.

Corresponding to each individual expected sales curve there is an expected marginal revenue curve, and a total common marginal revenue curve is attained upon summation. With the adopted assumptions about fixed relative prices and a given composition of production, this common expected marginal revenue curve corresponds to a marginal revenue curve calculated direct from the common expected sales curve.

The original expected marginal revenue curve $m.R. m.R.$ is indicated

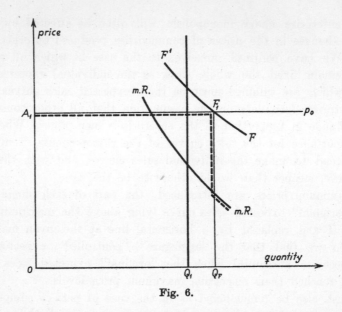

Fig. 6.

by an unbroken line in Fig. 6. The introduction of a maximum price leads to a change in shape of the expected marginal revenue curve, since it becomes horizontal at the level of the maximum price, as far as the original expected sales curve at the quantity Q_F. After that the curve turns vertically downward as far as the original expected marginal revenue curve, and then bends again and follows the original expected marginal revenue curve down to the right (the broken line in Fig. 6).

8. *The planned supply of commodities*

As in the case of perfect competition, we understand by the planned supply of commodities the expected sales of commodities (not expected possible sales), and since it is assumed that the entrepreneurs always wish to preserve their stocks intact, the expected sales of commodities cannot be greater than the planned production. As will be shown, the expected sales of commodities will in certain cases be determined from the original expected sales curve; in other cases, however, the original expected sales curve is irrelevant for this purpose.

Since we assume that the expected sales curve falls to the right throughout its length, and the expected marginal cost curve rises to

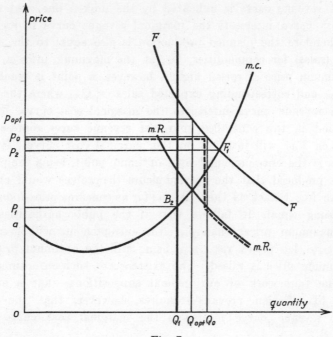

Fig. 7.

the right throughout its length, these two curves may intersect, at the price p_2, say.

It is easily seen that the price p_2 serves as a demarcation line between that range of prices where the expected sales of commodities is determined by the original expected sales curve, and the range of prices where the original expected sales curve is of no importance for the expected sales of commodities. At prices between p_1 and p_2, the horizontal part of the controlled expected sales curve continues to the right beyond the marginal cost curve, and the expected sales of commodities (= the planned production) are determined by the intersection of the price-line with the marginal cost curve, since the price-line here is the relevant part of the marginal revenue curve, without regard to how far to the right the original expected sales curve lies. For maximum prices higher than p_2 the controlled expected sales curve bends down to the right before the marginal cost curve is reached, and the horizontal part of the marginal revenue curve is therefore also finished before the marginal cost curve is reached. At the price p_0 the marginal revenue curve is indicated by the broken line, and the marginal cost curve intersects the marginal revenue curve in its vertical part. Therefore the planned production is also equal to the expected demand (sales) for commodities, Q_0, at the maximum price p_0. When the maximum price is raised higher, however, a point is reached at a price p_{opt} and corresponding expected sales $= Q_{opt}$ where the original marginal revenue curve intersects the marginal cost curve. Here the lower bend in the controlled marginal revenue curve represented by the broken line will just fall on the marginal cost curve. It is seen that this is the entrepreneurs' own optimum point, being the price and quantity produced that the entrepreneurs themselves would choose, if they were free to act as they like as far as concerns price-fixing, other things being equal. It follows that if the public authorities permit higher maximum prices than p_{opt}, the entrepreneurs will have no inducement to let prices rise, p_{opt} being still the optimum price when the maximum price is raised. The existence of such an optimum price within the framework of our general suppositions—that a monetary pressure of inflation prevails—requires, however, that the original marginal revenue curve intersects the marginal cost curve to the right of B_2.

So we have the result that, if the maximum price rises from p_1, the planned production will first rise with the price in a way determined by the intersection of the price-line with the marginal cost curve, until the price p_2 is reached. Thereafter the planned production will fall with rising maximum price in a way determined by the intersection of the price-line with the expected sales curve, until a price is eventually reached, which is the entrepreneurs' own optimum price p_{opt}. Further increase in the maximum price will not be followed by a raising of the price offered by the entrepreneurs, nor by a fall in the planned production. If such an optimum price is not attained, at last a maximum price will be reached for which the planned production is equal to the possible production Q_1.[1]

---

[1] It is very often asserted that price-control tends to have an expansive effect, due to the fact that price-control signifies lower prices than the optimum for the entrepreneurs and so a transfer of income to the workers who have a higher consumption-ratio than the entrepreneurs. However, it follows from what has already been said, that maximum prices also have an expansive effect in quite another direction, namely on planned production and so on the planned demand for labour-services.

9. *The planned demand curve*

The construction of the planned demand curve for commodities is carried out in much the same way as in the case of perfect competition, in that expected wage income and expected profits are determined for each individual price, whereupon, multiplying by the respective consumption-ratio's of workers and capitalists, we arrive at the demand for consumer-goods planned at the price concerned. When the volume of investment is determined in some way or other and added to this, the total demand for commodities results. We have to distinguish between two different cases.

When the price is between p_1 and p_2 (see Fig. 7), the determination of the planned demand curve is quite analogous to the perfect competition case, because in this price interval the original expected sales curve lies to the right of the marginal cost curve, so that the planned production and the expected profit are determined entirely by the horizontal part of the controlled expected sales curve. The system appears, in this interval, to be similar to perfect competition. For the position and shape of the planned demand curve, reference can therefore be made to the treatment under A, Section 5.

The calculation is somewhat different for prices between p_2 and (perhaps) p_{opt}. Whereas with perfect competition the expected gross profit is represented by an area between the ordinate axis, the marginal cost curve and the price-line, under monopolism, when the price is higher than p_2, the expected gross profit is represented by an area between the ordinate axis, the marginal cost curve, the vertical part of the controlled marginal revenue curve and the price-line. Since the vertical part of the marginal revenue curve moves to the left when the maximum price rises, the expected gross profit may obviously increase more or less sharply than the price, and the effect on the planned demand for commodities becomes uncertain.

For, if we assume in connection with Fig. 7, that the price is equal to p_{opt} to start with, the planned production being Q_{opt} and then maximum prices are introduced which are lower than p_{opt} (they must be lower as a rule, otherwise there is no point in introducing them), the result will be an *increase* in the planned production. It is only when the maximum price is fixed below the price which is determined by the intersection of the expected marginal cost curve and original expected marginal revenue curve that the planned production becomes less than Q_{opt}.

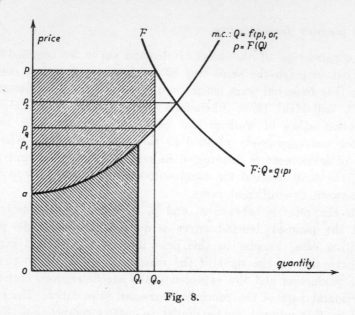

Fig. 8.

Therefore, we continue with the mathematical approach used in A, Section 5, for the calculation of the planned demand curve for prices between p_2 and p_{opt}. We now introduce a new function, which gives the quantity of commodities expected to be sold, Q, as a function of the price p:

$$Q = g(p), \qquad \text{(IV: 33)}$$

where

$$\frac{dQ}{dp} = g'(p) < 0. \qquad \text{(IV: 34)}$$

We have now, as before, that the workers' expected income (= actual payments of wages), which is indicated by the area shaded N.W.—S.E. in the figure, is given by

$$E_0^w = {}^l B_1^c = Q_1 \cdot p_1 - \int_a^{p_1} f(p)\,dp. \qquad \text{(IV: 35)}$$

On the other hand, the expected profit (the meaning of p_Q being seen from Fig. 8) is given by

$$E_0^c = p \cdot Q - \left(p_Q \cdot Q - \int_a^{p_Q} f(\tau)\,d\tau \right), \qquad \text{(IV: 36)}$$

which is denoted in the figure by the area shaded S.W.—N.E. Or, since $Q = g(p)$ and $p_Q = F(Q)$, and therefore

$$p_Q = F\left(g\left(p\right)\right): \tag{IV: 37}$$

$$E_0^c = g\left(p\right) \cdot p - F\left(g\left(p\right)\right) \cdot g\left(p\right) + \int_a^{F(g(p))} f\left(\tau\right) d\tau. \tag{IV: 38}$$

From this we have the demand equation for $p > p_2$:

$$D_0 = \frac{c^c}{p}\left(p \cdot g\left(p\right) - F\left(g\left(p\right)\right) \cdot g\left(p\right) + \int_a^{F(g(p))} f\left(\tau\right) d\tau\right) +$$

$$+ \frac{c^w}{p}\left(p_1 \cdot Q_1 - \int_a^{p_1} f\left(p\right) dp\right) + \frac{I_0}{p}. \tag{IV: 39}$$

Differentiating with respect to p we have (since we provisionally put $I_0 = Q_I \cdot p$, where Q_I is constant) that

$$\frac{dD_0}{dp} = \frac{c^c}{p^2} \cdot \left\{p^2 \cdot g'\left(p\right) - F\left(g\left(p\right)\right) \cdot g'\left(p\right) \cdot p + F\left(g\left(p\right)\right) \cdot g\left(p\right) - \int_a^{F(g(p))} f\left(\tau\right) d\tau\right\} -$$

$$- \frac{c^w}{p^2} \cdot \left\{p_1 \cdot Q_1 - \int_a^{p_1} f\left(p\right) dp\right\}, \tag{IV: 40}$$

from which it follows that

$$\frac{dD_0}{dp} \gtreqless 0, \tag{IV: 41}$$

according as

$$\frac{c^c}{{}^l B_1^c} \cdot \left\{{}^l B_0^c + p \cdot g'\left(p\right)\left[p - F\left(g\left(p\right)\right)\right]\right\} \gtreqless c^w. \tag{IV: 42}$$

It is seen at once that when $p \to p_2$ from above, $F\left(p\left(g\right)\right) \to p_2$, that is

$$\frac{c^c}{{}^l B_1^c}\left\{{}^l B_0^c + p \cdot g'\left(p\right) \cdot \left[p - F\left(g\left(p\right)\right)\right]\right\} \to c^c \cdot \frac{{}^l B_0^c}{{}^l B_1^c} \gtreqless c^w, \tag{IV: 43}$$

because $c^c < c^w$ and ${}^l B_0^c > {}^l B_1^c$.

In the neighbourhood of the price p_2 (from above) the planned demand curve can therefore have either positive or negative slope or be vertical. Furthermore, from comparison of (IV: 13) with (IV: 39) and (IV: 14) with (IV: 40), it follows that the planned demand curve is continuous and differentiable at the point $p = p_2$. dD_0/dp tends to the same value whether p_2 is approached from above (IV: 40) or from below (IV: 14), and the same applies to the value of D_0 (cf. (IV: 13) and (IV: 39)).

112

If $g'(p)$, which is < 0, does not tend to 0 for large p, we have, for p ($> p_2$) sufficiently large but less than p_{opt} that $g(p) = Q_1$ and therefore $^lB_0^c = {}^lB_1^c$, so that

$$\frac{c^c}{{}^lB_1^c} \cdot \{{}^lB_0^c + p \cdot g'(p) \cdot [p - F(g(p))]\} = c^c \cdot \left\{1 + \frac{p \cdot g'(p) \cdot [p - F(g(p))]}{{}^lB_1^c}\right\} < c^w,$$

(IV: 44)

c^c being $< c^w$, $g'(p) < 0$ and $p > F(g(p))$.

So, if p_{opt} is not reached before $g(p) = Q_1$, the planned demand curve must have a negative slope above a certain price.

If p_{opt} is reached before $g(p) = Q_1$, the entrepreneurs will not follow the rising maximum price, and therefore the planned demand curve cannot be drawn for prices higher than p_{opt}. In this case the planned demand curve may quite well rise to the right along the whole of its length.

Other cases may be considered, e.g. where I_0 is constant, or where Q_I increases with p, or possibly where $c^c > c^w > 1$. It will be seen that when Q_I increases with p and when $c^c > c^w$, the planned demand curve will tend to rise to the right throughout its length.

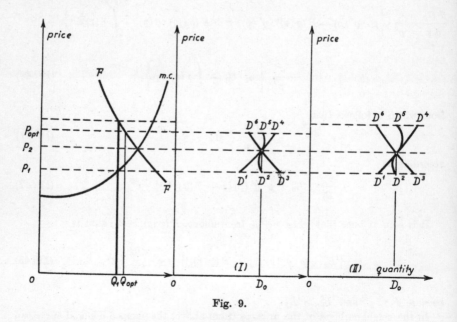

Fig. 9.

So, in both cases, where the maximum price allowed is between p_1 and p_2 (or equal to either), and where it is greater than p_2, we find that the planned demand curve exhibits the same behaviour as was mentioned in the case of perfect competition. If we now take as starting-point a certain given planned quantity in demand at the price p_2, we may indicate in Fig. 9 the following conceivable shapes of the planned demand curve at prices higher than or less than p_2. For the sake of clarity, the planned demand curves are drawn in separate partitions. (I) denotes the case in which p_{opt} is reached before $Q_F = Q_1$, and (II) indicates the case where p_{opt} is not reached before $Q_F = Q_1$.

The different possibilities are indicated by $D^1, \ldots, D^6$. For complete curves the possibilities are: $D^1 D^4$, $D^1 D^5$, $D^2 D^4$, $D^2 D^5$ and $D^3 D^6$. It is to be noticed that the planned demand curve, as mentioned before, will go "smoothly" through the point $p = p_2$, and will not have a bend at that point, as it might perhaps have been expected to have.

10. *The geometrical illustration of the gaps*

We have shown how the expected sales curve and the expected marginal revenue curve and the planned demand curve are dealt with when all-round monopolism in the commodity-markets is assumed, also how the planned production and planned payments of wages are determined. Now, for the sake of completeness we shall show the difference between planned investment and planned saving, assuming monopolism in the commodity-markets (it is further assumed that

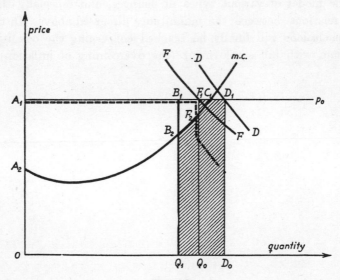

Fig. 10.

p_{opt} is not reached before $Q_F = Q_1$). We continue to assume, of course, that demand may be identified with planned purchases and supply with expected sales.

If the significance of symbols is taken from Fig. 10 (or from previous figures), it is seen that the *ex ante* factor-gap $= B_2 Q_1 Q_0 F_2$ and the *ex ante* commodity-gap $= F_1 Q_0 D_0 D_1$, so that

$$I_0 - S_0 = B_2 Q_1 Q_0 F_2 + F_1 Q_0 D_0 D_1,$$

which is the area shaded S.W–N.E.

The inflationary gap in the commodity-markets $= B_1 Q_1 D_0 D_1$, whereas the area $B_1 B_2 F_2 F_1$ is equal to the capitalists' unexpected loss of income.

It has now been shown how the geometric model is constructed, both when perfect competition is assumed everywhere in the commodity-markets, and when monopolism is assumed everywhere in the commodity-markets. We have also shown the functional connection and diagrammatic illustration of the decisive macro-economic magnitudes, $(I_0 - S_0)$, the factor-gap, the inflationary gap in the commodity-markets, etc., magnitudes of which the definitional relations were discussed in Chaps. II and III. In the following chapters we go on to show the effect on the geometric model of various types of changes, and especially the effect on the relations between the magnitudes discussed above. In this way some conclusions will finally be reached concerning the conditions for equilibrium with full employment (the overcoming of inflation) (Chap. IX).

CHAPTER V

REMOVAL OF THE EXCESS DEMAND UNDER REPRESSED INFLATION

A. The Removal of the Inflationary Gap in the Commodity-Markets when Maximum Prices and Wage-Rates Remain Unchanged

1. *Perfect competition*

We shall begin by considering an alteration which corresponds to an anti-inflationary policy often recommended, namely, a diminishing of the demand for commodities at fixed maximum prices and wage-rates in such a way that the inflationary gap in the commodity-markets is completely closed. We first deal with the case of *perfect competition*.

We use Fig. 11, with a marginal cost curve, an expected sales curve which is the price-line through A_1 and a planned demand curve $D'D'$ plotted as explained in Chap. IV, A. The significance of the symbols used is just the same as in Fig. 1.

As before, we have an inflationary gap in the commodity-markets which $= B_1 Q_1 D_0 D_1$, when $D'D'$ is the planned demand curve, and a factor-gap $= B_2 Q_1 Q_0 C_1$, since the planned production, and thus the expected sales, are equal to Q_0, with the value $A_1 O Q_0 C_1$.

Now suppose that, at the beginning of a period, by means of direct taxation the demand curve is moved from $D'D'$ to $D''D''$, so that it cuts the price-line in B_1. The planned purchases of commodities are thus reduced to $A_1 O Q_1 B_1$ (= the actually realizable production), and the inflationary gap in the commodity-markets disappears, i.e. $= 0$. It is therefore just possible to sell the quantity of commodities which are produced during the period at the prices prevailing.

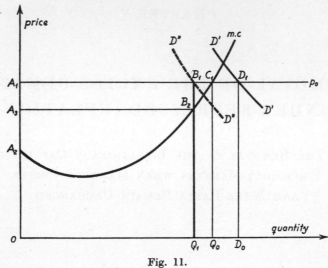

Fig. 11.

What about the factor-gap? We have assumed perfect competition and continuation of unchanged prices, so, as was earlier said, the entrepreneurs expect to be able to sell whatever they think fit to produce, and they will therefore, as always, plan to extend their production until expected marginal cost and expected marginal revenue (here equal to the price) are equal. This implies that planned production = Q_0, and the factor-gap = $B_2 Q_1 Q_0 C_1$. In other words, the factor-gap, with the assumptions stated, is quite unaffected by the magnitude of the inflationary-gap in the commodity-markets—anyway, so long as this magnitude is greater than or equal to zero. This follows from the assumption of perfect competition in the commodity-markets.

What happens in the period in which the inflationary gap in the commodity-markets is closed is then, that the actual production is just saleable at the expected prices, so that the commodity-market may be said to have attained equilibrium, *in a sense*. For, even if sales expectations were $A_1 O Q_0 C_1$, the production plans have miscarried, and what was actually produced was actually sold. None of the entrepreneurs (in their positions as entrepreneurs) had the opportunity to ascertain that the quantity of commodities $Q_0 - Q_1$ could not be sold if prices were to be maintained. It should be noticed that this conclusion is conditional upon no planned changes in stocks, or, at any rate, no

117

planned decrease in stocks, an assumption which will always be fulfilled when the stocks of commodities are completely empty, and is likely to be fulfilled in the case where stocks are subnormal, cf. below.

Since the inflationary gap in the commodity-markets has been nullified, in these circumstances a negative *ex ante* commodity-gap has arisen, which is numerically equal to the factor-gap *plus* the unexpected loss of income for the entrepreneurs. Saving is greater than investment (in the *ex ante* sense) by an amount which is equal to the unexpected loss of income for the entrepreneurs, since $I_0 - S_0$ continues to be equal to the *ex ante* commodity-gap plus the factor-gap. In spite of the excess saving, we have an upward pressure on prices in the factor-markets and equilibrium in the commodity-markets. The situation must therefore be called inflationary, according to the definition of monetary pressure of inflation used here. On the other hand, it is clear that the pressure of inflation has decreased, because decreased excess demand in the commodity-markets along with unchanged excess demand in the factor-markets implies decreased pressure of inflation (both monetary and quantitative), in accordance with our criterion of change in the pressure of inflation (cf. equations (I:4)—(I:6) and (I:7)—(I:9)).

In the next period, everyone may with good reason count on unchanged prices (the price-ceiling only fixes maximum prices, but there is nothing in the developments of the preceding period to induce anyone to expect lowered prices), and the entrepreneurs will, as before, plan a production equal to Q_0. The state of affairs will continue unaltered. In other words, equilibrium in the commodity-markets with disequilibrium in the factor-markets will recur.

However, the loss of income for the capitalists may have certain effects. In the first place there is the possibility that the entrepreneurs resign themselves and do not try to purchase the whole of the quantity of factors which they could profitably (*ex ante*) use in production. In this case the factor-gap will tend to decrease, and simultaneously, of course, the planned production and expected income of the capitalists decreases. Their unexpected loss of income thereupon also decreases. However, the question may be raised of whether such a development is really compatible with the assumption of perfect competition. If this behaviour of the market does not imply such a "tacit combination" that the entrepreneurs will continue not to demand more labour-power than exists as the control of wages is dropped, then this behaviour may be said to be in agreement with the assumption of perfect competition.

Secondly, the capitalists' purchases of consumer-goods may be a function of their expected income (in the construction of the model that has been reckoned with), and the demand for consumer-goods may thus fall with the decline in the income expectations caused by resignation about the possibility of obtaining sufficient labour-power. This will tend to diminish the inflationary gap in the commodity-markets, and the effect will not depend on whether or not the state has diminished or closed the inflationary gap in the commodity-markets beforehand. However, if the state has closed the inflationary gap in the commodity-markets, and subsequently the capitalists' expectations of income fall in the way mentioned above, the production Q_1 can no longer be sold at the prevailing prices (a deflationary gap arises), and since we have a situation of perfect competition, prices will fall (unless the policy of the state is to keep the inflationary gap in the commodity-markets just zero, and not positive or negative). This again will imply a decline in expectations of income, (how much will depend, among other things, on the price expectations, for, it is obviously now difficult to reckon that the elasticity of expectations will be equal to 1), and we may in this way think of successive adjustments leading to a fall in prices until equilibrium is reached.

Such a process of adjustment requires, however, that the plans for purchases of factors are subsequently diminished, and it may therefore be taken to be slow, at best.

There are other reasons to suggest that a downward process may take place, e.g. if the entrepreneurs have planned to diminish their stocks at the same time as the inflationary gap in the commodity-markets is closed. If the entrepreneurs try to sell not only their actual production but also part of their stocks, a fall in prices will occur. However, this case is of course excluded when there are no stocks of commodities and unlikely when stocks are below normal, and it can be disregarded.

Thus we see that, with the inflationary gap in the commodity-markets diminished to zero so that the demand for commodities is equal to the actual production of commodities, price-control may quite well be dropped, but not control of wages. If the control of wages were relaxed, the competition between entrepreneurs would force up wages until the marginal cost curve went through B_1. Then there would be equilibrium in the factor-market, but at the same time a new inflationary gap in the commodity-markets would perhaps arise, which would in turn force up prices in the commodity-markets and so on, unless the state all the time practised a tax-policy such that the inflationary gap in the commodity-markets was held at zero.

If instead of restricting the demand for commodities to make the inflationary gap in the commodity-markets zero, the demand for commodities were restricted to make planned investment and saving equal, the situation is not improved. For, with $D'D'$ as demand curve, the difference between planned investment and saving is represented by the area $B_2 Q_1 D_0 D_1 C_1$, and a restriction of the demand for commodities by this amount will still leave an inflationary gap in the commodity-markets equal in size to $B_1 B_2 C_1$. Consequently, the new planned demand curve will intersect the price-line to the right of B_1, and the factor-gap will not be affected, for the same reasons as were previously given. We arrive at a situation where $I_0 = S_0$ and there is an upward pressure of prices in both the commodity and factor markets.

It follows that, if it is desired to proceed directly from a situation in which the planned demand is equal to D_0 to the situation where there is complete equilibrium, the demand for commodities must be reduced, not only by an amount $B_1 Q_1 D_0 D_1$, but by $B_1 Q_1 D_0 D_1$ *plus* $A_1 A_3 B_2 B_1$. That is, the demand for commodities must be reduced not only by the amount which corresponds to the inflationary gap in the commodity-markets at the prevailing price, but further, by an amount which is equal to the actual production of commodities Q_1 multiplied by the difference $B_1 B_2$ between the prevailing price and the marginal costs at the greatest possible production, i.e. by Q_1 $(p_0 - Q_1 B_2)$.

It may be of interest to notice a concept introduced by Keynes in *A Treatise on Money*. If, with Keynes, we define "the 'normal' remuneration of entrepreneurs at any time as that rate which, ... would leave them under no motive either to increase or to decrease their scale of operations"[1], and add that their "scale of operations" is such that it gives full employment of labour-power, we see that the amount $A_1 A_3 B_2 B_1$ corresponds exactly to the "supernormal" profit

---

[1] J. M. Keynes, *A Treatise on Money*, Vol. I, p. 125.

9

ex post (or what Keynes in *A Treatise on Money* called "profit" out-right). In contrast to Keynes, for whom "profit" was a purely *ex post* concept, we may distinguish between *ex ante* and *ex post* "supernormal" profit. Whereas the *ex post* "supernormal" profit is equal to $A_1 A_3 B_2 B_1$, the *ex ante*, expected "supernormal" profit is greater and is equal to $A_1 A_3 B_2 C_1$. The "normal" profit, the "normal remuneration" of Keynes, is, on the contrary—*ex ante*—equal to $A_3 A_2 B_2$, which is also the "normal remuneration" *ex post* in an equilibrium situation. This distinction, which is significant of course, is not dealt with by Keynes. It seems as if he assumes that the results and also the profit for the one period are expected to recur in the next period.

2. *Monopolism*

A great deal of what has been · said in Section 1, may, without noteworthy alteration, be taken as applicable to the case of *monopolism in all the commodity-markets*.

In Fig. 12 two expected sales curves are drawn, one of which, the curve $F' F'$, intersects the price-line to the right of C_1, the other of which, $F'' F''$, intersects the price-line between B_1 and C_1. Also we have in the initial situation a planned demand curve $D' D'$. What is different here from the case of perfect competition, is that the entrepreneurs do not count on being able to sell indefinite amounts at the given maximum price. In the first case, with $F' F'$ as the expected sales curve, the planned production and expected sales of commodities are equal to $_1Q_0$; in the second case, with $F'' F''$ as expected sales curve, the planned production and expected sales of commodities are equal to $_2Q_0$. In the second case, it is seen that the entrepreneurs must necessarily plan to keep their stocks unchanged. On moving the planned demand curve from $D' D'$ to $D'' D''$, so that the inflationary gap in the commodity-markets is closed, the factor-gap will not be affected, unless the expected sales curve is affected by the closing of the inflationary gap in the commodity-markets. As long as this does not happen, the state of equilibrium in the commodity-market and disequilibrium in the factor-market may continue. If the demand for commodities is reduced only so much that $I_0 = S_0$, there will be, as in the case of perfect competition, excess demand and a consequent upward pressure on prices in both the commodity and factor markets. The remarks about a possible resignation on the part of the entrepreneurs

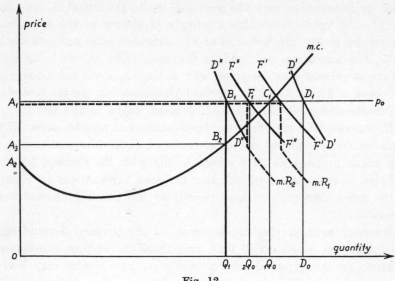

Fig. 12.

with respect to the demand for labour-power, together with the consequences mentioned, apply here as well as in Section 1. But a further possibility for a movement towards equilibrium in the factor-market presents itself, namely, that the expected sales curve may be displaced to the left.

As long as the expected sales curve intersects the price-line to the right of C_1 a displacement of the expected sales curve to the left does not alter the picture, because the planned production will remain $= {}_1Q_0$.

However, if the intersection of the price-line and the expected sales curve moves from the right to the left of C_1, or moves from a position already to the left of C_1 further to the left, this shift will be significant in two respects. It must be remembered that the planned demand curve is constructed on the assumption of a given expected sales curve. A displacement of the expected sales curve to the left must evidently also displace the planned demand curve to the left. This effect may be neglected if we suppose that the state continually, by means of its tax-policy, keeps the total demand for commodities at the given maximum price equal to the actual production, Q_1. The reason for the shifting of the planned demand curve is the change in the planned production, as a displacement to the left of the expected sales curve when its intersection with the price-line lies to the left of C_1 diminishes the planned production. If, accordingly, a closing of the inflationary gap results in the displacement of the expected sales curve to the left of C_1, the factor-gap will tend to decrease, other things being equal.

Various reasons may be given why a closing of the inflationary gap can cause a decrease in the expected possible sales. In the first place, the displacement of the planned demand curve to the left may, in itself, decrease the entrepreneurs' expectations of possible sales. If the displacement is achieved by interference of authorities and announced with much propaganda as a means to diminish the demand for commodities, it is quite conceivable that the sales expectations are changed at the same time (in the same period) as the planned demand curve is moved.

However, even if the displacement of the planned demand curve takes place in a concealed way, and therefore without simultaneous influence on the expected sales possibilities, later events may lead to a change of opinion about sales possibilities. For instance, if the entrepreneurs expect sales to be greater than the profitable production and expect stocks to be diminished by sales, they will discover, if the inflationary gap is closed, that they do not experience the expected decrease in stocks in spite of production being less than was planned. Evidently some sales expectations are disappointed, and that may lead to a displacement of the expected sales curve to the left. This case only arises, however, when the expected sales curve intersects the price-line to the right of C_1 and when there do exist stocks to be diminished. Also, if the entrepreneurs have decided not to meet the demand for commodities by selling more than the planned production, but to sell just that much, they are likewise liable to suffer disappointments of sales expectations. This case may also arise when the expected sales curve cuts the price-line between B_1 and C_1, still assuming, of course, that there are stocks.

If, on the other hand, the entrepreneurs have no stocks .at all, or have decided not to meet any demand by the sale of stocks (the important part of the entrepreneurs' policy is thus that they do not wish their stocks to decrease), the result of the period, when the inflationary gap has been closed, does not necessarily lead to changed opinions regarding sales possibilities. Certainly sales have been less than expected, but this may very well appear to the entrepreneurs as a result of the break-down of production plans and not of incorrect sales expectations.

If the entrepreneurs are accustomed to excess demand giving rise to lengthened order-lists or some other form of queueing, they will see, when the inflationary gap in the commodity-markets is closed, that the order-lists cease to become longer, and this may suggest that smaller sales are to be expected in the future.

Therefore, it may normally be considered that a closing of the commodity-markets' inflationary gap will sooner or later result in a displacement of the expected sales curve to the left, large enough for the planned production to fall, and the planned demand for labour-power along with it. Yet we cannot neglect the possibility that the closing of the inflationary gap in the commodity-market may leave the factor-gap unaffected.

Let us now suppose that the pleasant state of affairs arises in which the state by means of direct taxes fixes the demand for commodities at the price p_0 at Q_1, while simultaneously the entrepreneurs' sales expectations decrease just sufficiently for the expected sales curve to go through the point B_1, whereupon planned demand for commodities, expected sales and planned and actual production become equal. Then we have apparently the neatest possible equilibrium in the commodity-market. However, a closer examination of the factor-market will show that the equilibrium in the commodity-market is of such a character that if controls are abandoned, either a deflationary or an inflationary process can begin.

The case is illustrated in Fig. 13, where the planned demand curve DD goes through B_1 and the expected sales curve FF also goes through B_1. There are three conceivable possibilities for the original marginal revenue curve (dependent on the slope of FF), denoted by $m.R._1$, $m.R._2$, and $m.R._3$. The difference between them is that they cut the marginal cost curve to the right of, at, or to the left of B_2.

First we may consider the case in which the original marginal revenue curve $m.R._2$ cuts the marginal cost curve at B_2. In this case the controlled marginal revenue curve $A_1 B_1 B_2 m.R._2$ will have its lowest bend on the marginal cost curve. It will be seen that removal of both price and wage controls here will not result in any changes, since, in spite of controls, the entrepreneurs find themselves in just that position they themselves would choose as optimum if there were no

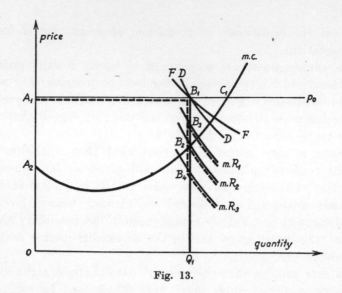

Fig. 13.

control of wages and prices. So there is equilibrium[1] in both the commodity and factor-markets, with full employment.

If we consider instead the case where the original marginal revenue curve $m.R_3$ intersects the marginal cost curve to the left of B_2, and where the marginal revenue curve $A_1 B_1 B_4 m.R_3$ consequently has its lowest bend below the marginal cost curve, it is seen at once that the given maximum price p_0 is lower than the entrepreneurs' optimum price, when the cost and expected sales relation is as given. A release of price-controls here would result in the actual marginal revenue curve ceasing to be the controlled marginal revenue curve for the entrepreneurs, and becoming the original marginal revenue curve, and so the entrepreneurs' optimum situation would be at a higher price than p_0 and a lower planned production than Q_1.[2] Consequently unemployment would occur and with it a tendency to contraction, which, however, cannot be dealt with on the assumptions of the model. But, in this situation, wage-controls might be relaxed without demand requirements leading to a tendency of wages to rise. For, as long as commodity prices are

---

[1] It should be noticed, however, that this equilibrium will be a stable equilibrium only if the planned demand curve DD and the expected sales curve FF coincide, not only in the point B_1, but in the whole of their lengths.

[2] We have here an obvious case of price-control having an expansive effect on planned production and on employment (cf. p. 108, note 1).

controlled, the factor-market is in a state of Marshallian neutral equilibrium.

Lastly, if we consider the third case, where the original marginal revenue curve $m.R._1$ intersects the marginal cost curve to the right of B_2, and where the lowest bend of the controlled marginal revenue curve $A_1 B_1 B_3 m.R._1$ is above the marginal cost curve, it is seen that this is a situation in which the entrepreneurs' optimum point must occur at a price which is lower than the permitted maximum p_0, and at a planned production which is larger than the possible production Q_1. So the case is impossible, since the entrepreneurs would have found it advisable, when the expected sales curve was moved to the left, to lower prices below the maximum. With a demand for commodities which is controlled by the state so that the possible production can always just be sold, this implies that we are situated in the case first mentioned, where we have an original marginal revenue curve which passes through B_2. However, if the entrepreneurs are resigned to asking for only the quantity of labour-power corresponding to the possible production, they will keep the "over-optimum" price p_0, as long as controls are enforced. In such a case price-control may be abandoned, but not wage-control, since if control of wages ceases, and the resignation along with it, the entrepreneurs will find it favourable to plan a greater production at lower prices, although this will force up wages. There is some reason for neglecting this case, however, because it is not very probable that maximum prices will be set higher than the entrepreneurs' optimum prices.

As in Section 1 we can also try to apply Keynes' concept of "normal profit" here. If we begin with the cases considered after Fig. 13, it will be seen that the profit is "normal" with $m.R._2$ as marginal revenue curve. Both the expected profit and actual profit of the entrepreneurs is then equal to $A_1 A_2 B_2 B_1$, and this is a profit which, with or without control "would leave them under no motive either to increase or to decrease their scale of operations". In this case no difficulty occurs in making use of the concept.

With $m.R._3$ as marginal revenue curve, both expected and actual profit which are still equal to $A_1 A_2 B_2 B_1$, will be "subnormal" in the sense that, if price-control ceases, the entrepreneurs will at once lower their "scale of operations" beneath the level of full employment. On the other hand, it is possible to say that the profit is 'normal' both *ex ante* and *ex post*, for, *while* control continues, the entrepreneurs have "no motive either to increase or to decrease their scale of operations" away from the level of full employment. Of course, there is no doubt that Keynes in *A Treatise on Money* thought exclusively about such cases as where the entrepreneurs are free to choose their own prices, but nowadays, when control is a very usual "environment" for the formation of prices, there is good reason to distinguish between a "free normal" and a "controlled normal".

The case in which $m.R._1$ is the marginal revenue curve was only conceivable when the entrepreneurs were supposed to have resigned themselves on the question of demand for factors. But it will be seen that the profit here, which is equal to $A_1 A_2 B_2 B_1$ both *ex ante* and *ex post*, is "supernormal" in the sense that if control of wages ceases, and the entrepreneurs' resignation along with it, the entrepreneurs will try to extend their "scale of operations" beyond full employment, and so force up wages. As long as control continues, however, the profit here is "controlled normal".

What is to be regarded as "controlled normal" profit when the expected sales curve passes through B_1 thus has no simple connection with the Keynesian "free normal". This is still clearer if we consider the more general case in which, at the given maximum price, the expected possible sales are greater than the possible production. It will be seen that here the planned production and planned employment will always be larger than possible production and employment, determined by the intersection of the price-line with either the expected sales curve or the marginal cost curve. The "controlled normal" profit may now be understood to mean that profit which would just make planned employment equal to the available amount of labour-services. Therefore, if there is excess demand for factors, the expected profit must in this sense necessarily be "supernormal" when there is control. However, whether expected and actual profits in such a case are above or below the "free normal" profit will be considered more closely in Section 7.

3. *Conclusions and modifications*

We have found that if we suppose the state to do away with the repressed inflation by closing the inflationary gap with the help of direct taxation, this will not necessarily lead to complete equilibrium.

When there was perfect competition we found that the factor-gap was not necessarily affected by the closing of the inflationary gap in the commodity-markets, apart from certain exceptional cases. When there was monopolism the factor-gap diminished only to the extent that the closing of the inflationary gap in the commodity-markets led to disappointed sales expectations. This was found to be most probable, but though the expected sales curve might move to the left, this did not ensure equilibrium in the factor-market, not even when planned demand, expected sales and actual production were equal.

As far as the difference between planned investment and saving was concerned, if it was zero this did not ensure equilibrium in either the commodity-market or the factor-market. $I_0 - S_0 = 0$ might occur together with excess demand and tendency to rise in prices in both the factor and commodity markets. However, the results must be modified to a certain extent, even in the model used.

For fixing the magnitude of the possible production $-Q_1-$ we began by dealing with usual cost diagrams and assumed, in accordance with the usual way of reasoning, that an arbitrarily chosen unit of production could not be produced without also producing all the units preceding it on the abscissa. This does not necessarily apply, however, if the cost curve is considered as arising from a summation of the cost curves of each of the individual enterprises. For, if there is no complete system of allocation of labour-power, the distribution of the labour-power available over the given profitable production, Q_0, at the given wage-rates, would be quite arbitrary (between the individual enterprises). So it is not possible to assume, as is done in all the figures, that it is necessarily the production with the highest marginal costs which is not started upon. The production which is not carried out because of lack of labour-power will be distributed over the whole of the interval $O Q_0$. This changes nothing in the size of the factor-gap, which must in all cases be as illustrated in the figures, but the size of the entrepreneurs' *ex post* profit is exaggerated and their unexpected loss of income consequently underestimated. A further result is that the produced quantity of goods will not be altogether unaffected by decrease or disappearance of the factor-gap. To the extent to which production at high costs, lying between Q_1 and Q_0, is fortunate in securing labour-power (in this case there are "holes" in the production between the origin and Q_1), a diminution of the factor-gap will imply that labour-power is freed for production by firms with lower costs. Diminishing of the factor-gap therefore tends to increase the quantity of commodities produced. This circumstance is an expression of what is perhaps one of the most serious drawbacks in repressed inflation with shortage of labour-power.

Furthermore, in deciding the size of the factor-gap we have always taken it that the control of investment does not imply any control of the amount produced but only a control of the demand for investment goods. If this were the case, however, planned production would obviously not be equal to optimum production.

The use of a common demand curve conceals the fact that when the inflationary gap in the commodity-markets increases or decreases, i.e. when the common planned demand curve is displaced, the demand for particular commodities will have different income-elasticity, or rather, when the inflationary gap is lessened by direct taxation, different income-*minus*-tax elasticity. If all commodities are perfectly substitutable for one another from a short-term point of view (meaning that if it is not possible to obtain one commodity at a given price, then another may be taken in order to spend the money), no disappointed sales can occur on any market as long as there is unsatisfied demand in other markets, and our assumption of a given composition of production would thus be justified. However, it is rarely possible to substitute commodities in this way, although there is that peculiar craze for buying which grips people in situation of severe shortage, so that it is a great satisfaction "to have got hold of something" even if there is no sensible use for what has been bought after it has been bought (apart from barter-trade with other people in a similar situation). It is therefore probable that even before the point of intersection of the planned demand curve and the price-line is jerked to the left of C_1, some profitable production begins to be unsaleable, so that the factor-gap may begin to decrease earlier than the figures suggest. Therefore we may say that only beyond that point where there are simultaneously unrealizable purchasing plans for commodities in all the individual markets, is the magnitude of the factor-gap wholly unaffected by the magnitude of the inflationary gap. It must also be remembered that in changing the composition of production the common cost curve is also changed, and we thus face the general problem of aggregation; we shall "look it firmly in the face and pass on".[1]

It has been assumed all the time—also in the preceding chapters— that labour-services cannot be directly used by the consumers, but only by the entrepreneurs (or possibly the state). This assumption is of course not quite realistic. If this were taken into account, by adding the planned direct consumption of labour-services to the demand for factors, a certain interdependence of the inflationary gap and the factor-gap would be introduced.

None of the three stated modifications is unimportant, but they will nevertheless be neglected in what follows. But it should always be borne in mind that this neglecting will limit the validity of the conclusions reached.

B. The "Red" Policy: Prices Fixed and Wages Free

4. *Perfect competition*

Under this heading we shall discuss a form of anti-inflationary policy and changes in the system which fixes prices and lets wages rise freely, while at the same time the demand relationships are left to themselves.[2]

With *perfect competition* it is at once obvious that if wage-rates are allowed to increase unhindered, while prices are fixed, the excess demand in the labour-market, the factor-gap, must tend to disappear, but the effects on the inflationary gap in the commodity-markets are not so certain. If we keep to Fig. 1, for instance, and suppose the marginal cost curve to move upwards because of rising wages until it passes through B_1, the profitable production will fall from Q_0 to Q_1, so that

---

[1] D. H. Robertson, "A Revolutionist's Handbook", *The Quarterly Journal of Economics*, Vol. LXIV, Febr. 1950, No. 1., p. 5.

[2] A policy of this sort seems to have been put into practise in Finland at one time after the armistice. This policy has also been explicitly suggested by the Swedish communists as an effective antiinflationary measure! A more sophisticated policy, of which the main points are the closing of the factor-gap by wage-rises and simultaneous maintaining of equilibrium in the commodity-markets with the help of a financial policy, was proposed by Gösta Rehn, "Ekonomisk politik vid full sysselsättning" ("Economic Policy at Full Employment"), *Tiden*, Stockholm, 1948, and further discussed by Erik Lundberg, "Lönepolitik under full sysselsättning" ("Wage-Policy under Full Employment"), *Ekonomisk Tidskrift*, 1950.

planned production is equal to realizable production and there is equilibrium in the factor-market. It is evident that this in itself may be regarded as essentially a good step, since production may hereby be forced to move from the less to the more productive firms.

What is important, however, is what effect this will have on the inflationary gap in the commodity-markets. If we wish to consider that, we may say that the possibility just mentioned of displacing of labour-power from less to more productive firms will increase the quantity of commodities and accordingly lessen the inflationary gap in the commodity-markets from the supply side. We are then left with the question of the effect on the demand for commodities.

Whereas in A we only went into the dependence of the factor-gap on changes in the inflationary gap in the commodity-markets, we must now deal with the dependence of the inflationary gap in the commodity-markets, the excess demand for commodities, on changes in the factor-gap, in particular, on a removal of the factor-gap. With a given volume of investment and consequently a given demand for investment commodities (control of investment is supposed to be retained), it becomes wholly a matter of the effect on the demand for consumer-goods. How large the total planned demand for consumer-goods by workers and capitalists will be is dependent partly on the total expected income, partly on its distribution, and partly on the respective consumption-ratio's of workers and capitalists. Since the economic subjects still have good reason to expect that existing prices continue unaltered, habits of saving may be taken as set and unaffected by these happenings.

When wage-rates rise, the marginal cost curve $m. c._1$ in Fig. 14 rises to $m. c._2$, which passes through B_1. The expected income of the workers and their actual income rises in accordance with the increase in wage-rates from $A_2 O Q_1 B_2$ to $A_4 O Q_1 B_1$, i.e. by an amount $A_4 A_2 B_2 B_1$. The capitalists' expected profit falls, however, by an amount greater than the increase in the workers' expected income, for the expected profit falls from $A_1 A_2 C_1$ to $A_1 A_4 B_1$, that is, by $A_4 A_2 C_1 B_1$, which is larger than the increase in the workers' expected income, with the amount $B_1 B_2 C_1$. Consequently the total expected gross income falls (the same applies, *a fortiori*, to the total expected net income). This connection is analogous to that previously mentioned in Chap. IV, Section 4, that with fixed wage-rate and rising price the expected

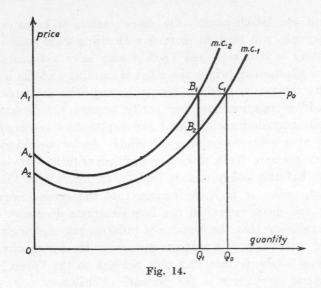

Fig. 14.

gross profit and the total expected income increase more sharply than the value of the realizable production.

As we still have the capitalists' consumption-ratio $= c^c$ and the workers' consumption-ratio $= c^w$ (where average and marginal ratio are taken to be equal), we have that

the change in planned consumption $= A_4 A_2 B_2 B_1 \cdot c^w - A_4 A_2 C_1 B_1 \cdot c^c$,

$c^c < c^w$ and $A_4 A_2 C_1 B_1 > A_4 A_2 B_2 B_1$, so that the change in the value of the planned demand for consumer-goods may be either negative or positive, and since prices are unchanged, the same applies to the change in the quantity of the planned demand for consumer-goods. Consequently it is not possible to say *a priori* whether the total demand for consumer-goods, and therefore the total demand for commodities and the inflationary gap in the commodity-markets, will increase or decrease as a result of the rise in wages.

If the entrepreneurs have initially resigned themselves completely over the demand for labour-power, and therefore only plan a production $= Q_1$ and only expect an income equal to $A_1 A_2 B_2 B_1$, increase in wages must certainly lead to an increase in the total demand for consumer-goods; at any rate, so long as $c^w > c^c$. Therefore, the greater the degree to which the entrepreneurs have resigned themselves on the question of demand for labour-power, the more certain it becomes that the inflationary gap will tend to increase with rising wage-rates. But what is interesting is that this "red" policy may have a favourable effect on both the factor-gap (where the effect is certain), and the inflationary gap in the commodity-markets, partly because the available quantity of commodities may increase, and partly because the demand for consumer-goods may decrease (without the explanation needing to depend on effects of a politico-psychological kind). As far as changes in the inflationary pressure (both monetary and quantitative) are concerned, it is seen that this policy cannot lead to an increase in the pressure of inflation, since it is quite certain that the excess demand (both monetary and quantitative) in the factor-markets decreases. There is a weak possibility that the pressure of inflation may definitely decrease because of a decrease of the excess demand in the commodity-markets, but what is likely is that this case belongs to the "open" category of the criteria of changes in the pressure of inflation.

If wages increase till $m.c_2$ is reached, the profit changes from "supernormal" to "controlled normal", which "controlled normal" is, however, the same as Keynes's "free normal" for perfect competition.

From time to time it is asserted from the trades-union side that a rise in profits must imply that there is room for a rise in wage-rates which does not need to result in price-increases if a sufficiently strong price-control (or financial policy with respect to the inflationary gap in the commodity-markets) is enforced. This may be said to be correct in a certain sense, since increased profits and unaltered wages must imply that the factor-gap increases, and that a certain wage-increase is therefore possible without it leading to unemployment. Such a rise in wages thus brings us nearer to equilibrium in the labour-market, and so there is indeed room for it at the given prices. But the result in the commodity-markets is more doubtful, even if it is not possible to maintain flatly that the disequilibrium will be intensified. In this sense also, it may be that there is "room" for wage-increases.[1]

On the other hand, increased profits with unchanged wages imply with certainty that, for instance, a tax on wages (proportional to the wages), or an ordinary indirect tax levied on the entrepreneurs at

---

[1] See Erik Lundberg, "Inflationsanalys och ekonomisk teori", p. 146—7. Cf. also Gösta Rehn, "Ekonomisk politik vid full sysselsättning", and Erik Lundberg, "Lönepolitik under full sysselsättning".

unchanged prices, brings the system nearer to equilibrium on both the factor and commodity markets. For, assuming that the receipts of such a tax does not give rise to increased public income-payments, such a tax must without doubt lessen both the entrepreneurs' demand for labour-power and the entrepreneurs' demand for consumer-goods. The same may be said for a wage increase which is subject to compulsory saving, although the possibility of the workers cutting down their customary saving makes the outcome in the commodity-market a little uncertain.

It should be mentioned, lastly, that if the labour-market is organized throughout, the marginal cost curve may of course be displaced even higher up than to the equilibrium point (by spontaneous wage increase) and we then have a situation in which there is unemployment at the same time as an inflationary gap in the commodity-markets.[1] This seems to have occurred in Finland at one time after the armistice.

5. *Monopolism*

With *monopolism in all the commodity-markets* the same reasoning applies as in the case of perfect competition. If wages are free, the excess demand will force up wages until the marginal cost curve goes through B_1 (see, for example, Fig. 12), whereupon equilibrium is obtained in the factor-market as long as there is control of prices, and the profit is "controlled normal". Here also the effect on the inflationary gap in the commodity-markets is uncertain; either an increase or a decrease may occur.

C. The "Liberal" Policy: Wages Fixed and Prices Free

6. *Perfect competition*

Although we are perhaps attributing wrong opinions to individual liberals, it is more or less justifiable to give the above heading to

---

[1] This point clearly illustrates that it is not possible, as has been suggested from several quarters (for instance, by Jørgen Gelting in *Finanstidende*, Copenhagen 1948, no. 42), to use the actual degree of employment as an indication of the pressure of inflation. Falling employment and rising strain of demand in the commodity-market can go together, even if there are no shortages of raw materials or bottle-necks to cause unemployment.

such a policy[1], where prices are allowed to rise, with the idea of achieving equilibrium in the commodity-market, while, on the other hand, wages are fixed, and the quantitative disequilibrium in the factor-markets is left to itself. This policy, or alteration in the system, may be illustrated by the figures previously used.

To maintain the assumption about fixed relative prices and expectations that prevailing prices will continue, we may assume that the control permits uniform price increases by jerks, so that control first ceases when it is considered that the price is one at which there is equilibrium. Then we consider what happens under *perfect competition* to the inflationary gap in the commodity-markets and the factor-gap respectively.

The development of the inflationary gap in the commodity-markets will depend on the shape of the planned demand curve. As we mentioned in Chap. IV, Section 5, the planned demand curve may have one of several different forms, illustrated in Fig. 2. Even if the planned demand curve at the first increases in prices rises to the left, so that increases in prices diminish the excess demand in the commodity-markets, the demand curve may turn back to the right at higher prices (like D^2 in Fig. 2), so that the excess demand in the commodity-markets begins to increase again upon further increase in prices. The inflationary gap in the commodity-markets will be closed only if the demand curve rises to the left until the gap is closed (as with curves D^6, D^5, and D^4). It should be noticed, though, that if prices in the initial situation are sufficiently high and the demand curve has a shape and position like D^4, for example, fall in prices may be necessary in order to close the inflationary gap in the commodity-markets.

Thus it is not certain that the price increase policy dealt with does lead to closing of the inflationary gap in the commodity-markets, or even to diminishing of it. It is moreover conceivable that a policy of price-lowering may be necessary in order to close the inflationary gap in the commodity-markets. But the planned demand curve may also be so placed that neither increases nor decreases in prices (above p_1) suffice to close the gap.

At best the inflationary gap in the commodity-markets will be closed; what about the factor-gap? It is easily seen that the development of the factor-gap here under perfect competition is completely

---

[1] O. Lange, *Price Flexibility and Employment*, The Principia Press, Inc., Bloomington, Indiana, 1944, p. 90.

without connection with the development of the inflationary gap in the commodity-markets. At each price the planned production will be determined by the intersection of the price-line with the expected marginal cost curve, and so long as the marginal cost curve is not vertical, the planned production, and with it the planned payments of wages, will rise with the price. The policy therefore leads to an increase in the factor-gap in any case. Only where a fall in prices is necessary to close the inflationary gap (as with the upper branch of D^4 in Fig. 2), and prices are actually lowered to achieve this, will the closing of the inflationary gap coincide with a decrease in the factor-gap.

Therefore we have as a result that this "liberal" policy will always heighten the disequilibrium in the factor-market and make an existing "supernormal" profit even more "supernormal", while it is uncertain whether it will move the commodity-market nearer to or farther from equilibrium. What may be said about the development of the pressure of inflation under this policy is, that it cannot normally diminish the pressure of inflation, and sometimes can increase it, but that the case otherwise belongs to the "open" category.

7. *Monopolism*

With *monopolism in the commodity-markets* the "liberal" policy gives altogether different results from the case of perfect competition. The development in both planned demand and expected sales with rising prices must be taken into account. Fig. 9 is suitable to use, and it is assumed that the expected sales curve is given and remains fixed, which was, it will be remembered, a basic assumption in constructing the planned demand curve.

As long as the initial price lies between p_1 and p_2 (in which interval the expected sales curve lies to the right of the marginal cost curve), price changes will have just the same effect as in the case of perfect competition. For instance it is possible that, with demand curves like D^2 or D^3, the inflationary gap in the commodity-markets is closed by increase of prices before p_2 is reached, and it may happen that lowering of prices is necessary (and sufficient) to close the inflationary gap in the commodity markets, if, for instance, the planned demand curve is like D^1. In any case the factor-gap increases when the price rises, and ꞓecreases when the price falls.

If the inflationary gap in the factor-market is not closed by rises

10

in the price below p_2, the price must rise above p_2. What was previously found to be the case applies also here, namely that expected sales, planned production, planned payments of wages and the factor-gap all decrease as the price rises and at a price sufficiently high the factor-gap becomes zero, that is, when the expected sales curve intersects the vertical line through Q_1. However, if the optimum price p_{opt} is reached before the expected sales have fallen to Q_1, the entrepreneurs will not, as long as the expected sales curve is fixed, have any inducement to set prices higher than the optimum price (if they do not resign themselves over the question of demand for labour-power), so that the factor-gap will continue to be positive. Therefore, if the optimum price is reached before the expected sales $= Q_1$ the factor-gap cannot be nullified merely by allowing price increase in the commodity-markets.

If we consider the development of the inflationary gap in the commodity-markets at prices higher than p_2, it will depend on the position and shape of the planned demand curve. It is seen that even if the expected sales curve rises to the left, as do D^6 and D^5 for instance, the inflationary gap in the commodity-markets is not necessarily closed, although prices may be allowed to rise right up to where the expected sales are equal to Q_1. In this case there will be a positive inflationary gap in the commodity-markets when the factor-gap has been closed by the price increases in the commodity-market. On the other hand it may be that, when the planned demand curve rises to the left, the inflationary gap in the commodity-markets is closed at a lower price than that at which the factor-gap is closed. If we now assume that the price-fixing authorities will never fix the price so high that the possible production (Q_1) is unsaleable, or so that unemployment occurs, we may summarize as follows.

The inflationary gap in the commodity-markets may be closed, that is, the planned demand curve may reach the vertical through Q_1, before the price has risen to that point at which a possible optimum price occurs, or that point at which the expected sales curve cuts the vertical through Q_1 if an optimum price is not reached. Then there will still be a positive factor-gap despite the closing of the inflationary gap in the commodity-markets. This factor-gap may be either greater or less than the initial factor-gap if the initial price lies between p_1

and p_2; it will always be less than the initial factor-gap if the initial price is greater than (or equal to) p_2.

If the inflationary gap in the commodity-markets is not closed before a possible optimum price is reached, it will be impossible to close the factor-gap and the inflationary gap in the commodity-markets by means of price increases alone, for the entrepreneurs will have no inducement to raise prices when the optimum price is reached.

The inflationary gap in the commodity-markets and the factor-gap will both be closed by price increases only if the former is just closed when the expected sales equal the greatest possible production, Q_1, that is, if the planned demand curve and the expected sales curve meet on the vertical through Q_1. This would be a very special case, but even if it does happen it does not imply that there is now such an equilibrium that both price and wage controls may be dropped. If it is to be possible to abandon price-control without disturbing the equilibrium, it is further necessary that the original expected marginal revenue curve cuts the marginal cost curve just on the vertical line through Q_1. Reference may be made in this connection to Section 2, Fig. 13, and the discussion following the figure.

The discussion above has been carried on with the assumption throughout that the expected sales curve is fixed and not affected by the price changes by themselves, and this is only natural since the expected sales curve is defined as that aggregate of points which shows the sales expectations of the entrepreneurs when control fixes various prices. Let us however suppose that the control has hit upon just such a price as closes the inflationary gap in the commodity-markets (the existence of this price is, of course, implied), and that at this price there is a positive factor-gap. When maximum prices and wages are fixed, cannot a displacement of the expected sales curve be brought about by the influence of what happens in one or more periods so that a tendency to closing of the factor-gap afterwards appears? As was suggested in Section 2, it is very likely that this will happen, and at best the expected sales curve will at last come to intersect the vertical through Q_1 at the same point as the planned demand curve. However, it should be remembered that a displacement of the expected sales curve to the left leads to a simultaneous displacement of the planned demand curve to the left. Therefore, if the controlling authority has first fixed a price at which the possible production can just be sold, then as soon as the expected sales curve begins to move to the left the possible production becomes unsaleable at the current price. The situation then becomes radically different, and a deflationary process begins.

Merely to set prices higher seems to provide little possibility of arriving at a situation of equilibrium such as will persist if controls cease, in the case of monopolism; whereas there is no possibility at all in the case of perfect competition, as we saw.

Finally, we shall consider what happens to the "normality" of profits here.

If the factor-gap is closed by price increases, the subsequent profit will be "controlled normal", and in that altogether special case where the original expected marginal revenue curve intersects the marginal cost curve on the vertical through Q_1, will be "free normal". This applies both to the expected and actual profit, which are equal when the factor-gap is closed. Whether the profit is "normal", in this or any other sense, has, however, nothing to do with whether the inflationary gap in the commodity-markets is closed at the same time.

If the factor-gap is not closed, the expected profit in all cases is "controlled supernormal", which does not, however, imply that the expected profit is larger than the "controlled normal", as would occur if prices rose so much that the expected sales became equal to Q_1. The quantitative relations between the magnitudes involved depends on the shape of the expected sales curve. However, the actual (*ex post*) profit corresponding to the expected "controlled supernormal" profit will always be less in magnitude than the "controlled normal" profit just mentioned.

With regard to the relation of the profit to the Keynesian "free normal", it may be said that this "free normal" exists only in the special case mentioned, the one where the expected sales curve is such that the marginal revenue curve cuts the marginal cost curve on the vertical through Q_1. If it is assumed that the expected sales curve is of this form, and a price exists at which the inflationary gap is closed, but at which the factor-gap is positive, the expected profit in this case, which is "controlled supernormal", may still be either larger or smaller than the "free normal" profit, while the *ex post* profit corresponding to the expected profit must be less than the "free normal".

CHAPTER VI

CHANGES IN PRODUCTIVITY UNDER REPRESSED INFLATION

1. *Introductory remarks*

During inflation, quite drastic changes in productivity may often be expected, brought about by the abnormal conditions which are behind an inflationary situation and also by the methods for repressing inflation. A *decline* in productivity is what usually occurs, as, for instance, in the Scandinavian countries during the first and the second World Wars. Therefore it is only the effects of a decline in productivity which are considered in what follows, but a rise in productivity could be treated in a similar manner. In dealing with the case of a decline in productivity it is also intended to illustrate the concept of *"knapphetsprisstegring"*, or, literally translated, "price increase due to scarcity", which has played an important part in the Scandinavian discussion of inflation from as far back as the days of Wicksell and Davidson[1]; also to throw further light on the Davidson norm for monetary policy. This chapter is of significance for the discussion in Chap. IX of what may best be understood by the much-discussed concept of "monetary equilibrium".

---

[1] The Swedish expression *knapphetsprisstegring* is itself of quite recent date, and furthermore quite a misleading expression. The voluminous literature on the subject includes the discussion in *Ekonomisk Tidskrift*, 1920, 1921, and 1922 on problems of inflation; in this discussion Wicksell and Davidson and Gustaf Åkerman, Sven Brisman and Bertil Ohlin took part; see also Axel Nielsen, "Er der inflation" ("Do We Have Inflation"), *Nationaløkonomisk Tidsskrift*, Copenhagen, 1941; Erik Lindahl "Sveriges penning- och prispolitik efter kriget" ("Sweden's Monetary Policy and Price Policy after the War"), *Ekonomisk Tidskrift*, Stockholm, 1943; Carsten Welinder, "Inflation contra knapphetsprisstegring" ("Inflation and price increases due to scarcity"), *Ekonomisk Tidskrift*, Stockholm, 1943, and Erik Lundberg, "Ekonomisk teori och inflationsanalys" ("Economic Theory and Inflation Analysis"), *Ekonomisk Tidskrift*, Stockholm, 1948.

2. *Changes in productivity defined. Effects on cost curves*

We start by the case of *perfect competition* and must begin by distinguishing between the two forms of decline in productivity which are different from one another in their duration, or rather, in their expected duration. Firstly there are those declines in productivity which are *permanent* in the sense that when the entrepreneurs first experience them they expect them to continue into the following periods. Then, secondly, we have the *temporary* declines in productivity, which the entrepreneurs do not expect to continue beyond the period in which they unexpectedly rise. Such a distinction is used by Lindahl in his work, *Penningpolitikens mål (The Ends of Monetary Policy)*, and later in *Penningpolitikens Medel (The Means of Monetary Policy)*[1], two books which are fundamental in the literature of this subject.

We consider first the *permanent* declines in productivity which are important in inflation and it should be noticed that we consider here, as, indeed, throughout the discussion, only general declines in productivity which affect all firms to a similar extent. In so far as only permanent declines are considered, this limitation may be justified, since these declines in productivity under inflation are connected with general disorganisation, among other things.

By a "decline in productivity" we shall understand that, with given quantities of factors—in the model used: given equipment and a given quan ity of labour-services per period—the quantity of goods produced decreases. The decrease in productivity is measured by the decrease in the quantity of goods produced.[2] If the total quantity of goods produced before the decline in productivity was equal to Q_1^1, and after the decline equal to Q_1^2, where $Q_1^1 > Q_1^2$, we may, if we designate the initial productivity as 1, express the productivity after the decline as $a = Q_1^2/Q_1^1$, where $a < 1$. The decline in productivity is then $1 - a$.

In the diagrams, this implies that the point Q_1^1, which gives the maximum realizable production before the decline in productivity, is shifted to the left to Q_1^2 (cf. Fig. 15 which follows). However, we still have that the area under the marginal cost curve in the interval be-

---

[1] Erik Lindahl, *Penningpolitikens mål (The Ends of Monetary Policy)* edited by Fahlbeckska Stiftelsen, XIV, Malmö 1929, p. 43 and p. 48, and Erik Lindahl, *Penningpolitikens medel (The Means of Monetary Policy)*, edited by Fahlbeckska Stiftelsen, XV, Malmö 1929, Chap. III.

[2] Lindahl, *Penningpolitikens mål*, p. 42.

tween 0 and the realizable production, now Q_1^2, will be equal to the total wages actually paid out, which are supposed to be unaltered since the hourly rate of wages and the quantity of available labour-services are given. The expected marginal cost curve must therefore be displaced upward when productivity decreases. In order to fix the new expected marginal cost curve, we suppose *the decline in productivity to be in the same proportion for all possible actual production magnitudes*, that is, that if a decline in productivity equal to $1 - \alpha$ occurs for a definite quantity of labour-services in combination with the given equipment, then a decline of productivity equal to $1 - \alpha$ must also occur for every other quantity of labour-services combined with the given equipment.[1] The new expected marginal cost curve $m.c._2$—which we represent by $p = \psi(Q)$, whereas the old one, $m.c._1$, is represented by $p = F(Q)$—must then be so situated that

$$\int_0^Q F(\tau)\, d(\tau) = \int_0^{\alpha \cdot Q} \psi(\tau)\, d(\tau), \qquad (\text{VI}: 1)$$

from which we get

$$F(Q) \cdot (1/\alpha) = \psi(\alpha \cdot Q). \qquad (\text{VI}: 2)$$

(VI: 2) says that the ordinate of the point on $m.c._2$ for which the abscissa is $\alpha \cdot Q$ is equal to $1/\alpha$ times the ordinate of the point on $m.c._1$ for which the abscissa is Q. This implies that the new marginal cost curve may be arrived at by first moving the old one upward so that any ordinate is $1/\alpha$ times the corresponding old ordinate, and then moving it to the left so that abscissae change in the ratio $\alpha : 1$.[2] If the decline in production is 10 %, i.e. $\alpha = 0.9$, for example, the new marginal cost curve is obtained by moving the old one $11\,1/_9$ % of the distance from the abscissa axis upwards and then 10 % of the distance from the ordinate axis to the left.

---

[1] It is clear that all the following results are conditioned by this assumption, but since it seems to be the simplest which can be chosen in relation to the problem dealt with, it is adhered to in what follows. If other assumptions are made on this point, the results become distinctly more complicated, and, as will be seen later, it is just this simplicity which is important in this connection, and therefore also one of the reasons for choosing the assumption of the text. Our assumption is equivalent to the case in the Lindahlian analysis where the marginal productivities of the productive agents are proportionally affected by the decline in productivity.

[2] It is not difficult to see that the average cost curve is moved in the same way.

142

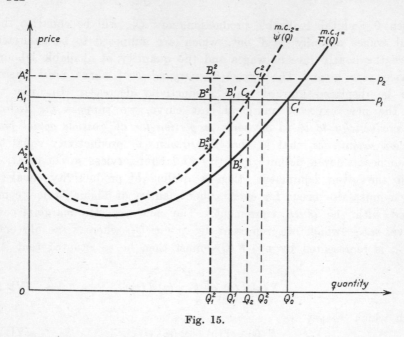

Fig. 15.

In Fig. 15 the expected marginal cost curve before the decline in productivity is denoted by $m.c._1$, and after the decline in productivity by $m.c._2$, and $m.c._2$ is constructed in the manner just explained. Q_1^1 is the realizable production before and Q_1^2 the realizable production after the decline in productivity. $Q_1^2 = a \cdot Q_1^1$.

Before the decline in productivity, at the price p_1, the factor-gap $= B_2^1 Q_1^1 Q_0^1 C_1^1$. The question of the inflationary gap in the commodity-markets, and the excess demand for commodities, and how these are affected, is taken up later on.

A "knapphetsprisstegring" (price increase "due to scarcity") is a price increase which is proportional to the decrease in productivity, that is, a price increase in the ratio $1 : a$. Let us suppose the price is raised to p_2, where $p_2 \cdot a = p_1$. The total monetary income at the new price is *ex post* $= p_2 \cdot Q_1^2 = (p_1/a) \cdot Q_1^1 \cdot a = p_1 \cdot Q_1^1$, that is, is unchanged from the initial situation. The distribution of this income in wages and profit is also unchanged from the initial situation, since the total wages actually paid out are constant ($= A_2^1 O \, Q_1^1 B_2^1 = A_2^2 O \, Q_1^2 B_2^2$), so that the total actual profit is also unchanged ($A_1^1 A_2^1 B_2^1 B_1^1 = A_1^2 A_2^2 B_2^2 B_1^2$).

After the decline in productivity and the increase of price ("due to scarcity"), the new planned production, Q_0^2, is determined by the point of intersection, C_1^2, of $m.c._2$ and the new price-line p_2. However, C_1^2 may also be arrived at by moving the point C_1^1 on $m.c._1$ upwards in the ordinate ratio $1 : a$, i.e. to the price-line p_2, and next to the left on the price-line p_2 in the abscissa-ratio $a : 1$, and so it is obvious that $a \cdot Q_0^1 = Q_0^2$, that is, that the planned production diminishes in the same proportion as the actually realizable production. It follows at once from equation (VI:1) that the total planned payment of wages previous to the decline in productivity and the increase of price ("due to scarcity") is equal to the total planned payment of wages after the decline in productivity and the increase in price ("due to scarcity"), i.e. $A_2^1 O Q_0^1 C_1^1 = A_2^2 O Q_0^2 C_1^2$. Since the wages actually paid are unaffected by these circumstances, the factor-gap, both monetarily and quantitatively, must be the same before and after the decrease of productivity and the increase of price ("due to scarcity"), i.e. $B_2^1 Q_1^1 Q_0^1 C_1^1 = B_2^2 Q_1^2 Q_0^2 C_1^2$. Furthermore, we have that $B_1^1 Q_1^1 Q_0^1 C_1^1 = B_1^2 Q_1^2 Q_0^2 C_1^2$, and the factor-gap is, as just explained, unaltered, so that $B_1^1 B_2^1 C_1^1 = B_1^2 B_2^2 C_1^2$, which leads to the result that the total expected monetary income is unaffected by the decline in productivity and increase of price "due to scarcity". Also, since $m.c._2$ rises to the right, it follows that if the price is not permitted to rise from p_1 to p_2, the decrease in productivity will lead to a decrease in the factor-gap, both monetary and real $(B_2^1 Q_1^1 Q_0^1 C_1^1 > B_2^2 Q_1^2 Q_2 C_2)$.

We can now sum up these results:

If there is a permanent decline in productivity affecting all production magnitudes in a certain given proportion, and

the price of commodities remains unaltered, the total actual (*ex post*) monetary income will fall in proportion to the fall in productivity, and this fall in the monetary income exclusively affects the profit. The total expected monetary income also falls, but more sharply than in a simple proportion to the decline in productivity and this also exclusively affects the profit. The workers' real wages, both actual and expected, remain unaltered. The factor-gap diminishes, both monetarily and quantitatively. If an

increase of price "due to scarcity" (a "knapphetsprisstegring") is allowed to take place in the same proportion as the decline in production, the total actual and expected monetary incomes, and their distribution in wages and profits will not be changed from the initial situation. The factor-gap is likewise unchanged, both monetarily and quantitatively.[1]

Actually it was these effects of the increase in prices, applied to an equilibrium situation, which lead Davidson and more especially Lindahl to put forward what is called the Davidson norm, that prices (of consumer-goods) shall vary in inverse proportion to productivity; but more of this later.

3. *Effects on the planned demand for commodities*

If the commodity price is kept fixed, both the total expected and the total actual monetary incomes fall, and this may lead to a fall in the value of the planned demand for commodities for consumption. The capitalists have to bear the decline in expected income, which decline is more than simply proportional to the decrease in productivity; and they—assumedly—have a marginal consumption-ratio which is less than 1. Therefore the value of the planned demand for consumer-goods may decline more or less than in a simple proportion. to the decline in productivity, and if it assumed that the total planned consumption of the capitalists and workers is less than the total production of commodities initially, the value of the demand for consumer-goods may decline, in an absolute sense more or less than the actually realizable production. The effects of the demand for investment-commodities are also important. If there is control of investment, everything depends on the reaction of the controlling authorities; it is conceivable that such a control will restrict the quantity of permitted investment further because of the reduced national product,

---

[1] From a consideration of Fig. 15 it is easily seen that it is really immaterial (disregarding debtor-creditor relationships) whether an increase of price ("due to scarcity") is permitted in the ratio $1/\alpha$ or whether a fall in wages instead occurs in the ratio $\alpha/1$. Because, if the marginal cost curve, as it is after there has been a decline in productivity, falls, that is, if the marginal cost curve $m.c._2$ sinks in the ratio $\alpha/1$, and the price remains unchanged at p_1, it may be seen that this lowered marginal cost curve cuts the price-line p_1 in the same point as the vertical through Q_0^2 intersects the price-line: it follows from this that the excess demand for labour power after the decline in productivity and increase of price ("due to scarcity") is equal to the excess demand for labour-power after the decline in productivity and fall in wages ("due to scarcity"). On the other hand, the factor-gap of course decreases (from the value point of view) in the same proportion as the fall in wages.

but it is equally well conceivable that the authorities will allow increased investments in the hope of overcoming the decline in production later on with the help of a bigger production apparatus. If there is no control of investment, the rate of interest is of some importance. If it is held fixed, there will perhaps be a tendency to lessening of the demand for investment commodities because of the smaller expected profit. Thus, it is necessary to confine ourselves to saying that the total planned demand for commodities (quantitatively) will probably decline to some extent, but it is uncertain whether it will decline in an absolute sense more or less than the decline in the actually realizable production.

With the commodity prices unaltered, the inflationary gap in the commodity-markets may thus decrease or increase or remain unaltered as the result of the decline in productivity. This also applies to the quantitative excess demand (in the inflationary-gap sense) in the commodity-markets.

If an increase in prices ("due to scarcity") which is proportional to the decline in productivity is allowed to take place, both the workers' and capitalists' expected incomes remain unchanged from the initial situation. Therefore, if we determine the demand for consumer-goods by multiplying the workers' and capitalists' expected incomes by the respective given consumption-ratio's (c^w and c^c, cf. equation (IV: 11)), the value of the total demand for consumer-goods must also remain unaltered. If the value of investments is constant, the value of the whole of the planned demand for commodities is unchanged, and since the value of the actually realizable production of commodities is also unchanged, the inflationary gap in the commodity-markets must be unchanged from the initial situation. But, this implies that the excess demand for commodities (in the inflationary-gap sense) must fall quantitatively in the same proportion as the productivity falls. Regarding the *ex ante* commodity-gap, that also remains unchanged, for planned production decreases in proportion to the decline in productivity. The *ex ante* excess demand in the commodity-markets therefore falls in proportion to the decline in productivity, so that its value remains unaltered.

Thus the *preliminary* conclusion is that a decline in productivity combined with increase in price ("due to scarcity") leaves both the factor-gap and the inflationary gap in the commodity-markets unchanged. Since the *ex ante* commodity-gap is also unchanged, the difference between planned investment and planned saving is unchanged. While the monetary situation is in this way unaltered, the excess demand in the commodity-markets quantitatively falls in proportion to the decline in productivity, but the excess demand in the factor-markets is unchanged.

In determining the total planned demand for commodities, we ought, however, to take into account that both the workers' and capitalists' real incomes have fallen (expected and actual), which may tend to cause an increase in the consumption-ratio's. Furthermore, investments may be fixed in quantity (or affected in some arbitrary fashion by controls). Therefore, although we can certainly conclude that the total demand for commodities falls quantitatively, we cannot be at all certain whether it falls absolutely more or less than the decline in the realizable (or in the planned) production. As far as the inflationary gap in the commodity-markets and the *ex ante* commodity-gap are concerned, however, we may quite definitely conclude that they will increase.

The *final* conclusion is thus—with a reservation for the reaction of authorities controlling investment—that a decline in productivity combined with an increase of prices ("due to scarcity") leaves the factor-gap unchanged but probably leads to an increase in the inflationary gap in the commodity-markets. The difference between planned investment and planned saving will also be likely to rise somewhat. This is the monetary aspect of the matter. Quantitatively, the excess demand in the factor-markets will remain unchanged, while the excess demand in the commodity-markets (in the inflationary-gap sense) may be considered either to increase or decrease relative to the initial situation. In addition, the demand for investment commodities may be considered as so regulated that either the inflationary gap in the commodity-markets or the excess demand in the commodity-markets remains unchanged. On the other hand, in general it cannot happen that both the inflationary gap in the commodity-markets and the excess demand in the same markets remain unchanged (this can be achieved only when the initial inflationary gap in the commodity-markets is zero, i.e. where there is equilibrium in the commodity-markets). This is of course a consequence of the increase in commodity prices.

4. *The Davidson norm*

It must now be emphasized that, whereas we have here considered all the commodity-markets in one (both commodities for consumption and investment), the *Davidson norm* in monetary policy, that prices shall vary in inverse proportion to the productivity, was originally formulated only with respect to consumer-goods. This distinction is not, however, a matter of principle (compare what follows). More important is that the Davidson norm takes as starting-point a situation in which there is complete equilibrium in both the commodity and factor markets. The idea behind the norm was that if a decline in productivity occurred in such an equilibrium situation, the equilibrium in the commodity and factor markets would be maintained if only the prices of commodities were permitted to rise in proportion to the fall in productivity, when money wage-rates remained unchanged. A necessary assumption in this way of reasoning is, however, as was pointed out by Lindahl[1], that the price-elasticity of the demand for commodities is equal to 1.[2] This is just the assumption which is made in the preliminary conclusion arrived at above, and if we add that complete equilibrium shall initially exist in both commodity and factor markets, it follows from the preliminary conclusion that the increase of prices ("due to scarcity") is just sufficient to maintain this equilibrium, monetarily and quantitatively. Certainly, one of the preliminary conclusions was that the excess demand in the commodity-markets falls

---

[1] *Penningpolitikens Mål*, p. 50, among others. However, Lindahl puts this forward only when he deals with partial changes in productivity, and only with respect to the demand for commodities for consumption. Where he speaks about general changes in productivity the question is not explicitly dealt with, but as I understand it, the conclusion follows from Lindahl's general assumptions. Lindahl all the time considers the loan-rate of interest to be the same as the "normal" rate of interest, which implies that if changes occur in planned monetary saving, then the loan-rate of interest is varied in such a way that planned investment changes monetarily in a similar manner to saving. However, this must mean that the total planned demand for commodities (for consumption and investment) remains unchanged when reckoned in value, and in this way the price-elasticity for the total planned demand for commodities is fixed at 1.

[2] It will be noticed that the elasticity which we are talking about here is not the same as the elasticity for the demand curve which occurs in the model we have been working with; for we now consider a comparison between two points on two different demand curves, because our demand curve is displaced when the expected marginal cost curve is displaced.

in proportion to the decline in productivity, but if the excess demand in the commodity-markets is zero before the decline in productivity it will remain that after the decline in productivity.

It must also be stressed, still adhering to the assumption which is behind the preliminary conclusion, that even if it is found desirable, as a result of that conclusion to let prices vary in inverse proportion to the productivity (or possibly, wages in direct proportion to the productivity) if there is complete equilibrium in the initial situation, it does not necessarily follow that it is also desirable to let prices vary in inverse proportion to the productivity when the initial situation is an inflationary disequilibrium with excess demand in both the commodity and factor markets, such as is dealt with here.

The main point with the Davidson norm, as explained and rationalized by Lindahl, disregarding the problem of justice, is that there shall be, as far as possible, equilibrium in both the commodity and factor markets. If therefore, the initial situation is one of disequilibrium, the right policy according to the line of reasoning leading to the Davidson norm is that policy which brings the system nearer to equilibrium, and we are definitely nearer to equilibrium (monetary or quantitative) if the excess demand (monetary or quantitative respectively) in both commodity and factor markets decreases. But whether this is equivalent to allowing prices to rise or not where a decline of productivity occurs must be decided from the effects of alternative forms of price policy pursued by the controlling authorities.

If prices are not allowed to rise, the factor-gap and the excess demand in the factor-market decrease. It follows from this that if prices are not allowed to rise the decline in productivity can never definitely increase the pressure of inflation, neither monetarily nor quantitatively; but it may quite well be supposed that it will decrease the pressure of inflation and bring the system nearer to equilibrium. This depends on the development in the commodity-markets. Taking everything into consideration, at unchanged prices the inflationary gap and excess demand in the commodity-markets may be considered either to increase or decrease (or remain unchanged) as a result of the decline in productivity. So, if prices are not allowed to rise, there is the possibility that the pressure of inflation (monetary and quantitative) will decrease, whereas, on the other hand, it cannot increase.

If an increase in prices ("due to scarcity") is permitted, the factor-gap and the excess demand for factors will be unchanged. According to the development in the commodity-markets, the pressure of inflation may consequently be considered as either increased, decreased or unchanged. As a consequence of the assumptions behind the preceding preliminary conclusion (cf. Section 3), the inflationary gap in the commodity-markets should be unaffected by a decrease in productivity and an increase in prices ("due to scarcity"), while the quantitative excess demand corresponding to the inflationary gap in the commodity-markets must decrease. If this is correct, the quantitative pressure of inflation must definitely decrease. However, taking more realistic assumptions into consideration, the final conclusion reached above was that the excess demand in the commodity-markets may be considered either to decrease or to increase, or remain unchanged, and the result is therefore that the pressure of inflation (monetary and quantitative) may increase, decrease or remain unchanged. It is not possible to say anything about which of these possibilities is most likely without making wider assumptions. It thus seems that of the two alternatives —unchanged prices and increase of prices ("due to scarcity")—the first is to be preferred, for that does at any rate exclude all possibility of an increase in the pressure of inflation. This may also be expressed by saying that the one thing that is quite certain about the effect of a decline in productivity is that, if prices are kept fixed, the excess demand in the factor-markets will be less than in the initial situation, and if an increase in prices ("due to scarcity") is permitted the excess demand in the factor-markets will remain unchanged from the initial situation. But a condition which is absolutely necessary for the achievement of complete equilibrium without inflation is that the factor-gap shall disappear, and that is just what is brought about by a decrease in productivity without increase of prices ("due to scarcity"). So, a decline in productivity may be said to be a favourable circumstance for combatting inflation!

This may also be expressed by the use of the concept of "normal" profit. The existence of an excess demand in the factor-markets is, under perfect competition, equivalent to the profit being "supernormal" both *ex ante* and *ex post*. A decline in productivity without increase of prices ("due to scarcity") decreases the expected and the actual profit and therefore brings the system nearer to equilibrium. This mode of expression is in agreement with Lindahl's line of argument, which just uses "gains" as indicators of disequilibrium.

A permanent rise in productivity may be dealt with in an analogous fashion to a decline in productivity and has precisely the opposite effects, that is, certainly results in an increase of the factor-gap, if prices are kept unchanged, whereas a fall in prices proportional to the increase in productivity leaves the factor-gap unaltered. Thus in the case of an increase in productivity, there seems to be some inducement to follow the Davidson rules and lower prices in accordance with the increase of productivity in the disequilibrium situation dealt with here. And the motive for this asymmetric policy is quite simply that the achievement of the desired equilibrium always requires prices to decrease relative to wages—when productivity is unchanged.[1]

5. *Temporary changes in productivity*

What is characteristic of occasional, temporary falls in productivity is that they occur unexpectedly in a period (i.e. the actual marginal cost curve is higher than the expected marginal cost curve), and are expected to disappear at the beginning of the following period. Therefore, the expected marginal cost curve is not affected in any period. If no price increases are allowed, the entrepreneurs will suffer an unexpected loss as a result. Their total unexpected loss—the difference between *ex ante* and *ex post* profit—consequently becomes $A_2^2 A_2^1 C_1^1 B^2 B_2^2$ instead of merely $B_2^1 C_1^1 B_1^1$ (see Fig. 15). But the factor-gap is not affected by this, neither in this nor in any later period. This is due to the fact that the decline in productivity is not permanent. The inflationary gap in the commodity-markets and the excess demand for commodities therefore increases for the same period by the same absolute amount as the actual production of commodities decreases, but this increase in the inflationary gap in the commodity-markets disappears in the next period, unless later periods are affected by "postponed demand". But if prices are allowed to rise during the period—and this rise in prices must be an unexpected one for everyone except the controllers of prices—the factor-gap will not be affected, neither

---

[1] It is quite possible to extend this method of reasoning to a case which is on the other side of the equilibrium position, that is, where there is unemployment. Opposite results are then obtained.

during the period concerned, where the planned production is fixed on a basis of the incorrect expectations about the cost curve and prices, nor during some future period, supposing the entrepreneurs to count on the prices for the next period being the same as the old prices. On the other hand, the entrepreneurs' actual profit is, of course larger than it would have been if no increase of prices ("due to scarcity") had been permitted during the period, and the entrepreneurs' *ex post* profit is unchanged despite the decline in productivity. As far as the effects on the inflationary gap in the commodity-markets are concerned, it should be noticed that the demand for commodities at the new higher price cannot be determined from the planned demand curves of the model, for these only say how much those who demand plan to buy at alternative expected prices, assuming these price expectations to be correct. However, if the price is other than was expected, the question is one of how much those who demand will then be prepared to spend. What is usually assumed at this point in the theory is that the purchasers have decided what sums of money they will spend, whatever the price turns out to be. Such an assumption is equivalent to reckoning with a demand elasticity equal to 1 for this case, and it follows from this that if an increase in prices ("due to scarcity") is permitted, the inflationary gap in the commodity-markets will be the same as it would have been if a decline in productivity and increase of prices ("due to scarcity") had not occurred. This of course implies that the excess demand in the commodity-markets has decreased. So the consequence of permitting a price increase ("due to scarcity") is in this case that the factor-gap and excess demand in the factor-markets in the period is unchanged, and the inflationary gap in the commodity-markets is unchanged, but the excess demand for commodities is less than it would have been if there had been no decline in productivity and no price increases ("due to scarcity"). Therefore the system approaches nearer to equilibrium in the period concerned. The following periods are unaffected.

However, this result is only obtained by assuming a demand elasticity equal to 1. If this is not the case, and prospective purchasers would rather try to carry out the quantitative planned demand, the quantitative excess demand in the commodity-markets could be supposed either to increase, decrease or remain unchanged, even it is taken for granted that the quantitative demand which it is sought to carry out may fall to some extent because of increase in prices ("due to scarcity"). In this case, we have that an increase in prices ("due to scarcity") may increase, decrease or leave unaltered the pressure of inflation.

The reasoning is quite analogous for temporary increases in productivity.

The result of permitting price increases ("due to scarcity") if the decline in productivity is only temporary is thus uncertain, but this much does seem certain, that the excess demand in the commodity-markets cannot be larger within the period if price increases ("due to scarcity") are permitted, than if they are not permitted, and it may decrease somewhat. So we almost certainly come nearer to equilibrium within the period if prices increase ("due to scarcity"), and this would seem to provide a reason for allowing a temporary fall in productivity to be accompanied by a temporary rise in price. On the other hand it is seen that there is reason to keep commodity prices fixed and not to carry out a lowering of prices when a temporary increase in productivity occurs. Thus it seems desirable here also to practise an asymmetric policy with regard to changes in productivity, in order to come nearer to equilibrium. But it is seen that the reasonable policy for temporary changes in productivity is precisely the opposite of what seemed to be reasonable for permanent changes in productivity. When productivity decreases, fixed prices seem to be advisable if the decrease is permanent; if it is temporary, price increases ("due to scarcity") seem to be preferable. And conversely as regards increases in productivity.

When the initial situation is one of disequilibrium such that there is excess demand in both the factor and commodity markets, we find no simple rule of price-policy. But, as already explained, that does not in any way contradict the Davidson norm that if there is equilibrium in the initial situation, in order to retain equilibrium it is best to regulate prices in inverse (or wages in direct) proportion to the productivity.

6. *Effects on the cost curves and on planned supply under monopolism*

We turn to the case of *monopolism* and first consider *permanent* declines in productivity, proportional for all production magnitudes, and this is illustrated, from the cost point of view, by just the same displacement of the expected marginal cost curve upward and to the left as was described in Section 2. As in the preceding chapters, different cases must be distinguished. There is the case in which the price before the decline in productivity and price increase ("due to scarcity") is lower than p_2 (see Fig. 16), which is the price determined by the intersection of the expected marginal cost curve before the decline in productivity—$m.c._1$—and the expected sales curve FF. There is also the case in which the price before the decline in productivity and price increase "due to scarcity" is higher than p_3 (Fig. 16), which is the price determined by the intersection of the expected marginal cost curve after the decline in productivity—$m.c._2$—and the expected sales curve FF, which we take to be unaffected by the decline in productivity. Lastly, there is the case in which the price before the decline in productivity and price increase ("due to scarcity") is between p_2 and p_3. For the sake of simplicity we suppose that the price never rises above p_{opt} (cf. Fig. 7).

The first of these cases is quickly dealt with, since it is characteristic of this that the controlled expected sales curve is horizontal over the whole of the relevant interval (both before and after price increase "due to scarcity"), so that this case behaves just like the corresponding one with perfect competition.[1] All the reasoning used in that case may be carried over to this case of monopolism.

But, in the next case, where the initial price is higher than p_3, the results from the case of perfect competition cannot be used. As already mentioned, we take the entrepreneurs total expected sales curve FF to be unaffected by the decline in productivity. The case may then be illustrated in Fig. 16 which follows.

If the initial price, p_0, is higher than p_3, which is, as explained, determined by the intersection of the curves $m.c._2$ and FF, the planned production will not be affected by the decline in productivity, for both $m.c._1$ and $m.c._2$ cut the controlled marginal revenue curve in its vertical part. Since the actually realizable production falls, however, from Q_1^1 to Q_1^2, the factor-gap must increase from $B_2^1 Q_1^1 Q_0^1 C_1^1$ to

---

[1] However, if increase in price ("due to scarcity") cause the price to rise above p_2, this does not apply if the price elasticity of the expected sales curve is significantly greater than 1 at the price p_2.

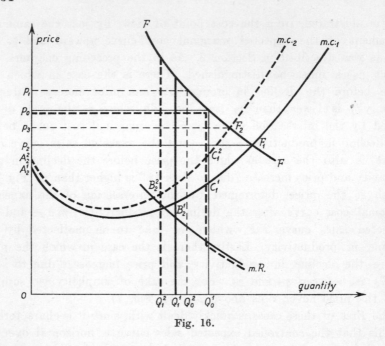

Fig. 16.

$B_2^2 Q_1^2 Q_0^1 C_1^2$ when the price remains p_0. The excess demand for factors rises correspondingly.

If an increase of price ("due to scarcity") from p_0 to p_1 is allowed, in the same proportion as the decline in productivity, the planned production will fall from Q_0^1 to Q_0^2. If the elasticity for the expected sales curve FF is everywhere just equal to 1, the planned production will fall in the same proportion as the productivity, and the factor-gap and excess demand for factors remains unchanged from the initial situation. If the elasticity mentioned is greater than 1, the factor-gap and the excess demand for factors will be less than initially, and if the elasticity is less than 1, greater than initially.

It is seen that the relationship is just the opposite of what we had in the case of perfect competition. There, with fixed prices the factor-gap diminished, and when prices increased ("due to scarcity") the factor-gap remained unchanged from the initial situation; but here, with fixed prices the factor-gap increases, and when prices increase ("due to scarcity") the factor-gap (possibly) remains unchanged from the initial situation.

If the initial price is between p_2 and p_3, the decline in productivity will lead to a certain decline in the planned demand for factors. For, whereas with prices in this interval the curve $m.c._1$ intersects the controlled marginal revenue curve in its vertical part, the curve $m.c._2$ will intersect the controlled marginal revenue curve in its horizontal part, and this must imply a reduction of planned production. If the initial price is p_2, the planned production will decrease more sharply than in simple proportion to the decrease in productivity (cf. the perfect-competition case), so that the factor-gap and the excess demand for factors must be less than initially. If the initial price is as high as p_3, the planned production will be unaffected by the decline in productivity, and the factor-gap and excess demand for factors must increase relative to what they were initially. Thus there must obviously be a price between p_2 and p_3—let us call it p_{ind} where ind signifies "indifferent"—at which price, when fixed, the decrease in productivity neither increases nor decreases the factor-gap and the excess demand for factors. If an increase in price ("due to scarcity") is permitted, and if the elasticity for the expected sales curve is equal to 1, the factor-gap and the excess demand for factors remain unchanged wherever the initial price is in the interval between p_2 and p_3. If the initial price is less than p_{ind}, a decline in productivity, considered by itself, leads to a decline in the factor-gap and excess demand for factors, but price increase ("due to scarcity"), considered by itself, leads to a corresponding increase in the factor-gap and excess demand for factors. If the initial price is higher than p_{ind}, the converse applies; and if the initial price is just p_{ind}, neither decline in productivity nor price increase ("due to scarcity"), considered by themselves, will lead to any alteration in the factor-gap or excess demand for factors.

If the results for the initial price lower than p_2 or higher than p_3 are borne in mind, we may summarize the effects on the factor-gap and excess demand for factors in the following way: Between p_2 and p_3 there is a price p_{ind}, at which the factor gap and excess demand for factors are unaffected by a decline in productivity unaccompanied by an increase in prices; at all fixed prices below p_{ind} a decrease in productivity leads to a decrease of the factor-gap and the excess demand for factors; at all fixed prices above p_{ind} a decrease in productivity leads to an increase of the factor-gap and the excess demand for factors. If a price increase ("due to scarcity") is allowed, the factor-gap and excess demand for factors remains unchanged from the initial situation for all initial prices, assuming the elasticity for the expected sales curve FF to be equal to 1. If the elasticity for the expected sales curve is different from 1, the factor-gap and excess demand for factors may be either larger or smaller than initially after a decline in productivity and price increase ("due to scarcity"), depending on the shape of the expected sales curve and the initial price. It is clear that there will always be a price at which the factor-gap and excess demand for factors remain unchanged from the initial situation, but the increase of price will then not be proportional to the decrease in productivity.

7. *Effects on the demand for commodities under monopolism*

From a consideration of the effects of a decline in productivity and price increase ("due to scarcity") on expected incomes of capitalists and workers similar to that made in the case of perfect competition, it will be seen that there is nothing else to be said than that the excess demand for commodities can either decrease or increase, both when prices are kept fixed and when price increases ("due to scarcity") are permitted. Unless special assumptions are made like the ones advanced in the case of perfect competition, there is no reason to suppose that a decline in productivity combined with price increases ("due to scarcity") should leave either the inflationary gap in the commodity-markets or the excess demand for commodities unchanged at the initial values.—

Now, we only have to go into the matter of the effects of a decrease in productivity and increase in prices ("due to scarcity"), when the initial situation is such that there is complete equilibrium in both the commodity and factor markets under monopolism. Here, as in the case of perfect competition, if the price is fixed, an excess supply of factors will arise and (probably) an excess demand for commodities. If prices are allowed to increase ("due to scarcity"), the excess supply of factors will disappear and equilibrium will be achieved in the factor-market, *if* the expected sales curve has unit elasticity. If it is also true that the planned demand for commodities during this change has a price elasticity equal to 1, the price increases ("due to scarcity") will just cause the excess demand for commodities to disappear, so that complete equilibrium is established. So, it is necessary that not only the price elasticity of the planned demand for commodities, but also of the expected sales, should be equal to 1 (which is equivalent to the entrepreneurs' sales expectations being correct at all prices), in order that Lindahl's reasoning may be extended to the case of monopolism.

Finally, we consider *temporary* decreases in productivity. These are characterized by the expected cost curve being unaffected in all periods, so that neither the demand for factors nor the excess demand for factors is affected. The effects are apparent only in the commodity-markets and the reasoning which was applied to these effects in Section 5, may be carried over to the case of monopolism.

8. *Policies against the effects of changes in productivity under monopolism*

When it comes to deciding, from this reasoning, what price-policy is advisable under monopolism when there is a change in productivity, from the general viewpoint that it is desirable to approach as near as possible to monetary equilibrium in both the commodity and factor markets, the result is much more complicated than with perfect competition.

For temporary changes in productivity, however, just the same reasoning applies as under perfect competition. But for permanent changes in productivity it is another matter. In what follows, it is only a decrease in productivity which is dealt with, but the argument for an increase in productivity is analogous.

Since the effects upon excess demand for commodities of both a permanent decline in productivity at fixed prices and a permanent decline in productivity when price increases ("due to scarcity") are permitted are uncertain (unless more precise assumptions can be made), we must direct our attention to the factor-gap and the excess demand for factors. In these circumstances we can only be certain that we have not come definitely farther away from equilibrium if the factor-gap and the excess demand for factors is less than in the initial situation. The "right" policy seems to be that which lessens the factor-gap as much as possible. Here the shape of the expected sales curve is of decisive importance. If the expected sales curve is unaffected by changes in productivity, and if its price elasticity is everywhere equal to 1, we get the simple result that a decline in production coupled with price increases "due to scarcity" always leaves the factor-gap unchanged from the initial situation. If the price before the decline in productivity is lower than p_{ind}, the excess demand becomes less than in the initial situation when the price is fixed, and therefore it is preferable to keep the price fixed rather than to allow an increase in price ("due to scarcity"). If the price before the decline in productivity is higher than p_{ind}, on the other hand, the excess demand becomes greater than in the initial situation when the price is fixed, and it is therefore preferable to allow an increase of price ("due to scarcity"). Lastly, if the price before the decline in productivity is equal to p_{ind}, it is immaterial whether the price is allowed to rise or not, because the excess demand for factors remains unchanged in either case with this initial situation.

If it is not possible to maintain the above-mentioned assumptions about the sales curve, these relatively simple rules cease to hold, and here again it is important that, whereas it is probably reasonable to assume that the expected sales curve is unaffected by the fall in productivity by itself, there is no reasonable ground for assuming that the price elasticity of the expected sales curve is everywhere equal to 1. If the shape of the expected sales curve is known, it is of course always possible to calculate whether it is the fixed price or the permitted increase of price ("due to scarcity") which makes the excess demand for factors a minimum, but it is no longer possible to put forward a simple rule for the matter. Moreover, in choosing the "right" price-policy to deal with a decline in productivity under monopolism, it is necessary to take into consideration which form of equilibrium is considered desirable; one in which all controls may cease, or one in which controls are maintained.

CHAPTER VII

ON OPEN INFLATION: SIMPLE MODEL

1. *Introductory remarks*

In order to give a complete account of the problems of open inflation, it would be necessary to deal with the whole of the dynamic
theory, but this cannot be attempted here. However, in extending the
preceding discussion it is necessary to show how the magnitudes considered, such as the inflationary gap in the commodity-markets, the
factor-gap, the speed of the rise in prices, etc., may react upon one
another in a simple case, when it is assumed that the governing
authorities do not put any restraints on the development of prices
and wages.

Therefore, in Section 2 a very simple dynamic model is set up,
which shows the ratio of price to wage-rate, the excess demand for
commodities and labour-services and the speed of the rise in prices of
commodities and in wage-rates, under inflationary conditions. In Sections 3, 4, 5, and 6 the effects of various changes of data in this
model are considered; in Section 7 the importance of monopolism is
briefly reviewed, and finally in Section 8, how this simple dynamic
model may be regarded as a special case of a more general model,
which covers both the case of inflation and the case where there is
no inflation in the system. This more general model, however, is itself
of quite a simple nature, but Chap. VIII is devoted to the analysis
of a very general model, of which the models used in this and the
previous Chaps. IV to VI may be regarded as special cases.

2. *A simple dynamic model for inflation*

We assume that there is perfect competition in all markets unless
something is said to the contrary, and that the expectations are that
the prices of the moment will persist in the future. It is further

assumed that only one commodity is produced, for which only one (variable) factor, labour-services, is used. The quantity of labour-services per unit of time is a given magnitude, and there is thus a given actual production, which, as before, is called Q_1;

$$Q_1 = \text{constant.} \qquad \text{(VII: 1)}$$

With given equipment and technique and with expectations as described above, the volume of planned production Q_0 is a function of the relation between price p and wage-rate w, (p/w), such that the higher the price is relative to the wage-rate, the larger is the attempted (= planned = optimum) production.[1]

$$Q_0 = \varphi\left(\frac{p}{w}\right),^2 \qquad \text{(VII: 2)}$$

$$\varphi' > 0. \qquad \text{(VII: 3)}$$

Since we are at present considering only the case of inflation in which the total real income is constant (at a maximum), the demand for consumer-goods may be regarded as a function of the price-wage ratio, such that the higher the price is relative to the wage-rate, the less is the demand for consumer-goods. This is due to the fact that the higher (p/w) is, the greater is the capitalists' share of the total national income, and that the capitalists' consumption-ratio is less than the workers'; and we neglect the possibility dealt with in Chap. IV, Section 5, that the expected income of the capitalists increases so strongly when prices rise, that demand increases with rising price-wage ratio. The demand for investment commodities is taken to be constant (for example, determined by a given rate of interest), and the state's de-

---

[1] The distinction pointed out in Chaps. II and III between what is to be taken as optimum, what it is attempted to carry out, and what is planned is therefore disregarded here. In principle, in this chapter demand should however be understood to mean active attempts to purchase.

[2] If w is kept constant, the Q_0-curve is obviously the expected marginal cost curve of the models for repressed inflation in Chap. IV, i.e. $Q_0 = \varphi\,(p/w)$ becomes identical with $Q = f\,(p)$, (IV: 5). When only wage-costs enter into the variable costs, a rise in wage-rates of k per cent will move the marginal cost curve upwards with k per cent. A simultaneous price rise in the same proportion will accordingly leave the planned production unaltered. So, equation (VII: 2) is a generalized version of equation (IV: 5).

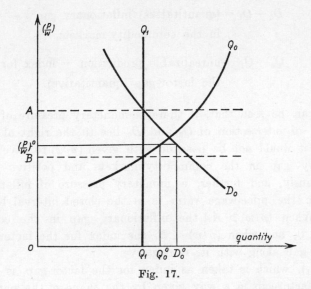

Fig. 17.

mand for commodities (and "production of commodities" = demand for labour-services) is taken to be constant (fixed by the budget), and we therefore find the total quantitative planned demand for commodities, D_0, to be given by

$$D_0 = \Phi\left(\frac{p}{w}\right),^1 \qquad\qquad (\text{VII}:4)$$

$$\Phi' < 0. \qquad\qquad (\text{VII}:5)$$

In Fig. 17, with the quantity of commodities as abscissa and the price-wage ratio as ordinate, the actual production, the planned production and the planned demand for commodities are indicated.

We now have, reading horizontally, that

---

[1] If w is kept constant, the D_0-curve becomes identical with the planned demand curve of Chap. IV, see equation (IV:13). If the assumption of constant wage-rate applied in Chap. IV is removed, it is easily seen that a proportional change in price and wage-rate will leave the planned demand, D_0, of (IV:13) unchanged. For if both p and w change to $k \cdot p$ and $k \cdot w$, respectively, we have to substitute in (IV:13), $k \cdot p$ for p, $k \cdot p_1$ for p_1, and $k \cdot \int_a^p f(\tau)\, d\tau$ for $\int_a^p f(\tau)\, d\tau$. So, equation (VII:4) is to be regarded as a generalized version of equation (IV:13).

$$D_0 - Q_1 = \text{(quantitative) inflationary gap} \atop \text{in the commodity-markets,} \qquad \text{(VII: 6)}$$

$$Q_0 - Q_1 = \text{unrealizable production} = \text{index for} \atop \text{the factor-gap (quantitative).} \qquad \text{(VII: 7)}$$

So it can be seen that, if there is monetary pressure of inflation, the point of intersection of Q_0 and D_0 lies to the right of Q_1, since otherwise it would not be possible with given (p/w) to have a positive inflationary gap in the commodity-markets and positive factor-gap simultaneously, and further, a monetary pressure of inflation exists only when the price-wage ratio is in the closed interval between A and B. When $(p/w) > A$, the inflationary gap in the commodity-markets < 0, and when $(p/w) < B$, the index for the factor-gap, and the factor-gap along with it, is negative.

$(Q_0 - Q_1)$, which is taken as index for the factor-gap, is connected with the factor-gap in a way given by the shape of the marginal cost curve. $(Q_0 - Q_1)$ is thus an unambiguous index for the factor-gap, since $(Q_0 - Q_1) = 0$ implies that the factor-gap is zero, and larger $(Q_0 - Q_1)$ always implies a larger factor-gap, and *vice versa*. This is all we need to know in what follows.

If the equations (VII: 1), (VII: 2), and (VII: 4), and in addition the two conditions of equilibrium:

$$D_0 - Q_1 = 0, \qquad \text{(VII: 8)}$$

$$Q_0 - Q_1 = 0, \qquad \text{(VII: 9)}$$

are considered as a static equilibrium system in the magnitudes Q_1, Q_0, D_0 and (p/w), the system obviously is overdetermined and inconsistent. This is nothing to be downhearted about, however, since we do not wish to treat the system statically.

Equations (VII: 8) and (VII: 9) are thus not to be used, but we introduce two dynamical equations, firstly

$$\frac{dp}{dt} = f(D_0 - Q_1), \qquad \text{(VII: 10)}$$

where

$$f(0) = 0 \qquad \text{(VII: 11)}$$

and
$$f' > 0, \tag{VII:12}$$

and secondly
$$\frac{dw}{dt} = F(Q_0 - Q_1), \tag{VII:13}$$

where
$$F(0) = 0 \tag{VII:14}$$

and
$$F' > 0, \tag{VII:15}$$

t denoting time.

Equations (VII:10) and (VII:13) with the properties described have often been used in the literature[1], and will be discussed more thoroughly in Chaps. VIII and IX. Yet it should be remarked that (VII:13) should really have the form $dw/dt = G(g(Q_0 - Q_1))$, since $Q_0 - Q_1$ is only an index for the factor-gap, so that the factor-gap $= g(Q_0 - Q_1)$, but since the function g may be supposed to have similar properties to the function G (namely $g(0) = 0$ and $g' > 0$), $G(g(Q_0 - Q_1))$ may be replaced by $F(Q_0 - Q_1)$, a monotone function of a monotone function being itself a monotone function, and $G(g(0))$ being equal to 0 from $G(0) = 0$ and $g(0) = 0$. The function F thus preserves the properties which are characteristic of G.

For the price-wage ratio we have

$$\frac{d\left(\dfrac{p}{w}\right)}{dt} = \frac{w \cdot \dfrac{dp}{dt} - p \cdot \dfrac{dw}{dt}}{w^2} = \frac{f(D_0 - Q_1) - \left(\dfrac{p}{w}\right) \cdot F(Q_0 - Q_1)}{w}, \tag{VII:16}$$

from which it follows that the condition for the ratio of price to wage-rate to be constant, that is, for

$$\frac{d\left(\dfrac{p}{w}\right)}{dt} = 0, \tag{VII:17}$$

is that

$$\left(\frac{p}{w}\right) = \frac{f(D_0 - Q_1)}{F(Q_0 - Q_1)}, \tag{VII:18}$$

assuming $F(Q_0 - Q_1) \neq 0$ and also p and $w \neq 0$ and positive.

---

[1] Cf., for instance, Paul A. Samuelson, *Foundations of Economic Analysis*, Ch. IX, and O. Lange, *Price Flexibility and Employment*, Appendix.

Equation (VII: 18) may now be used as a condition[1] of what in the following will be called *quasi-equilibrium*, so we now have the quasi-equilibrium system given by:

$$Q_1 = \text{constant} \tag{VII: 1}$$

$$Q_0 = \varphi\left(\frac{p}{w}\right) \tag{VII: 2}$$

$$D_0 = \Phi\left(\frac{p}{w}\right) \tag{VII: 4}$$

$$\left(\frac{p}{w}\right) = \frac{f(D_0 - Q_1)}{F(Q_0 - Q_1)} \tag{VII: 18}$$

in the four unknowns Q_1, Q_0, D_0 and (p/w). With the help of (VII: 10) and (VII: 13) we next find the speed of the rise in the price, dp/dt, and the speed of the rise in the wage-rate, dw/dt. From (VII: 18) it is at once evident that, in quasi-equilibrium,

$$\frac{p}{w} \cdot \frac{dw}{dp} = 1, \tag{VII: 19}$$

i.e., the wage-elasticity of the price, or, if preferred, the price-elasticity of the wage-rate, is equal to 1.

On considering the functions φ, Φ, f and F, restricted according to (VII: 3), (VII: 5), (VII: 11), (VII: 12), (VII: 14), and (VII: 15), it is not difficult to see that there is one and only one solution of the system; and the value of (p/w) given by the solution is in the open interval AB. It follows directly from this that both the excess demand for commodities and the excess demand for factors are positive, so that both price and wage-rate will follow a persistent upward trend. Since there is accordingly a quasi-equilibrium solution for this system, it may be shown that this quasi-equilibrium is stable in the sense that, whatever price-wage relation we start with, there will be forces at work which tend to bring the system back to the quasi-equilibrium position.

---

[1] When $F(Q_0 - Q_1) = 0$ the condition of quasi-equilibrium must be written as

$$f(D_0 - Q_1) - \left(\frac{p}{w}\right) \cdot F(Q_0 - Q_1) = 0. \tag{VII: 18'}$$

We will call the quasi-equilibrium values of (p/w), D_0 and Q_0 respectively $(p/w)^0$, D_0^0 and Q_0^0, and we then get

$$\frac{d\left(\dfrac{p}{w}\right)^0}{dt} = \frac{f\,(D_0^0 - Q_1) - \left(\dfrac{p}{w}\right)^0 \cdot F\,(Q_0^0 - Q_1)}{w} = 0. \qquad \text{(VII:20)}$$

We now wish to show that when $(p/w) < (p/w)^0$, then $d\,(p/w)/dt > 0$, and conversely, when $(p/w) > (p/w)^0$, then $d\,(p/w)/dt < 0$, for these are the conditions that any movement away from the quasi-equilibrium position is always accompanied by a tendency to return to that position.

It is now assumed that $(p/w)^1 < (p/w)^0$, and we have that D_0^1 is the demand and Q_0^1 is the planned production at $(p/w)^1$, and accordingly

$$\frac{d\left(\dfrac{p}{w}\right)^1}{dt} - \frac{f\,(D_0^1 - Q_1) - \left(\dfrac{p}{w}\right)^1 \cdot F\,(Q_0^1 - Q_1)}{w} > \frac{d\left(\dfrac{p}{w}\right)^0}{dt} = 0 \qquad \text{(VII:21)}$$

because $f\,(D_0^1 - Q_1) > f\,(D_0^0 - Q_1)$, $(p/w)^1 < (p/w)^0$, $F\,(Q_0^1 - Q_1) < F\,(Q_0^0 - Q_1)$ and lastly w, whose numerical value is admittedly undetermined, is positive. In the same way it may be seen that when $(p/w) > (p/w)^0$, $d\,(p/w)/dt < 0$. We have thus shown that the quasi-equilibrium is stable.[1]

In Fig. 17 the quasi-equilibrium position is indicated by $(p/w)^0$, the excess demand in the commodity-market being $D_0^0 - Q_1$, and the excess demand in the labour-market being $Q_0^0 - Q_1$ (index). It is evident that this quasi-equilibrium position need in no way coincide with the point of intersection of the curve for demand, D_0, and the curve for supply,

---

[1] The stability is, of course, conditioned by the fact that we have only considered a demand curve with negative slope. If other possibilities for the shape of the demand curve are taken into account—see Chap. IV, Section 5—it may well happen that the quasi-equilibrium is unstable, and even that the system has no quasi-equilibrium solution at all. However, we shall not examine the questions arising in these circumstances.

It should also be noticed that the assumptions made here about the slopes of the curves are sufficient, but in no way necessary, conditions for the system to be stable. It is seen that a necessary and sufficient condition for stability is

$$f' \cdot \Phi' - \left(\frac{p}{w}\right) \cdot F' \cdot \varphi' < F.$$

Q_0. Therefore, although the system does certainly tend to a fixed relation between excess demand for commodities and excess demand for labour-services, it is not such that the excess demand for labour-services "corresponds" to the excess demand for commodities in the sense that there is just such an excess demand for labour-services as would be necessary to· produce the amount of the excess demand for commodities. The planned production which cannot be carried out, $Q_0^0 - Q_1$, may be greater than or smaller than the excess demand for commodities, depending on whereabouts in the interval AB the quasi-equilibrium price-wage ratio is, and the quasi-equilibrium position is itself a matter depending on the functions f, F, φ, and Φ.

It is also intuitively evident that the system must move towards such a quasi-equilibrium position. If we consider Fig. 17 and begin with a price-wage ratio A, the excess demand for commodities at this price-wage ratio will be zero, whereas the excess demand for labour-services will be positive. The price will consequently be constant, while the wage-rate tends to rise, which means that the price-wage ratio at A tends to fall. When the price-wage ratio has become a little lower, an excess demand for commodities will begin to appear, while the excess demand for labour-services simultaneously decreases. The price therefore begins to rise, and the speed of the rise in the wage-rate is retarded, which retards the fall in the price-wage ratio. In this way the price-wage ratio will fall—increasingly slowly—to a level where the excess demand for commodities "corresponds" to the excess demand for factors in the sense that the percentage rise of the wage-rate per unit time which is thus brought about is equal to the percentage rise of the price per unit time. Corresponding reasoning could be put forward if we started from the price-wage ratio B instead.

When we prefer to speak about quasi-equilibrium instead of equilibrium, it is of course because this quasi-equilibrium is no static equilibrium, since both price and wage-rate rise without interruption and excess demands are not zero. There is equilibrium only in the sense that the price-wage ratio, excess demand for commodities and for labour-services, and along with them the speeds of the rise in the price and the wage-rate are constant.

That the system moves towards such a quasi-equilibrium may be taken as a dynamic proof for the Keynesian proposition that the ratio of prices to wages tends to be constant, so that a certain rise in money-wages is accompanied by a corresponding rise in prices, that is, so that the real wages of the workers tend to remain constant, despite possible attempts to raise them by raising the money wages. But this result applies here only in respect of a tendency which does not have effect until quasi-equilibrium is reached. And the movement towards quasi-equilibrium takes time, depending on the functions f and F. Therefore, if we suppose that a position of dynamic quasi-equilibrium has been attained with price-wage ratio $(p/w)^0$ and constant speeds for the rise in the price and the rise in the wage-rate, and further suppose that the wage-rate at some moment suddenly increases with a jump faster than the value of the speed of the rise in the wage-rate which follows from the given excess demand for labour-services, (we thus suppose that a spontaneous wage-rise occurs, which is superimposed on the induced (continuous) increase in wages, cf. Chap. I, Section 7), (p/w) will be displaced downwards below the quasi-equilibrium value $(p/w)^0$. This will lead to a fall in the excess demand for labour-services and a rise in the excess demand for commodities; the new price-wage ratio immediately begins to rise again, (the price-elasticity of the wage-rate becomes < 1), so that it approaches the old quasi-equilibrium position after a time, but until quasi-equilibrium is reached, the workers evidently have the benefit of a rise in the real wage.[1]

Thus it is seen that through an uninterrupted series of spontaneous rises in the wage-rate, the workers are in a position to keep the price-wage ratio permanently below the quasi-equilibrium value and so to maintain real wages permanently higher than the quasi-equilibrium value. This will not cause unemployment, so long as the price-wage ratio continues to be within the interval $A B$. The system is still inflationary, but it is clear that the workers only win the race between the price and the wage-rate at the cost of heightened pressure of inflation, since both price and wage-rate must rise faster than the quasi-equilibrium speeds if spontaneous rises in the wage-rate are added to the other rises. This is only mentioned in passing, however, since when spon-

---

[1] The real wage will be taken to be wage/price. Whether or not the workers also increase their real consumption is another matter, which depends on who—workers or capitalists—are best able to avoid unrealizable plans for the purchase of consumer-goods (when there are no stocks of consumer-goods). Most probably it will be the capitalists.

taneous rises in the wage-rate are introduced the assumption of perfect competition in the labour-market is dropped. The question then arises of what will happen if we also drop the assumption of perfect competition in the commodity-market, so that there is also the possibility of spontaneous rise in the price.

However, it is perhaps of interest to say something about the effect on the model of a regulation of the wage-rate according to a cost-of-living index, which is an important form of spontaneous rise in wages. The wage-rate is taken to be regulated according to the commodity price, say each three months. To do this as easily as possible, we assume that there is open inflation, in such a way that the quasi-equilibrium position of the price-wage ratio, $(p/w)^0$, has been reached, cf. Fig. 17. Then regulation of the wage-rate according to the cost-of-living is introduced, which regulation is based on the price-wage ratio B. If the monetary pressure of inflation has been caused by a displacement to the right of the D_0-curve while the Q_0-curve remained fixed, this will be the price-wage ratio at the beginning of the inflationary process. The cost-of-living adjustment applied in Denmark October 1939 to May 1940, was of just this type.

So we are assuming that the functions f and F express a continuous induced rise in the price and wage-rate, and that a discontinuous displacement of the price-wage ratio to B, occurring at fixed intervals, disturbs this induced rise. Spontaneous rises in the price are neglected. The development of the system may be illustrated by Fig. 18.

Let adjustment according to the cost-of-living be introduced at time t_0, until which time the magnitudes (p/w), dp/dt, $(D_0 - Q_1)$, dw/dt, and $(Q_0 - Q_1)$ are constant at the quasi-equilibrium level. At t_0 (p/w) falls from $(p/w)^0$ to B, whereupon the excess demand for labour-services completely disappears (see Fig. 17), so that the speed of the rise in the wage-rate becomes zero. At the same time the excess demand for commodities rises, so that the speed of the rise in the price increases. As a result, when (p/w) has spontaneously fallen to B, (p/w) begins to rise. The period until the next wage-adjustment is then characterised by a rising price-wage ratio, which is caused by the smaller excess demand for labour-services and the larger excess demand for commodities than existed in the initial quasi-equilibrium situation. However, between t_0 and t_1 the excess demand for labour-services rises so that the speed of the rise in the wage-rate becomes positive and rising, whereas the excess demand for commodities and the speed of the rise in prices falls; this follows from the rising price-wage ratio. If the original quasi-equilibrium is not attained before the next wage-adjustment (and in principle it is not, since the movement towards the quasi-equilibrium position will be asymptotic, see Chap. VIII), we have $(p/w) < (p/w)^0$ immediately previous to that adjustment, whereas the excess demand for labour services and the speed of the rise in the wage-ratio are less than the quasi-equilibrium values, and the excess demand for commodities and the speed of rise in the price are greater than the quasi-equilibrium values. So the workers' real wages are all the time higher than the quasi-equilibrium value, and the workers thus gain permanently when wage-adjustment according to the cost-of-living is introduced.

At the next adjustment time t_1, the price-wage ratio is again displaced downwards to B, and the whole process which took place between t_0 and t_1 is repeated between t_1 and t_2, and so on.

If we apply our criterion of changes in the (quantitative) pressure of inflation, we reach the result that, since the excess demand for labour-services is permanently less than the quasi-equilibrium value and the excess demand for commodities is greater than the quasi-equilibrium value, the case should be included in the "open" category of the criterion, where it cannot be decided whether the pressure of inflation has risen or fallen. It might be regarded as a deficiency in the criterion for changes in the (quantitative) pressure of inflation that it can tell us nothing about this case in which it is given that the speeds of the rises in both price and wage-rate are increased if the discontinuous spontaneous rises in the wage-rate are added to the induced rises, but this apparent deficiency arises, of course, from the fact that the criterion was set up solely with *induced* rises in prices and wage-rates in mind.

In this description of the effect of wage-adjustment according to the cost of living, it is assumed that the adjustment is carried out in such a way that "induced" rises in the wage-rate which have taken place since one adjustment are taken into account at the next adjustment.

Often, however, negotiations on regulation according to the cost-of-living include a clause, enforced more or less strictly, which states more or less directly that the wage-rate shall be unaltered between the adjustment times. If effective, this alters Fig. 18 by making

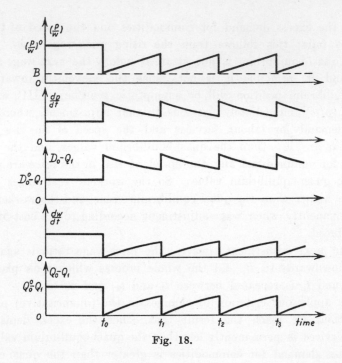

Fig. 18.

$dw/dt = 0$ within the intervals $t_0 - t_1$, $t_1 - t_2$, etc. (the function F $(Q_0 - Q_1)$ is now equal to zero for all values of $(Q_0 - Q_1)$). This causes dp/dt to be greater within the intervals $t_0 - t_1$, $t_1 - t_2$, etc., and therefore (p/w) to rise faster towards the quasi-equilibrium value, $(p/w)^0$, within t_0 to t_1, t_1 to t_2, etc.

There may be wage-regulation according to the cost-of-living which does not adjust the ratio of price to wage-rate to a certain basis, that is, does not give 100 % compensation with respect to some basis, but only compensation for a part of the current rise in price, for instance, gives compensation for half the rise in price since the preceding adjustment, and this adjustment may also be taken to be such that the wage-rate is constant between the adjustments. Such a wage-adjustment was applied in Sweden during the first part of the war. In this case the price-wage ratio steadily rises despite the discontinuous lowering of (p/w), since (p/w) must now rise more between any two adjustments than it is lowered at the second of them. (p/w) must therefore, (see Fig. 17), approach the value A, where the excess demand for commodities is zero, and where dp/dt is consequently also zero. Here the price and the wage-rate will remain constant unless so-called black-market wage-sliding appears, as is very likely. The pressure of inflation is not removed, since an excess demand for labour-services persists.

In Finland at one time since the war (introduced October 1947), there was compensation which was so arranged that it could be greater or smaller than 100 %. A cost-of-living adjustment which gives more than 100 % compensation for the price increase between two adjustments must lower (p/w) to the value B, (see Fig. 17), since the discontinuous fall in (p/w) at each adjustment is always greater than the rise in (p/w) induced by the excess demand for commodities—between the former adjustment and the one in question. At B the excess demand for labour-services is zero, but there remains an excess demand for commodities and therefore the price rises, so that (p/w) at the next adjustment falls below B and unemployment ensues. It may be noticed that while all this is going on the speed of the rise in price is becoming larger and larger.

It should be remarked that, whereas the system was inconsistent when regarded as static, i.e. conditioned by the equilibrium conditions (VII: 8) and (VII: 9), sometimes this inconsistency is removed by making the position of the curve for demand, D_0, a function of the absolute price-level, which is introduced into the system by making the demand for commodities a function of the real cash-holdings[1], in such a way that smaller real-cash tends to displace the D_0-curve to the left, whereupon a continued rise in the price moves the D_0-curve to the left until it cuts the Q_0-curve at the possible production Q_1, and complete static equilibrium is achieved. Moreover, use is often made of the relation pointed out by Keynes[2], that rising prices with a given quantity of money tend to cause a rise in the rate of interest, since the need of money for transactions increases; this diminishes the demand for investment commodities and moves the D_0-curve to the left as the level of prices rises. If the state's purchases of commodities is fixed in money and not in quantity, that will affect matters in the same direction, and something similar can be made out with reference to foreign trade. But it should be remembered that there is also a tendency to moving of the D_0-curve higher (to the right), since the permanent excess demand for commodities causes either a steady depletion of

---

[1] A. C. Pigou, *Employment and Equilibrium*, MacMillan & Co., London, 1941.
[2] J. M. Keynes, *The General Theory*, for instance, p. 253.

stocks or an accumulation of orders, and both these will have the effect of raising the D_0-curve. Which of these displacing tendencies has the strongest effect it is impossible to say *a priori*, and we have therefore altogether disregarded them in setting up the model. It would also be possible for the curves to move if there is the earlier-mentioned resignation about obtaining the desired commodities or labour-services.

3. *Increased purchases of commodities by the state*

Most of the more important inflations seem to have been caused by a sharp increase in the state's purchases of goods or labour-services. We shall therefore introduce into the model of Section 2 an isolated increase of the state's purchases of commodities ("isolated" means that it is not financed by taxation or raising of interest rates), and it is assumed that the state is always able to carry out the (quantitative) purchases it wishes to make. Increased state purchases of commodities of this character may be introduced most easily as a decrease in the supply of commodities by the amount Q_s, cf. Fig. 19.

We have now, reading horizontally, that

$D_0 - (Q_1 - Q_s)$ = the inflationary gap in the commodity-market

(quantitative), $\hspace{4cm}$ (VII: 22)

$Q_0 - Q_1$ = index for the factor-gap (quantitative), $\hspace{2cm}$ (VII: 7)

and

$$\frac{dp}{dt} = f(D_0 - Q_1 + Q_s), \hspace{3cm} \text{(VII: 23)}$$

$$\frac{dw}{dt} = F(Q_0 - Q_1), \hspace{3cm} \text{(VII: 13)}$$

and the condition of quasi-equilibrium (VII: 18) is altered in accordance with this.

Suppose now that the system before the increase in state purchases of commodities was in quasi-equilibrium with the price-wage ratio equal to $(p/w)^0$, demand for commodities D_0^0, and planned production Q_0^0, that is

$$\frac{1}{w} \cdot \left\{ f(D_0^0 - Q_1) - \left(\frac{p}{w}\right)^0 \cdot F(Q_0^0 - Q_1) \right\} = 0. \hspace{1cm} \text{(VII: 20)}$$

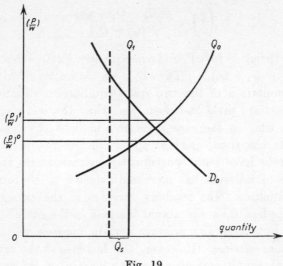

Fig. 19.

The first thing that happens when the state increases its purchases of commodities is that

$$\frac{d\left(\dfrac{p}{w}\right)}{dt} > 0, \tag{VII: 24}$$

with (p/w) unchanged at $(p/w)^0$, because

$$f\,(D_0^0 - Q_1 + Q_s) > f\,(D_0^0 - Q_1). \tag{VII: 25}$$

The increase in the state's purchases of commodities in itself obviously implies an increase in the (quantitative) pressure of inflation, since the excess demand for commodities rises at the same time as the excess demand for labour-services remains unchanged (cf. the criterion for an increase in the (quantitative) pressure of inflation in Chap. I, Section 5). According to (VII: 24), this leads to a rise in the price-wage ratio, so that the system must move towards a new position of quasi-equilibrium at the price-wage ratio $(p/w)^1$, where

$$\left(\frac{p}{w}\right)^1 > \left(\frac{p}{w}\right)^0, \tag{VII: 26}$$

with the demand for commodities D_0^1 and the supply Q_0^1.

However, in the new quasi-equilibrium position

$$\left(\frac{p}{w}\right)^1 = \frac{f(D_0^1 - Q_1 + Q_s)}{F(Q_0^1 - Q_1)} \qquad \text{(VII: 27)}$$

and moreover $(p/w)^1 > (p/w)^0$, and consequently $F(Q_0^1 - Q_1) > F(Q_0^0 - Q_1)$, so that $f(D_0^1 - Q_1 + Q_s) > f(D_0^0 - Q_0)$, on comparison with (VII: 20).

From a comparison of the two quasi-equilibrium situations we have that the price-wage ratio has risen, and thus the real wage has fallen, at the same time as the excess demand in both the commodity and factor markets has risen, and the speeds of the rise in the price and in the wage-rate have both consequently increased. So the (quantitative) pressure of inflation has increased relative to the original quasi-equilibrium situation. The resulting increase in the excess demand for commodities is less than the actual increase in the state's purchases of commodities, but there also arises a certain increase in the excess demand for labour-services. However, the increase in the excess demand for labour-services only corresponds to the increase in the excess demand for commodities in the sense that they cause the same percentage rise per unit of time in the wage-rate and price respectively.

A decrease in the state's purchases of commodities may be treated in just the same way and leads to the opposite result, with a fall in the price-wage ratio and in the speeds of the rises in the price and in the wage-rate.

4. Decline in productivity

Another important companion of inflation is often a decline in productivity. It might seem that such a decline in productivity may be illustrated in much the same way as was the increase in the state's purchases of commodities, for what happens in both cases is that there is a smaller supply of commodities available from the same input of labour-power to meet the private demand for commodities. The relationships will certainly be of this type if the decline in productivity is temporary, for example, a bad harvest, but even in this case the reasoning of Section 3 cannot be applied, because the temporary decline in productivity must in the nature of the matter be something which does not last and is not expected to last either (just as with an unexpectedly bad harvest).

What we wish to deal with is the effect of a permanent decline in productivity which the entrepreneurs expect to persist in the future.

In this case the vertical Q_1-line, which indicates the possible production of commodities, is moved to the left, and simultaneously the Q_0-curve, which indicates the planned production, is moved still farther to the left so that with the price-wage ratio unchanged at $(p/w)^0$, the excess demand for labour-services decreases. This is due to the fact that when the price-wage ratio remains unchanged, a raising of the marginal cost curve is accompanied by a decrease in planned production and demand for labour-services (cf. Chap. VI, Section 2). So we have as first effect that the speed of the rise in the wage-rate decreases.

If the D_0-curve is not affected, the excess demand for commodities will evidently rise, and consequently the speed of the rise in the price will increase. But we cannot count on the D_0-curve being unaffected by all this. In constructing the D_0-curve we began by assuming a constant total real income (net national product), so that D_0 may be taken to be a function dependent on (p/w) and on nothing else. After there has been a change in productivity and thereupon a fall in the real national income, it may be assumed that the same applies, only that the D_0-curve will have been moved to a new position. Two opposing tendencies operate here. The fall in real income will by itself tend to push the curve to the left, because when the real income decreases the real demand for consumer goods will probably decline (though perhaps not quite so much as the fall in real income). But on the other hand, with the price-wage ratio unchanged, a larger part of the income will go to the workers, and this by itself tends to move the curve to the right. Moreover, the effect on the demand for investment commodities is uncertain, whereas it is quite certain that the state's real demand for commodities will usually not diminish. Nothing certain can be said about the resultant of these forces, other than that it does not seem likely that the demand for commodities will fall as much as the actual supply of commodities (Q_1). Thus, the excess demand for commodities may be taken to increase, when the price-wage ratio is taken to be unchanged at $(p/w)^0$, so that the speed of the rise in the price must be greater.

The immediate result—with (p/w) still unchanged—is therefore that the excess demand for labour-services falls, whereas the excess demand for commodities rises, so that we cannot decide whether the pressure of inflation has increased or decreased.

With the situation in the commodity and labour markets altered in this way, the price-wage ratio must tend to rise, so that the excess demand for labour-services and the speed of the rise in the wage-rate also rises, but the excess demand for commodities and the speed of the rise in the price falls. As a consequence the system takes up a new quasi-equilibrium position at a price-wage ratio which is higher than it was previously (i.e. the real wage has fallen). In this quasi-equilibrium situation one of the following cases will be valid:

(a) Both the excess demand for commodities and the excess demand for labour-services are greater than in the initial "equilibrium" situation (before productivity fell).

(b) Both the excess demand for commodities and the excess demand for labour-services are less than in the initial quasi-equilibrium situation.

(c) Both the excess demand for commodities and the excess demand for labour-services remain unchanged from the initial quasi-equilibrium situation.

(d) The excess demand for commodities is greater and the excess demand for labour-services is less than in the initial quasi-equilibrium situation.

(e) The excess demand for commodities is less and the excess demand for labour-services is greater than in the initial quasi-equilibrium situation.

Any of these possibilities may arise, since the only thing we know—unless precise assumptions are made about the position of the D_0-curve and Q_0-curve in relation to Q_1, before and after the change in productivity, and about the functions f and F—is that the new quasi-equilibrium position occurs through an increase in an excess demand for labour-services, which had become less than in the initial quasi-equilibrium situation, and through a decrease in an excess demand for commodities, which had become greater than in the initial quasi-equilibrium situation.

The final result when the new quasi-equilibrium is achieved, is, as far as the (quantitative) pressure of inflation goes,[1] that in case (a) the pressure of inflation becomes definitely greater than in the initial quasi-equilibrium situation, in case (b) definitely smaller, and in case

---

[1] By considering only the commodities (and services) market, Erik Lundberg, "Ekonomisk teori och inflationsanalys", also comes to the conclusion that a change in productivity may lead to either increased or decreased inflationary pressure.

(c) definitely unchanged, whereas cases (d) and (e) belong to the open category of the criterion for changes in the pressure of inflation, so that nothing definite can be said about them. The only thing that is certain is that the price rises relative to the wage-rate.

5. *The removal of the pressure of inflation by diminishing the inflationary gap in the commodity-markets*

Now, with the help of the model, we will consider the possibility of removing the pressure of inflation and bringing about a true equilibrium with full employment by doing away with the excess demand in the commodity-markets.

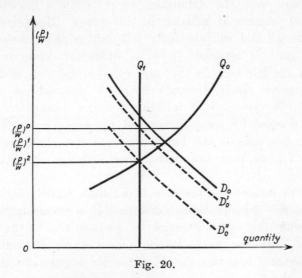

Fig. 20.

The curves for the initial situation are Q_0, D_0, and Q_1. Quasi-equilibrium is supposed to have been reached at the price-wage ratio $(p/w)^0$. If we further suppose that a statistical calculation of the inflationary gap in the commodity-markets is made, our statistician arrives at the magnitude $D_0^0 - Q_1$ (multiplied by the current price), which is the horizontal distance between D_0 and Q_1 at $(p/w)^0$. The state wishes to overcome inflation, and therefore displaces the curve D_0 to the left, so that it cuts Q_1 at the height $(p/w)^0$, i.e. to D_0'. Then the inflationary gap in the commodity-markets is closed. This displacement of the curve D_0 may be accomplished by the state by, for instance, allowing increased imports equal in quantity to $D_0^0 - Q_1$, so that this amount of the demand for commodities is diverted from the home-market (we suppose for the sake of simplicity that prices abroad rise in the same proportion as those at home). Or, the same object could be achieved by a suitable direct taxation of income.

It is seen at once from Fig. 20 that, with the D_0'-curve for the demand for commodities, the excess demand for labour-services and with it the speed of the rise in the wage-rate remain unchanged from the initial situation, when the price-wage ratio is $(p/w)^0$, whereas the excess demand for commodities and the speed of the rise in the price are less than in the initial quasi-equilibrium situation, both being zero. In accordance with the definition, there is still a monetary (and a quantitative) pressure of inflation in the system. The price-wage ratio will tend to fall and will obviously fall until a new quasi-equilibrium price-wage ratio is attained—$(p/w)^1$— where the conditions of quasi-equilibrium are fulfilled. In this new quasi-equilibrium situation there are still positive excess demands for both commodities and labour-services. So the pressure of inflation has not disappeared, but both the excess demand for commodities and the excess demand for labour-services are less than in the initial situation (for proof, consider equation (VII: 27)), so that the pressure of inflation (quantitative) has diminished.

In order to remove the pressure of inflation entirely by means of a decrease in the demand for commodities, it is necessary not only to do away with the excess demand for commodities at the price-wage ratio $(p/w)^0$, but also to create an excess supply of commodities at $(p/w)^0$ sufficiently large for the D_0''-curve for demand for commodities to intersect the Q_0-curve at Q_1. Thus a deflationary gap in the commodity-markets must be created, which is illustrated in Fig. 20 by the horizontal distance between D_0'' and Q_1 at $(p/w)^0$ (we assume that the D_0-curves may be extended to the left of Q_1, cf. Section 8 below).

When there is an excess supply in the commodity-markets, the speed of the rise in the price is negative, while there continues to be excess demand in the labour-market and a positive (unchanged) speed of the rise in the wage-rate at $(p/w)^0$. Therefore, the price-wage ratio falls, until a price-wage ratio $(p/w)^2$ is reached at which the excess supply of commodities is zero and the excess demand for labour-services is zero. Here there will be complete, true equilibrium with full-employment and without either inflation or deflation. $(p/w)^2$ is constant, dp/dt and dw/dt are both equal to zero.

This result is in agreement with the result obtained in the analysis of repressed inflation with perfect competition (Chap. V, Section 1). If the pressure of inflation is to be removed merely by decreasing the demand for commodities, this demand must decrease by an amount larger than the existing inflationary gap in the commodity-markets, actually by so much more that the price is forced down so far in relation to the wage-rate that the excess demand for labour-services also disappears. The mere removal of the inflationary gap in the commodity-markets once and for all is not sufficient to bring about equilibrium when there is perfect competition.

Reasoning based on more crude Keynesian models usually leads to the result that to do away with inflation a lowering of real wages and increase of profits is necessary, because wage-earners have a higher consumption-ratio than the profit-earners. It follows from the above that this result does not hold in general.

6. *The removal of the pressure of inflation by diminishing the factor-gap*

In Section 5 we dealt with setting up of equilibrium with full employment and constant absolute price and wage-rate, by a movement of the D_0-curve to the left so that it intersects the Q_0-curve just on the vertical Q_1-line. However, if we return for a moment to Fig. 17, we see, from a purely formal point of view, that there is another way of bringing about equilibrium, namely, by causing a displacement of the Q_0-curve to the left so that it intersects the unchanged D_0-curve on the vertical Q_1-line. In this case as well, equilibrium with full employment and constant prices is obtained, but the price-wage ratio is greater than it was in the initial quasi-equilibrium situation, i.e. the real wage has fallen. Is this method, formally open to us, also economically possible, that is, is it reasonable to suppose that the Q_0-curve may be moved without affecting the Q_1-line and the D_0-curve?

In Section 5 we assumed that the Q_0-curve and the Q_1-line were independent of movements of the D_0-curve, and the economic reasonableness of this was bound up with the assumption that the supply of labour-services was fixed and independent of the workers' **real** wages, and with the fact that the direct taxation (for example) which caused the displacement of the D_0-curve did not affect the en-

180

trepreneurs on the production margin, and so did not cause any alteration in the entrepreneurs' planned production. These underlying assumptions are not in any way economically unreasonable; indeed, this
is the traditional way of treating the effects of direct taxes.

When it comes to bringing about such a displacement of the Q_0-
curve as leaves both the D_0-curve and the Q_1-line unaffected, the
matter is somewhat more difficult. Certainly, in Section 4 we did
deal with a displacement of the Q_0-curve to the left which was due
to diminished productivity, but the characteristic thing about that
change was that it did not leave the D_0-curve and the Q_1-line unaffected. However, such an effect as the one desired may be brought
about by indirect taxation. Let us now suppose that the price-wage
ratio is the ratio between the price *including* indirect tax and the
wage-rate. Then it is obvious that, with perfect competition, the price
must rise by the amount of the tax per article, if the entrepreneurs
are to be willing to continue the same production as before the introduction of the tax. This means that if we suppose an indirect tax
to be levied on the entrepreneurs, then, at a given price-wage ratio,
the planned production is less after the tax is levied than it was before. So the introduction of an indirect tax leads to a displacement
of the Q_0-curve to the left. Assuming the supply of labour-services to
be given and unaffected by changes in the real wage, the actually realizable production—represented by the Q_1-line—is unaffected by the
introduction of the tax. On the other hand, the D_0-curve will not be
unaffected by the tax. Because, at a particular price-wage ratio, the
state claims a part of the capitalists actual profit, and this means
that the D_0-curve is shifted to the left. However, this obstacle may
be overcome by supposing the state to pay the whole of the amount
of the indirect tax back as subsidies to the capitalists (of, course, in
some way which is not connected with the way in which the tax is
taken from them). In this way, at a given price-wage ratio the quantity
of consumer-goods in demand remains the same as it was before the
tax was levied on the entrepreneurs; still assuming, of course, that
the demand for consumer-goods is a function of actual income rather
than expected income.

Thus, if an indirect tax is levied on the entrepreneurs and the whole
of the revenue from it is paid out to those persons who receive their
incomes from the enterprises' profits, the Q_0-curve will be moved to

the left, while the Q_1-line and the D_0-curve are left unchanged. Obviously then, by making the indirect tax sufficiently large, the Q_0-curve may be moved so much to the left that it intersects the D_0-curve on the Q_1-line, and in this situation there is true equilibrium with full employment at the price-wage ratio A (see Fig. 17). The real wage is clearly lower in this equilibrium situation than it was in the initial quasi-equilibrium situation.

If we now combine what has been said in this and the preceding section, it is clear that the state, by means of a suitable combination of direct and indirect taxation, can bring about complete equilibrium with full employment without a monetary pressure of inflation—and so without a tendency to induced changes in prices or wage-rates—and with the real wage at whatever level is desirable, if real wage is understood in the sense (wage-rate)/(price including indirect taxes).

7. *Monopolism*

In the preceding sections we have assumed that the entrepreneurs always work under conditions of perfect competition. The question arises as to what alteration in the reasoning is necessary if the entrepreneurs work under conditions of monopolism. In the case of repressed inflation this lead to quite radical changes in the reasoning in many places, but it will appear that this is not the case when the inflation is open. What makes the case of monopolism so different from that of perfect competition with repressed inflation is the special change in the entrepreneurs' marginal revenue curve brought about by the introduction of maximum prices, the marginal revenue curve acquiring the special form in which the first part is horizontal, followed by a vertical part and lastly by a part falling to the right. It is not difficult to see that most of the qualitative inequalities between the results under perfect competition and monopolism in the case of repressed inflation depend on just that fact that the marginal revenue curve becomes vertical at a certain point. But this peculiarity does not arise in the case of open inflation (unless the situation is introduced through "kinked" expected sales curves). If the functional relations used for the model in Section 2 are considered again, it will be seen that they may perhaps be preserved under the assumption of monopolism in the commodity-markets. The doubtful points are the equation for planned production, in which expected sales ought to be introduced explicitly, and the equation for price-reaction.

8. *Inflation as a special case of a more general model*

We shall now see how the model of Section 2 may be regarded as the inflation-case of a more general model which also covers the case in which there is no inflation. This model is one, which, regarded statically, is inconsistent in the general case, but which may be shown to have a tendency to move towards a dynamic quasi-equilibrium. Since some of the arguments used are just the same as those in Section 2, in these cases we will just refer back to Section 2, if a more precise treatment is not required.

It is still assumed that there is perfect competition and expectations that the current price and wage-rate will continue to hold in the future. Only one commodity is produced, with the aid of one variable factor, labour-services, and a fixed production equipment.

We begin with the supply curve, that is, the curve for planned production Q_0. As in Section 2, this is regarded as dependent on (p/w) and nothing else (the state's "production" ($=$ the state's purchases of labour-services) is taken to be constant and fixed by the budget), cf. the assumptions about perfect competition and about expectations:

$$Q_0 = \varphi\left(\frac{p}{w}\right), \tag{VII:2}$$

where

$$\varphi' > 0. \tag{VII:3}$$

It is also desirable to introduce a function, called Q_{max}, which denotes the maximum production which can be carried out. This, according to the present assumptions, is determined by the quantity of labour-services which the workers are willing to supply, and the supply of labour-services may itself be regarded as a function of the real wage (w/p), so that we may write

$$Q_{max} = \psi\left(\frac{p}{w}\right), \tag{VII:28}$$

where the only assumption we shall make about the function ψ is that it intersects the Q_0-curve from below.

Q_{max} corresponds to the line Q_1 in Fig. 17, where it was assumed that the supply of labour-power was constant and where only the case of planned production $>$ actually realizable production was considered.

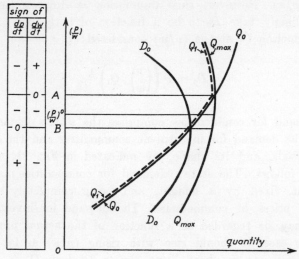

Fig. 21.

In just the same way as in Section 2, we may say, reading horizontally, that

$$Q_0 - Q_{max} = \text{excess demand for labour-services (index),} \quad \text{(VII: 29)}$$

so that when $(Q_0 - Q_{max}) > 0$, the excess demand for labour-services is positive, and when $(Q_0 - Q_{max}) < 0$, the excess demand for labour-services is negative. $Q_0 - Q_{max}$ is thus an index for excess demand for labour-services or for involuntary unemployment.

When (p/w) rises, the production of commodities actually carried out, which, as before, we call Q_1, follows the Q_0-curve from below as far as the point of intersection of the Q_0-curve and the Q_{max}-curve and afterwards follows the Q_{max}-curve. Below this point of intersection the actual production is less than the maximum production, and there is involuntary unemployment; above the point of intersection the actual production is less than the planned production and there is excess demand for labour-services and some production plans must break down.

These three curves are shown in Fig. 21, where the dotted curve denotes the Q_1-curve.

The D_0-curve for commodity-demand is also included in Fig. 21. In the model in Section 2 the (real) net national product was taken to be constant, and the D_0-curve could then be regarded as dependent only on (p/w). However, this assumption is dropped here, and we may accordingly take D_0 to be a function of both (p/w) and of the actual production Q_1 at the (p/w) considered:

$$D_0 = \Phi\left(\left(\frac{p}{w}\right), Q_1\right).^1 \qquad \text{(VII: 30)}$$

The demand for commodities comprises the state's demand for commodities, the demand for investment commodities and the demand for consumer-goods, and its shape, as indicated in Fig. 21, may be explained as follows. The state's demand for commodities may be taken as constant, fixed by a budget, and being completely elastic with respect to prices of commodities. The demand for investment commodities may be regarded as a function of the actual production; if this is the case, it should rise with rising (p/w) as far as A, and afterwards fall, as we here have chosen to draw Q_{max}. Interest is supposed to be kept constant, but with constant interest-rates the demand for investment commodities will probably also rise with (p/w), that is, with a rising average profit margin. It is therefore probably justifiable to make it a function of the planned production Q_0, in which case it will rise with (p/w) throughout. The demand for consumer-goods may, for the sake of simplicity, be regarded as a function of the total real income actually obtained (real taxes are supposed to be kept constant), and of its division between workers and capitalists. As (p/w) rises, the rise in Q_1 as far as A will cause a rise in the demand for consumer-goods, whereas the simultaneous fall in the real wage will cause a decrease in the demand for consumer-goods. The rise in Q_1 is taken to be the decisive factor. When $(p/w) > A$, both circumstances tend to diminish the demand for consumer-goods.

As final result therefore, D_0 has been drawn as rising up to A, and afterwards falling, but it is obvious that the D_0-curve could be supposed to have other shapes.

Reading horizontally, we now have that

$$D_0 - Q_1 = \text{the excess demand for commodities,} \qquad \text{(VII: 31)}$$

---

[1] Since Q_1 is itself a function of (p/w), (VII: 30) could be written as $D_0 = \Phi_1$ (p/w), but for the following discussion we shall write it as in the text.

and it is apparent that when $(p/w) < B$ the excess demand for commodities is positive, and when $(p/w) > B$, negative.

From the way in which Q_0, Q_{max}, Q_1, and D_0 appear in Fig. 21, it is seen that there is no static equilibrium solution such that simultaneously

$$Q_0 - Q_{max} = 0 \qquad \text{(VII: 32)}$$

and

$$D_0 - Q_1 = 0. \qquad \text{(VII: 9)}$$

However, it may be assumed that

$$\frac{dp}{dt} = f(D_0 - Q_1) \qquad \text{(VII: 10)}$$

and

$$\frac{dw}{dt} = F(Q_0 - Q_{max}), \qquad \text{(VII: 33)}$$

where f and F have the properties which are given by (VII:11), (VII: 12) and (VII: 14), (VII: 15).

What we now require is the quasi-equilibrium where (cf. (VII: 18)),

$$\left(\frac{p}{w}\right) = \frac{f(D_0 - Q_1)}{F(Q_0 - Q_{max})}. \qquad \text{(VII: 34)}$$

This quasi-equilibrium occurs in an interval for (p/w) in which dp/dt and dw/dt are either both positive or both negative. A table is attached to Fig. 21 showing the sign of dp/dt and dw/dt when $(p/w) < B$, $= B$, $> B$ and $< A$, $= A$, and $> A$; this table shows that only in the open interval between A and B is there a quasi-equilibrium position to be found, since here both dp/dt and dw/dt are negative. From the shape given to the curves in the figure it is easily seen that here also only one solution exists, and an examination of the signs of dp/dt and dw/dt in other intervals makes it clear that this quasi-equilibrium position is stable (the stricter proof of this proceeds as in Section 2).

So, left to itself, the system will arrive at a quasi-equilibrium at $(p/w)^0$, let us say, where there is an excess supply of commodities and involuntary unemployment. In this quasi-equilibrium situation the system is in a state of permanent deflation with price and wage-rate continually falling in proportion to one another.

This is of course not the Keynesian equilibrium with involuntary unemployment, since that is a static equilibrium with price and wage-rate constant. If might be asked whether the system might be modified so that it is possible to reach static equilibrium with price and wage-rate constant. This may be done, as mentioned in Section 2, by making the position of the D_0-curve a function of the absolute price-level, so that a falling price moves the D_0-curve to the right, whereupon it will eventually intersect the Q_0-curve in the point where $Q_1 = D_0 = Q_0 = Q_{max}$, that is, where $(p/w) = A$. However, an excess supply of commodities leads to an accumulation of stocks of commodities, which leads to a displacement of the D_0-curve to the left (intended changes of stocks being reckoned in demand). Therefore, if the curves are in the beginning situated as shown in Fig. 21, it is not possible *a priori* to maintain that the curves will tend to be displaced in such a way that static equilibrium is achieved. The displacement may be in the opposite direction.

However, even if it were supposed that such a displacement of the D_0-curve took place that complete static equilibrium with $D_0 = Q_1 = Q_0 = Q_{max}$ was at last reached, neither is this equilibrium the equilibrium with which Keynes worked. In this case there is no involuntary unemployment. Therefore solutions of this sort never lead to static equilibrium with involuntary unemployment.[1]

So it is either necessary to give up the idea that there should be a static equilibrium with involuntary unemployment, or to make special assumptions about the properties of the function (VII: 33), e.g. that $F = 0$ when $(Q_0 - Q_{max}) \leqq 0$, and $F > 0$ when $(Q_0 - Q_{max}) > 0$, with corresponding changes in the property of F' which has hitherto been used (i.e. $F' > 0$). If this is done, the quasi-equilibrium will occur when the price-wage ratio is B, the excess demand for commodities is zero and therefore $dp/dt = 0$ as well, simultaneously with involuntary unemployment. The quasi-equilibrium is then a Keynesian equilibrium, but it is obvious, that it is based on an assumption of a special trade-union policy, which may or may not correspond to reality.

Another device was thought out by Joan Robinson,[2] who points out that it is reasonable to suppose that there is a certain critical

---

[1] See also Chap. VIII, Section 4.

[2] Joan Robinson, *Essays in the Theory of Employment*, MacMillan & Co., London, 1937, p. 7 et seq.

level of employment, somewhat less than full employment, at which the wage-rate begins to rise. This corresponds to the introduction of a critical production Q_{crit}, such that (reading horizontally)

$$\frac{Q_{crit}}{Q_{max}} = \text{constant} < 1, \qquad (VII:35)$$

so that

$$\frac{dw}{dt} = F(Q_0 - Q_{crit}), \qquad (VII:36)$$

and $F(0) = 0$ and $F' > 0$.[1] With this function there is one—but only one—position of the D_0-curve which gives rise to static equilibrium

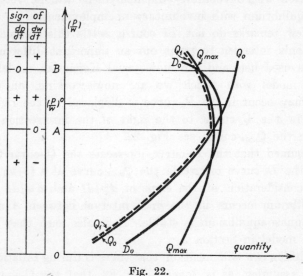

Fig. 22.

with involuntary unemployment, and this static equilibrium arises in the case when the Q_{crit}-curve, Q_0-curve and D_0-curve intersect in the same point.

But neither does this overcome the difficulty, for Keynes considered that there could be equilibrium at all possible levels of employment, whereas with the function (VII: 36) it is possible to have quasi-equilibrium with involuntary unemployment and either permanent decreases

---

[1] Joan Robinson thinks that $F = 0$ within an interval, so that there is an upper and a lower critical employment, but for the sake of simplicity we neglect this here.

in the price and wage-rate or increases, depending on whether the D_0-curve intersects the Q_0-curve to the left or to the right of the intersection of the Q_0-curve with the Q_{crit}-curve. If we introduce an additional assumption about the function (VII: 36), namely that $F' > 0$ but is very small within a certain "usual" interval around $Q_0 - Q_{crit} = 0$, the quasi-equilibrium will occur at a position where there are only mild processes of rise or fall in price and wage-rate, and where there is only a very small excess demand for or excess supply of commodities, but where involuntary unemployment may be significant. The quasi-equilibrium position will consequently be at a value of (p/w) lying very near B. In these circumstances the dynamic quasi-equilibrium solution with involuntary unemployment will be very similar to a static equilibrium with involuntary unemployment.

These few remarks do not, of course, settle this complex problem; they are only intended to point out an important difference between the models used here and the more usual Keynesian models.

In the model with which we are now working, an inflationary situation may occur if the D_0-curve is displaced to the right, so that it intersects the Q_0-curve to the right of the intersection of the Q_0-curve with the Q_{max}-curve, see Fig. 22.

It is assumed that the D_0-curve intersects the Q_0-curve from below, and that the D_0-curve intersects the Q_{max}-curve at a (p/w) sufficiently large. A consideration of the signs of dp/dt and dw/dt shows that quasi-equilibrium occurs in the open interval between A and B, and that this quasi-equilibrium is stable. It is also seen that Fig. 22 includes the model in Section 2.

In conclusion we will mention that there is during inflation a special reason for assuming, as is done in Fig. 22, that the Q_{max}-curve turns back when (p/w) is sufficiently large. Both excess demand for labour-services by itself (which places the individual worker in a very strong market-position), and excess demand for commodities by itself (which leads to difficulties for the workers in spending their money incomes in some reasonable way), make the workers inclined not to work so much. This situation has become well known in most countries since the second World War.

CHAPTER VIII

ON OPEN INFLATION (CONT.):
A GENERAL QUASI-EQUILIBRIUM SYSTEM

1. *The inconsistency of the models used in Chaps. IV to VII*

All the models used in Chaps. IV to VII are inconsistent when regarded as static equilibrium models, because they do not in general have equilibrium solutions in which, without state control, the excess demands in all markets are simultaneously zero. As will be shown, this is not accidental, neither does it depend on a special choice of the models, but is intimately connected with the following two circumstances.

Firstly, it depends on the fact that we have always made demand and supply functions of the ratio between the price and the wage-rate, so that demand and supply only depend on the relative price (price-wage ratio), while the absolute price-level (and wage-level) is without significance. Mathematically, this means that our supply and demand relations have been homogeneous of degree zero in the absolute prices.[1] It may be seen at once that this is the case for the models in Chap. VII, and it is—as earlier mentioned—implied in the models of Chap. IV[2]. However, as is well-known, it has recently been pointed out[3] that homogeneity of degree zero in the absolute prices causes the Walras system to be inconsistent (or, better, the number of equations obtained to be one more than the number of unknowns, cf. below), unless special assumptions are made.[4] The general *quasi-equilibrium*

---

[1] A function $F = F(x, y, z, \ldots)$ is said to be homogeneous of degree r in x, y, z, ..., if $F(kx, ky, kz, \ldots) = k^r \cdot F(x, y, z, \ldots)$, where k is a real number.

[2] See, p. 160, note 2 and p. 161, note 1.

[3] Don Patinkin, "The Indeterminacy of Absolute Prices in Classical Economic Theory", *Econometrica*, Vol. 17, No. 1, Jan. 1949.

[4] W. Leontief, "The Consistency of the Classical Theory of Money and Prices", *Econometrica*, Vol. 18, No. 1, 1950, and articles by W. Braddock Hickman and Cecil G. Phipps in the same issue of *Econometrica*.

190

theory put forward in this chapter gives *one* possible answer to this problem of homogeneity by dropping the customary equilibrium conditions (that all excess demands shall be zero), and introducing instead another set of conditions, which include the customary equilibrium conditions as a special case. In this way we arrive at a dynamic system whose general properties may be studied—among them its reactions to changes of data—and which includes the usual Walras system and its reactions to changes of data as a special case. It also provides a certain possibility of investigating the extent to which the previous chapter's one-commodity, one-factor analysis of inflation may be broadened to a more general applicability, when several goods are taken into consideration. Thus the theory of static equilibrium and the theory of inflation (deflation) both become special cases of a more general dynamic theory, which may well be an advantage.

Secondly, the interpretation of the concept of excess demand which was used in the preceding chapters has some significance for the inconsistency. The inflationary gap interpretation of Chap. III of the concept of excess demand must in general (quite apart from the question of homogeneity) lead to models which are statically inconsistent, models without a static equilibrium solution. In order to prove this result an ordinary Walras system of a simple character will first be considered, and the proof is demonstrated by showing that the inflationary gap interpretation of the concept of excess demand must lead to the result that the so-called Walras's Law cannot be taken as an identity. This is done in Sections 2 and 3 which follow.

2. *A simple Walras system*

The Walras system which we shall consider is a simplified system of the type used of late in the discussion of the general equilibrium theory by, for example, J. R. Hicks, P. A. Samuelson, O. Lange and J. Mosak.[1]

---

[1] J. R. Hicks, *Value and Capital*, p. 314 et seq.; Paul A. Samuelson, *Foundations of Economic Analysis*, Chap. IX; Oscar Lange, *Price Flexibility and Employment, Appendix*, and also, "Say's Law: A Restatement and Criticism", *Studies in Mathematical Economics and Econometrics*, Ed. by O. Lange etc., The University of Chicago Press, Chicago, Ill., 1942, p. 49 et seq.; Jacob Mosak, *General-Equilibrium Theory in International Trade*, The Principia Press Inc., Bloomington, Indiana, 1944, Chap. II.

The system is supposed to be closed, with perfect competition, and there are $n + 1$ goods (commodities, factor-services, claims etc.), for which the demand equations have the form

$$D_r = D_r(p_1, p_2, \ldots, p_{n+1}), \quad (r = 1, 2, \ldots, n + 1), \quad \text{(VIII: 1)}$$

where D_r is the quantity of the rth good in demand, and $p_1, p_2, \ldots, p_{n+1}$ are the prices of the $n + 1$ goods, all expressed in a *numeraire*.

Similarly, there are $n + 1$ supply equations

$$Q_r = Q_r(p_1\ p_2, \ldots, p_{n+1}), \quad (r = 1, 2, \ldots, n + 1), \quad \text{(VIII: 2)}$$

where Q_r is the quantity of the rth good supplied.

The conditions of equilibrium are expressed by

$$D_r = Q_r, \quad (r = 1, 2, \ldots, n + 1), \quad \text{(VIII: 3)}$$

that is, the quantity supplied and the quantity in demand are equal, or in other words, the excess demands for all goods are zero.

Here we have $3n + 3$ unknowns, namely D_r, Q_r, and p_r (where $r = 1, 2, \ldots, n + 1$), and $3n + 3$ equations, namely $n + 1$ equations in each of (VIII: 1), (VIII: 2), and (VIII: 3). If we let the $n + 1$th good be the *numeraire* and also the money, we have, identically,

$$p_{n+1} = 1, \quad \text{(VIII: 4)}$$

which causes the number of equations to be greater than the number of unknowns ($3n + 4$ and $3n + 3$ respectively). However, this difficulty may be overcome if we show that one of the equations (VIII: 3) may always be derived from the other equations in (VIII: 1), (VIII: 2), and (VIII: 3); then there are at most $3n + 3$ independent equations, and the system can be solved for the quantities of goods and the absolute prices concerned. That one of the equations may be derived from the others depends on what Lange has called *Walras's Law*. This well-known "law" will be stated and discussed in Section 3.

Meanwhile, it may be remarked that the equilibrium position which is determined by (VIII: 1), (VIII: 2), (VIII: 3), and (VIII: 4) can be regarded as the stationary solution of a dynamic system, in which the n independent conditions of equilibrium in (VIII: 3) are replaced by, for instance, the n dynamic equations[1]

---

[1] Samuelson, *Foundations in Economic Analysis*, p. 269 et seq.

$$\frac{d\,p_r}{d\,t} = f_r(D_r - Q_r), \ f_r(0) = 0, \ f_r' > 0, \quad (r = 1, 2, \ldots, n). \quad \text{(VIII: 5)}$$

In consequence of (VIII: 4), $d\,p_{n+1}/d\,t = 0$. If the system represented by (VIII: 1), (VIII: 2), (VIII: 4), and (VIII: 5) has a stationary solution for which $d\,p_r/d\,t = 0$, this equilibrium solution will be identical with the equilibrium determined by (VIII: 1), (VIII: 2), (VIII: 3), and (VIII: 4).[1]

As regards the question of whether or not a given system of simultaneous equations has a solution (of economic relevance), we assume that a necessary condition for the given system of equations to have a solution is that the number of equations shall not be larger than the number of unknowns. But, as is known, this criterion is in general neither a necessary nor a sufficient condition for the system to be consistent. Mathematicians are therefore justifiably accustomed to regarding this counting of equations and unknowns as a rather empty procedure in the case of such general and unspecified systems of equations as are used here, but the following reasoning is presented in a manner which is not affected by this, so far as I can see.

3. Walras's Law

Walras's Law arises from the consideration that the only way in which an individual may count on aquiring—that is, may demand—money (the $n + 1$th good) is by offering some of the other n goods; and the only way in which an individual may count on disposing of —that is, may supply—money, is by demanding other goods. Therefore, we have that

$$D_{n+1} = \sum_{r=1}^{n} Q_r \cdot p_r, \quad \text{(VIII: 6)}$$

and

$$Q_{n+1} = \sum_{r=1}^{n} D_r \cdot p_r, \quad \text{(VIII: 7)}$$

from which

$$Q_{n+1} - D_{n+1} = \sum_{r=1}^{n} (D_r - Q_r) \cdot p_r. \quad \text{(VIII: 8)}$$

---

[1] It should be noticed, however, that other dynamic equations have the same stationary solution. For instance, the equations

$$d\,p_r/d\,t = p_r \cdot f_r(D_r - Q_r), \ f_r(0) = 0, \ f_r' > 0,$$

and

$$d\,p_r/d\,t = p_r \cdot f_r((D_r - Q_r)/Q_r), \ f_r(0) = 0, \ f_r' > 0.$$

Equation (VIII: 8) is *Walras's Law*, and it follows at once from this that if

$$D_r - Q_r = 0, \quad (r = 1, 2, \ldots, n) \quad \text{(VIII: 9)}$$

then

$$Q_{n+1} - D_{n+1} = 0. \quad \text{(VIII: 10)}$$

This means that as soon as any n of the $n + 1$ conditions of equilibrium are fulfilled the remaining condition of equilibrium is also fulfilled, and we can therefore do away with one of the equations (VIII: 3) as being dependent on the other n equations.[1]

It should be mentioned that equation (VIII: 8) is also valid when the system is not in equilibrium, in other words, when (VIII: 3) do not apply. Accordingly, (VIII: 8) is an expression of the identity previously mentioned:

excess supply of money = value of the excess demand for all goods

other than money. (VIII: 11)

The idea behind Walras's Law is most clearly seen by considering the form of Walras's Law which is to be found in Lindahl's cash-equations.[2] Rewriting slightly, we have for each individual in a closed system that

planned decrease in cash = planned purchases of commodities and
factors and claims *minus* expected sales
of commodities and factors and claims,

or, more simply, (VIII: 12)

planned payments   planned purchases
minus   = *minus* (VIII: 13)
expected receipts   expected sales.

---

[1] (VIII: 8) may also be written $\sum_{r=1}^{n+1}(D_r - Q_r) \cdot p_r = 0$. If it is also true that $\sum_{r=1}^{n}(D_r - Q_r) \cdot p_r = 0$, i.e. that $Q_{n+1} = D_{n+1}$, Lange says that *Say's Law* applies. Say's Law is not identically true, but if it is obeyed, it is obviously possible to do away with yet another of equations (VIII: 3), as being dependent on the others. This is a fact which has been used in the discussion of homogeneous systems. However, we shall assume that Say's Law does not apply.

[2] Lindahl, *Studies* ..., p. 79 and 113. See also J. Mosak, *General-Equilibrium Theory in International Trade*, p. 36 et seq.

The correctness of these equations depends only on the assumption that the cash budgets of the economic subjects are consistent (that the individual cash budgets are valid). On adding together all the economic subjects' cash budgets, we arrive at an equation like (VIII: 13) for the whole community, and if we interpret planned purchases *minus* expected sales on the right-hand side of this equation as the value of the excess demand for all goods other than money, and planned payments *minus* expected receipts on the left-hand side as excess supply of money, it is clear that (VIII: 13) becomes precisely Walras's Law.

But it follows at once from this that if it is found convenient to define (the value of) the excess demand for only one commodity, factor or claim in any way other than as the difference between planned purchases and expected sales, using these magnitudes in the sense in which they enter individual cash budgets, i.e. in the true *ex ante* sense, then it is necessary

either to dismiss Walras's Law,

or to define the excess supply of money in another way than as the planned payments *minus* the expected receipts, in the sense in which these magnitudes enter individual cash budgets.

Let us begin with the latter possibility. At least one $Q \cdot p$ in (VIII: 6) is now to be defined in some way other than expected sales. (VIII: 6) must then be considered as the *definition* of the demand for money, instead of as an identical relationship which arises from the consistency of the individual cash budgets. In the same way, if at least one $D \cdot p$ in (VIII: 7) is now defined in another way than as planned purchases, (VIII: 7) must be considered as a *definition* of the supply of money. (VIII: 8), and with it (VIII: 10), continues to be valid (given (VIII: 9)), but this is so only because we have dropped the definition of money according to which the supply of money is equal to planned payments and the demand for money is equal to expected receipts (in the *ex ante* sense). However, this *ex ante* definition of the excess supply of money is economically relevant, but the definition of excess supply of money arrived at by means of (VIII: 6) and (VIII: 7) is not necessarily so.

It has been pointed out in the preceding chapters, (see Chap. I, Section 9, and the whole of Chap. III), that there may be good reason to use the inflationary gap interpretation of the concept of excess demand. This interpretation of the concept of excess demand is different from the difference between planned purchases and expected sales, in the first place in that the supply in the inflationary gap sense is a smaller magnitude than the expected sales by an amount depending on the extent to which production plans break down. Therefore, if the demand for money is defined as the expected receipts, but the supply of goods is defined as the actual supply in the inflationary gap sense (for those goods for which this is of importance), we find that

$$D_{n+1} \geqq \sum_{r=1}^{n} Q_r \cdot p_r. \tag{VIII: 14}$$

Similarly, in the second place, there was found to be good reason to identify demand with something other than planned purchases, since it may quite well be supposed, for example, that binding offers to purchase may occur without being included in the cash budgets of those who make them. If this is taken into account, and the supply of money is considered as planned payments, we have that

$$Q_{n+1} \leqq \sum_{r=1}^{n} D_r \cdot p_r. \tag{VIII: 15}$$

It follows from this that the inflationary gap interpretation of the concept of excess demand leads to

$$Q_{n+1} - D_{n+1} \leqq \sum_{r=1}^{n} (D_r - Q_r) \cdot p_r. \tag{VIII: 16}$$

That is, the use of the inflationary gap interpretation of the concept of excess demand implies that, if the supply of money continues to be taken as the planned payments and the demand for money as the expected receipts, Walras's Law is not valid *in general*, that is, is not identically valid.

The reason for supposing that it may be preferable to use the inflationary gap interpretation of the concept of excess demand, instead of the purely *ex ante* interpretation, is that the excess demand which is involved in the price-reaction equations (VIII: 5) may be the excess demand in the inflationary gap sense (active attempts to purchase *minus* quantity of goods available). Although it is possible to give certain reasons for this preference, it is of course a question of empirical verification as to which interpretation of $(D_r - Q_r)$ is to be considered best, that is, which interpretation makes the equations (VIII: 5) agree with actual observations.—

The preceding may be summarized as follows: Consider a closed system with $n + 1$ goods, of which the $n + 1$th is money and *numeraire*, and where the $n + 1$th price is therefore 1, and with the equations for demand

$$D_r = D_r(p_1, p_2, \ldots, p_n), \quad (r = 1, 2, \ldots, n + 1), \quad \text{(VIII: 1)}$$

and equations for supply

$$Q_r = Q_r(p_1, p_2, \ldots, p_n), \quad (r = 1, 2, \ldots, n + 1), \quad \text{(VIII: 2)}$$

and equations for the price-reactions, e.g.

$$\frac{dp_r}{dt} = f_r(D_r - Q_r), \ f_r(0) = 0, \ f_r' > 0, \quad (r = 1, 2, \ldots, n). \quad \text{(VIII: 5)}$$

If, D_r and Q_r $(r = 1, 2, \ldots, n)$ are defined in a way appropriate for the use of $(D_r - Q_r)$ in equations (VIII: 5), and D_{n+1} and Q_{n+1} are defined as expected receipts and planned payments respectively (in the *ex ante* sense), the equation

$$Q_{n+1} - D_{n+1} = \sum_{r=1}^{n} (D_r - Q_r) \cdot p_r \quad \text{(VIII: 8)}$$

is not necessarily fulfilled.

However, as soon as Walras's Law is not identically valid, it cannot be used to show that the number of independent equations is not greater than the number of unknowns in the system (VIII: 1), (VIII: 2), (VIII: 3), and (VIII: 4). For, if Walras's Law is now added to the system, in which case one of the equations (VIII: 3) may certainly still be deleted, then Walras's Law itself becomes an independent restriction on the system.

Another thing is that the system (VIII: 1), (VIII: 2), (VIII: 3), and (VIII: 4) may have a solution even if the number of equations exceeds the number of unknowns and it is not possible to show in general that the equations are not all independent (this may happen by accident). If the system is in equilibrium, Walras's Law will naturally apply, but to use this fact to prove that the system is in general consistent is to argue from the particular to the general.

It may be remarked in conclusion that the criticism of Walras's Law which has been put forward does not imply anything in the way of "holistic" mysticism, that the Whole should be something other than can be determined from the single economic subjects' behaviour. The reasoning is built only on the fact that such dealings of the individuals which do not appear in their consistent cash budgets, may also be of relevance for the development of prices.

4. *The problem of homogeneity*

If it is assumed that the Walras system is homogeneous of degree zero in all absolute prices, and if Walras's Law as identically valid is abandoned, the question arises as to whether it is possible to treat the system of $2n + 2$ simultaneous equations for demand and supply in such a way that definite conclusions are derived as to the general properties of the system and its reactions to changes in data.

Let us first consider the case in which we, for *economic* reasons, take Walras's Law as valid, but in which all equations for supply and demand, for all the first n goods, are homogeneous of degree zero in the n absolute prices. If we use the equations for demand (VIII: 1) and supply (VIII: 2) and $p_{n+1} = 1$, together with the equilibrium conditions $D_r = Q_r$ $(r = 1, 2, \ldots, n + 1)$, we have as many equations as unknowns, because Walras's Law says that one of the equations may be deleted. However, because of the homogeneity, it is not the n absolute prices $p_1, p_2, \ldots, p_n$ which are the unknowns, but only the $n - 1$ relative prices $y_1, y_2, \ldots, y_{n-1}$, where $y_r = p_r/p_n$. So we still have one equation too many.

This problem has hitherto been cleared up in a way which can hardly be regarded as satisfactory. For example, one of the conditions $D_r = Q_r$, such as $D_n = Q_n$, is merely scrapped. If the nth good is labour-services, the static equilibrium system obtained in this way is such as does not require equality of the supply of and the demand for labour-services, that is, is a Keynesian system.[1] This method is clearly suspect, and implies in fact that the theory is deprived of its unity. It corresponds more or less to supposing that, if a child is born with three legs it may be made into a normal two-legged child just

---

[1] See, for instance, J. Mosak, *General-Equilibrium Theory in International Trade*, p. 152 et seq.

by cutting off one of the legs. Another way of resolving the problem is to assume that the absolute price of one of the goods enters into at least one of the equations for demand or supply, for example, to assume that the supply of labour-services is a function of the money wage. But it is not possible to solve what is purely a problem of homogeneity by assuming inhomogeneity.[1] A third possibility is to assume the validity of Say's Law; but its validity is just a question of economics, to be decided only from empirical considerations. If Say's Law is valid it is possible to do away with one more equation, since $\sum_{r=1}^{n}(D_r - Q_r) \cdot p_r = 0$.[2] But it should be noticed that in this case we actually have no real demand and supply conditions for money; here the money is only involved as a quite formal unity, which is not in any real way related to the system.

A simple way of solving this problem is, of course, to assume that the system has a solution in spite of the equations being one more than the unknowns. However, the most natural way of disposing the problem of homogeneity is to give up the static treatment, and we shall do this by formulating $n-1$ conditions different from the usual n equilibrium conditions, and *these other conditions are the dynamic conditions that the $n-1$ relative prices remain constant through time.* Thus we arrive at a system in which the absolute prices are not in general constant, but are always either rising or falling through time.[3]

If Walras's Law does not hold on economic grounds, we get one

---

[1] The whole of this problem is dealt with by Trygve Haavelmo, "Økonomisk likevekt og økonomisk velferd" ("Economic Equilibrium and Economic Welfare"), *Statsøkonomisk Tidsskrift*, Oslo, 1949, and Don Patinkin, "Involuntary Unemployment and the Keynesian Supply Function", *The Economic Journal*, 1949. See also W. Leontief, "Postulates: Keynes' General Theory and the Classicists", *The New Economics*, Ed. S. E. Harris, Alfred A. Knoph, New York, 1947, p. 232 et seq.

[2] See, for instance, W. Leontief, "The Consistency of Absolute Prices in Classical Economic Theory".

[3] Trygve Haavelmo, *The Notion of Price Homogeneity*, Rough Draft, Universitetets Socialøkonomiske Institut, Oslo, Stensil.-memo., 6 January, 1949, has shown how it is possible, in another way than that attempted here, to treat those homogeneous systems which have too many equations from the statical point of view by introducing certain dynamic relations. Haavelmo's model is different from the one used here in that, among other things, it gives a dynamic solution in which the excess demand for each single good is zero, but where absolute prices are nevertheless either continually falling or rising.

equation more of course, but the analysis in what follows is carried out in such a way that, in spite of this, there is no inconsistency from this cause.

In Section 5, the system and its conditions are set up and the general character of the system is considered. An important thing is to examine the stability conditions of the system and the effects of changes in data. A rigorous enquiry into these matters requires the use of some mathematics. Although the mathematics applied is rather well-known in economic theory it is, nevertheless, convenient to put it into an appendix (Appendix to Chapter VIII), and devote Section 7 to a looser verbal description of the results obtained in the appendix. In Section 6 some remarks are made about the price reaction equations, and the consequences of an alternative hypothesis examined.

5. *General properties of the quasi-equilibrium system*

In order to simplify the presentation somewhat, we write (since $p_{n+1} = 1$)

$$X_r = X_r(p_1, p_2, \ldots, p_n) \qquad \text{(VIII: 17)}$$
$$= D_r(p_1, p_2, \ldots, p_n) - Q_r(p_1, p_2, \ldots, p_n), \quad (r = 1, 2, \ldots, n + 1).$$

Further,

$$y_r = \frac{p_r}{p_n}, \quad (r = 1, 2, \ldots, n - 1). \quad \text{(VIII: 18)}$$

We assume that the excess demand equations for the first n goods are homogeneous of degree zero in all the absolute prices, so that these equations may be written as

$$X_r = X_r(y_1, y_2, \ldots, y_{n-1}), \quad (r = 1, 2, \ldots, n). \quad \text{(VIII: 19)}$$

Provided that Walras's Law is valid, it follows from this that the excess demand for money (the $n + 1$th good) is homogeneous of degree one in all the absolute prices. In this case therefore, the excess demand for the first n goods depends only on the relative prices, whereas the excess demand for money is a function of the absolute prices.

The equations for the price reactions are here taken to be

$$\frac{dp_r}{dt} = f_r(X_r), \; f_r(0) = 0, \; f_r' > 0, \quad (r = 1, 2, \ldots, n). \quad \text{(VIII: 20)}$$

14

200

There are $n-1$ relative prices $y_r = p_r/p_n$, so that it is possible to formulate $n-1$ necessary and sufficient conditions for the relative prices to be constant with respect to time. Then (cf. Chap. VII, Section 2),

$$\frac{d\left(\dfrac{p_r}{p_n}\right)}{dt} = \frac{p_n \cdot \dfrac{dp_r}{dt} - p_r \cdot \dfrac{dp_n}{dt}}{p_n^2} = 0, \quad (r = 1, 2, \ldots, n-1). \quad \text{(VIII:21)}$$

t represents time.

It follows that

$$f_r(X_r) - y_r \cdot f_n(X_n) = 0, \quad (r = 1, 2, \ldots, n-1). \quad \text{(VIII:22)}$$

The equations for the excess demand (VIII:19) and the *conditions of quasi-equilibrium*[1] (VIII:22) constitute $2n-1$ equations in the $2n-1$ unknowns $X_1, X_2, \ldots, X_n$ and $y_1, y_2, \ldots, y_{n-1}$. We shall now assume that this system has a unique solution in the relative prices and the excess demands, where the excess demands will not in general be zero, but may be zero as a special case.

The absolute prices will not in general be constant, so, if Walras's Law is valid, the excess demand for money at the instant t, X_{n+1}^t, is given by (the absolute prices being linear functions with respect to t, cf. Section 6)

$$- X_{n+1}^t = \sum_{r=1}^{n} p_r^t \cdot \overline{X}_r = \sum_{r=1}^{n} \{f_r(\overline{X}_r) \cdot (t - t_0) + p_r^{t_0}\} \cdot \overline{X}_r, \quad \text{(VIII:23)}$$

where $\overline{X}_r$ are the excess demands for the first n goods, as determined by the equations (VI:19) and (VI:22), and p_r^t and $p_r^{t_0}$ are the absolute prices of the rth good at the instants t and t_0, respectively.

When Walras's Law is not valid, we have that

$$X_{n+1} = X_{n+1}(p_1, p_2, \ldots, p_n). \quad \text{(VIII:24)}$$

But since the relative prices are constant in the position of quasi-equilibrium, whereas the absolute prices are functions of time (cf.

---

[1] If the quasi-equilibrium conditions (VIII:22) are to be both necessary and sufficient conditions for the ratio's (p_r/p_n) to be constant, p_n must be non-zero for all values of t considered, see Edouard Goursat, *Cours d'Analyse Mathématique*, Paris, Gauthier-Villars, 1943, Tome I, p. 37, note (1). This assumption is, however, also necessary for *economic* reasons, see below.

Section 6), we may write—*assuming* that X_{n+1} is homogeneous of degree one in all the absolute prices—e.g.,

$$X_{n+1}^t = \{f(\overline{X}_n) \cdot (t - t_0)/p_n^{t_0} + 1\} \cdot X_{n+1}(p_1^{t_0}, p_2^{t_0}, \ldots, p_n^{t_0}), \quad \text{(VIII: 25)}$$

where the p^{t_0}'s are the absolute prices at the instant t_0.

$\overline{X}_r \neq 0$. When the excess demands in the n good-markets are different from zero, the conditions of quasi-equilibrium (VI: 22) may be written as

$$y_r = \frac{p_r}{p_n} = \frac{f_r(X_r)}{f_n(X_n)}, \quad r = 1, 2, \ldots, n-1),$$

or,

$$\frac{p_r \cdot d\, p_n}{p_n \cdot d\, p_r} = 1, \quad (r = 1, 2, \ldots, n-1), \quad \text{(VIII: 26)}$$

from which it follows that all the absolute prices rise or fall in the same proportion.

$\overline{X}_r > 0$. If $\overline{X}_r > 0$, it follows at once from (VIII: 22), together with (VIII: 20), that $\overline{X}_n$ is also > 0 (and conversely). For, if $\overline{X}_r > 0$, $f_r(\overline{X}_r)$ is also > 0, and since $\bar{y}_r > 0$, $f_n(\overline{X}_n)$ must also be > 0, so consequently $\overline{X}_n > 0$. It follows that all $\overline{X}_r > 0$ $(r = 1, 2, \ldots, n)$. There is thus quasi-equilibrium with excess demand in all the n good-markets and rising absolute prices everywhere. The system is clearly characterized by the existence of a pressure of inflation. The excess demand for money is negative, if Walras's Law is valid (cf. (VIII: 23)), and this excess supply of money increases steadily. If Walras's Law is not valid, the excess demand for money may be either positive or negative, but will in any case increase numerically (cf. (VIII: 25)).

$\overline{X}_r < 0$. If $\overline{X}_r < 0$, we have, as before, that all $\overline{X}_r$ $(r = 1, 2, \ldots, n)$ are < 0. So there is quasi-equilibrium with excess supply in all n good-markets and falling absolute prices everywhere. The system is clearly characterized by a pressure of deflation. For the excess demand for money, the equivalent of what was said above applies. However, if all $\overline{X}_r < 0$, the absolute prices will fall steadily by a constant amount per unit of time, and must therefore become negative sooner or later. Thus, on economic grounds we should exclude the case where all $\overline{X}_r < 0$, cf. Section 6.

$\overline{X}_r = 0$. In the special case where $\overline{X}_r = 0$, the $n-1$ conditions of quasi-equilibrium may be replaced by the n customary conditions of equilibrium (not all being independent)

$$X_r = 0, \qquad (r = 1, 2, \ldots, n), \qquad \text{(VIII: 3')}$$

whereupon the system becomes identical with the usual Walras system solved as if $X_{n+1} = 0$ were satisfied by (VIII: 3'). The absolute prices are here constant, and the quasi-equilibrium degenerates to equilibrium. We find that $X_{n+1} = 0$, if Walras's Law holds. If Walras's Law does not hold, the excess demand for money is a constant positive or negative magnitude, since the coefficient of $X_{n+1} (p_1^{t_0}, p_2^{t_0}, \ldots, p_n^{t_0})$ in (VIII: 25) is here 1. —

In the preceding part of this section it was assumed that the excess demand equations for all the n goods are homogeneous of degree zero in all the absolute prices. If one of the goods is claims, this assumption is not unreservedly a good one, since if we, with Lange[1], assume that the excess demand equation for claims is homogeneous of degree 1 in all the absolute prices, and if we take the nth good to be claims, then the excess demand equations for the other $n-1$ goods are homogeneous of degree zero only in the absolute prices of the first $n-1$ goods. If these assumptions are made, we arrive at a well known case by supposing that there is an economic subject ("the bankers") who always buy or sell claims in such a way that the price of claims is constant. The price of claims may then be put equal to unity, and the excess demand equation for claims lumped together with that for money. If Walras's Law now holds, we have (cf. Chap. II, Section 6) that

$$I_0 - S_0 = -X_{n+1}^t = \sum_{r=1}^{n-1} \{f_r(\overline{X}_r) \cdot (t - t_0) + p_r^{t_0}\} \cdot \overline{X}_r. \qquad \text{(VIII: 27)}$$

If the system is inflationary, I_0 is then $> S_0$, and the difference between them increases steadily (but the "real" value is constant), and similarly, if the system is deflationary, $I_0 < S_0$. In the special case when there is static equilibrium, $I_0 = S_0$.

It is easy to see that the quasi-equilibrium system is now a generalized and continuous counterpart to Wicksell's model in *Geldzins und Güterpreise*, with the only difference, unimportant here, that whereas in the

---

[1] O. Lange, *Price Flexibility and Employment*, p. 16.

quasi-equilibrium system the absolute prices rise (fall) linearly (cf. below), the absolute prices in Wicksell's model rise (fall) exponentially. But what is common to them is that they both involve a continuous self-generating process, which does not imply any tendency to approach static equilibrium.

6. *An alternative system*

Some remarks on equations (VIII: 20) will not be out of place. Of course, these equations constitute only one among many reasonable hypotheses concerning the relation between the speed of the rise in prices and the excess demand. That used here has been adopted, for one reason, in order to bring the discussion into line with the more recent discussion of the Walras system, but it is inconvenient in one important respect, namely that the solutions of the quasi-equilibrium system when $\overline{X}_r < 0$ are *economically* unreasonable, since $\overline{X}_r < 0$ causes the absolute prices p_r to be negative sooner or later. This is a consequence of the fact, which has already been mentioned, that the absolute prices in this case vary linearly with time. For, if we solve the equations

$$\frac{d p_r}{d t} = f_r(\overline{X}_r), \qquad (r = 1, 2, \ldots, n) \qquad \text{(VIII: 20)}$$

we obtain (a result which has already been used in equations (VIII: 23) et seq.)

$$p_r^t = f_r(\overline{X}_r) \cdot (t - t_0) + p_r^{t_0}, \quad (r = 1, 2, \ldots, n),$$

where $f_r(\overline{X}_r) < 0$, and p_r^t and $p_r^{t_0}$ are the absolute prices at times t and t_0. Even if $p_r^{t_0}$ for economic reasons is chosen > 0, it can be seen that the absolute prices must become negative when t is sufficiently large.

This difficulty may be avoided by choosing, instead of hypothesis (VIII: 20), the **hypothesis**

$$\frac{d p_r}{d t} = p_r \cdot f_r(X_r), \ f_r(0) = 0, \ f_r' > 0, \quad (r = 1, 2, \ldots, n). \quad \text{(VIII: 20')}$$

If this relation is introduced into (VIII: 21), we obtain the conditions of quasi-equilibrium

$$f_r(X_r) = f_n(X_n), \quad (r = 1, 2, \ldots, n-1), \quad \text{(VIII: 22')}$$

which together with (VIII: 19) now constitutes the system. It is still true that in quasi-equilibrium

$$\frac{p_r \cdot d p_n}{p_n \cdot d p_r} = 1, \quad (r = 1, 2, \ldots, n-1). \qquad \text{(VIII: 26)}$$

So far the character of the system has not changed. However, if equations (VIII: 20′) are solved (X_r put equal to $\overline{X}_r$), we get

$$p_r^t = p_r^{t_0} \cdot \exp\left\{f_r(\overline{X}_r) \cdot (t - t_0)\right\}, \qquad (r = 1, 2, \ldots, n).$$

$p_r^{t_0}$ is chosen positive, and it will be seen that, for $\overline{X}_r > 0$, $p_r^t \to \infty$ as $t \to \infty$. For $\overline{X}_r < 0$, $p_r^t \to 0$ as $t \to \infty$.

Thus the hypothesis (VIII: 20′) is *a priori* preferable to hypothesis (VIII: 20), in so far as it makes it economically reasonable for the quasi-equilibrium system to be either in inflation or in deflation. Also, since with hypothesis (VIII: 20′) the absolute prices rise (fall) exponentially with respect to time, we thus have a perfect counterpart to Wicksell's model. Furthermore, (VIII: 20′) has the advantage that it is not necessary later on to make an unlikely approximation in order to simplify the treatment of the system (see equation (VIII: 38)). The reason we have kept hypothesis (VIII: 20) in this chapter, in spite of all this, is partly that we are interested here in the inflationary situation and partly, as already mentioned, that we wish to bring the analysis as close as possible to the most recent treatments of the Walras system.

7. *Multi-market analysis versus one-commodity, one-factor analysis*

The quasi-equilibrium system described in Section 5 is characterized by the fact that in the general case it is in disequilibrium in the sense that demand and supply are not equal, and do not tend to become equal. The absolute prices will therefore always be moving upwards (or downwards). So the quasi-equilibrium system has the property that it cannot escape a permanently recurring disequilibrium. In this respect it might be designated unstable. On the other hand, it is quite reasonable to talk about stability for such a system, in the sense that there may be stability in the movement of the absolute prices and in the disequilibrium on the various markets such that if the quasi-equilibrium is disturbed for some reason, there will still be forces internal to the system which will tend to re-establish quasi-equilibrium.

In Chap. VII we considered the question of stability for the simplest possible system, with only two goods and consequently only one relative price (the price-wage ratio), and showed that the assumptions formulated in Chap. VII, Section 2 concerning the shape of the curves for planned demand and planned supply were sufficient to ensure stability. But these assumptions were in no way necessary for the stability of that simple system.

It is obvious that, if we go on to study the conditions of stability for a system with several markets, the relationships will be considerably more complicated and impossible to understand intuitively in the same way as was possible in the two dimensional case. However, it is evident that the circumstances decisive for stability will be of much the same sort as in the case of the general Walras system, namely, the question of whether the various goods are substitutable or complementary, and of the reaction of prices. Since our quasi-equilibrium system includes the Walras system as a special case, it may be expected that the conditions of stability for the quasi-equilibrium system will include as a special case the customary conditions of stability for the Walras system which have been given by J. R. Hicks and others.[1] This is actually the case, as will be apparent from the Appendix to this chapter.

The reason for taking an interest in the conditions of stability for such general systems is not, however, due to the interest of the conditions themselves, so much as to the fact that the conditions of stability can be used to determine the effects of changes in the data of the system. In the one-commodity, one-factor model in Chap. VII, we were interested, among other things, in the effect on the price-wage ratio of a primary (partial) change in the excess demand for either commodities or labour, and arrived at the conclusion that a primary decrease of the excess demand for commodities will lead to a fall in the price-wage ratio, whereas a primary decrease of the excess demand for labour will lead to a rise in the price-wage ratio—both parts of the conclusion arising from the comparison of the quasi-equilibria before and after the change concerned.

It appears that similar conclusions are reached in the case of the general quasi-equilibrium system, assuming it to be stable. As is shown in the Appendix to this chapter, if a change of data occurs in the form of an increase (decrease) of the excess demand for a good, this increase (decrease) in the excess demand will lead to a rise (fall) in the relative price of the good concerned, assuming the system to be stable and governed by a certain symmetry, and taking all the repercussions throughout the system into account. If, in addition, all goods are substitutable, not only the relative price of the good directly affected will rise, but also *all* other relative prices.

These results are well-known from the Walras system[2], and are

---

[1] J. R. Hicks, *Value and Capital*, Chap. V and the Mathematical Appendix, Appendix to Chapter V.

[2] See, for instance, J. Mosak, *General-Equilibrium Theory in International Trade*, p. 45 et seq.

actually one of the few important results which have been derived from the Walras system. What might perhaps not have been expected is thus shown to be true, namely, that these results from the Walras system hold good even if the assumption of static equilibrium is abandoned. It is the stability properties of the system which are decisive in this respect, and not the possible property of being a static equilibrium system.

Another circumstance of significance for the conclusions in Chap. VII was that an increase (decrease) in the excess demand in one market causes a certain increase (decrease) of the excess demand in the other market, that is to say, a certain change in the excess demand in the one market "moves over" to the other market, in such a way that when a new quasi-equilibrium is achieved, the resultant change in the excess demand in the market where the primary change took place is less than the primary change; but there is a corresponding change in the same direction in the other market's excess demand.

For the general quasi-equilibrium system, it is possible to show that an increase (decrease) in the excess demand in one market will lead to increases (decreases) in the excess demands of the other markets; but possible only if we make the assumption that all goods are substitutes, which is hardly in accordance with reality. Furthermore, it is not possible to prove that the resultant alteration in the excess demand in the market where the primary change occurs is less than the primary change itself.

This latter circumstance makes it necessary to put a question-mark against the conclusions reached in Chap. VII, Sections 3 to 6, and it must be admitted that we have had only a limited success in carrying over the results of the one-commodity, one-factor analysis of Chap. VII to the general quasi-equilibrium system, and the assumptions which made that possible were not such as could be taken as economically reasonable. However, this is not necessarily the same as saying that the analysis of Chap. VII (and earlier) is worthless. For, although it has proved difficult to adapt results to the general quasi-equilibrium system which we have been considering, it should be remembered, on the one hand, that this quasi-equilibrium system is *very* general in character. For instance, no special conditions for production have been given for the system, so that the distinction between commodities and factors is really quite empty in such a system. On the other hand, it must also be remembered that even if it is impossible to carry over the results to a multi-market system in such a way that the results of the one-commodity, one-factor analysis still hold exactly for each single good in the multi-market system, it may well be that the results of the one-commodity, one-factor analysis may apply to a multi-market system, if the markets are lumped together in a suitable manner by means of indices.

No attempt will be made to establish a more complicated system in which an effective distinction between commodities and factors can be made,* nor to solve the general aggregation problem which occurs here. For, the object of the analysis of this chapter was, *inter alia*, to show how it is possible in general to overcome the difficulty of the inconsistency of our models when treated statically. That object has been accomplished.

Appendix to Chapter VIII

1. *Introductory*

In this appendix we shall assume that a unique solution of the quasi-equilibrium system given by equations (VIII: 19) and (VIII: 22), does exist; and we shall begin by establishing conditions for the quasi-equilibrium system to be stable.

There are two methods of procedure available. The first corresponds to the Hicksian treatment of the conditions for stability of the static Walras system. This method will be called *Hicks's Method*. A more attractive method, however, is one analogous to Samuelson's and Lange's treatment of the conditions for stability of the Walras system. This method is derived from the classical mathematical treatment of this type of problems. It will be called *Samuelson's Method*.[1]

In order to make the treatment easier a rather special assumption is introduced, and this makes the conditions of stability which we arrive at only approximate.

2. *Conditions for stability: Hicks's method*

Following Hicks, we start by considering the system to be in quasi-equilibrium, and suppose that there is an infinitesimal change dy_r in one of the relative prices

---

[1] The exposition is very near to that followed by O. Lange in *Price Flexibility and Employment, Appendix.*

y_r. Then we define stability by saying first that the system is stable if[1]

$$\left.\begin{array}{l} \dfrac{d}{d\,y_r}\{f_s\,(X_s) - y_s \cdot f_n\,(\overline{X}_n)\} = 0 \quad (s \neq r) \\[3mm] \dfrac{d}{d\,y_r}\{f_r\,(X_r) - y_r \cdot f_n\,(\overline{X}_n)\} < 0. \end{array}\right\} \qquad (\text{VIII: } 28)$$

It should be noticed that, in this, we are assuming that

$$\frac{d\,p_n}{d\,y_r} = 0, \qquad\qquad (\text{VIII: } 29)$$

which is only possible if the excess demand in the nth market is unaffected by the infinitesimal change in y_r. As a consequence of this, we must write in the relations (VIII: 28) $\overline{X}_n$ instead of X_n, since the bar over a symbol means that the symbol has the quasi-equilibrium value. So our approximation (VIII: 29) consists in supposing that the excess demand in the nth market, in the quasi-equilibrium position, may be regarded as relatively unaffected by such changes of the relative prices as we are here dealing with.[2] Something further is said about this under *Samuelson's Method* and in Section 6.

The meaning of (VIII: 28) is that when all relative prices other than the rth are adjusted so that all conditions of quasi-equilibrium other than the rth are fulfilled, a rise (for example) of y_r above the quasi-equilibrium value must cause $d\,y_r/d\,t$ to become negative if the system is to be stable. The analogy with Hicks's treatment in *Value and Capital* is evident.

We now have that

$$\frac{d}{d\,y_r}\{f_s\,(X_s) - y_s \cdot f_n\,(\overline{X}_n)\} = f'_s\,(\overline{X}_s) \cdot \sum_{j=1}^{n-1} \overline{X}_{s,\,j} \cdot \frac{d\,y_j}{d\,y_r} - f_n\,(\overline{X}_n) \cdot \frac{d\,y_s}{d\,y_r},$$

$$(s = 1,\,2,\,\ldots,\,n-1), \qquad (\text{VIII: } 30)$$

where $\overline{X}_{s,\,j} = \partial\,X_s/\partial\,y_j$ evaluated at the quasi-equilibrium position. To save space we will now write

$$b_{s,\,j} = f'_s\,(\overline{X}_s) \cdot \overline{X}_{s,\,j}, \qquad\qquad (\text{VIII: } 31)$$

whereupon, on applying (VIII: 28) $(s \neq r)$, we arrive at the system of equations

---

[1] It is assumed that all functions are well-behaved, so that all the operations which follow are permissible.

[2] For the simple case with only two goods, considered in Chap. VII, this approximation means that the Q_0-curve is taken to be vertical and situated to the right of the Q_1-line, see for instance Fig. 17.

$$- b_{1,r} = \left\{ b_{1,1} - f_n(\overline{X}_n) \right\} \cdot \frac{d\,y_1}{d\,y_r} + b_{1,2} \cdot \frac{d\,y_2}{d\,y_r} + \cdots + 0 + \cdots +$$

$$+ b_{1,n-1} \cdot \frac{d\,y_{n-1}}{d\,y_r}$$

$$- b_{2,r} = b_{2,1} \cdot \frac{d\,y_1}{d\,y_r} + \left\{ b_{2,2} - f_n(\overline{X}_n) \right\} \cdot \frac{d\,y_2}{d\,y_r} + \cdots + 0 + \cdots +$$

$$+ b_{2,n-1} \cdot \frac{d\,y_{n-1}}{d\,y_r}$$

. . . .

$$- b_{r,r} + f_n(\overline{X}_n) = b_{r,1} \cdot \frac{d\,y_1}{d\,y_r} + b_{r,2} \cdot \frac{d\,y_2}{d\,y_r} + \cdots + \frac{d\left\{ f_r(X_r) - y_r \cdot f_n(\overline{X}_n) \right\}}{d\,y_r} +$$

$$+ \cdots + b_{r,n-1} \cdot \frac{d\,y_{n-1}}{d\,y_r}$$

. . . .

$$- b_{n-1,r} = b_{n-1,1} \cdot \frac{d\,y_1}{d\,y_r} + b_{n-1,2} \cdot \frac{d\,y_2}{d\,y_r} + \cdots + 0 + \cdots +$$

$$+ \left\{ b_{n-1,n-1} - f_n(\overline{X}_n) \right\} \cdot \frac{d\,y_{n-1}}{d\,y_r}. \qquad \text{(VIII: 32)}$$

Solution gives

$$\frac{d}{d\,y_r} \left\{ f_r(X_r) - y_r \cdot f_n(\overline{X}_n) \right\} = \frac{J}{J_{r,r}} < 0, \qquad \text{(VIII: 33)}$$

where

$$J = \begin{vmatrix} b_{1,1} - f_n(\overline{X}_n) & b_{1,2} & \cdots & b_{1,n-1} \\ b_{2,1} & b_{2,2} - f_n(\overline{X}_n) & \cdots & b_{2,n-1} \\ \cdots \cdots \cdots \cdots \cdots \cdots \cdots \cdots \cdots \cdots \\ b_{n-1,1} & b_{n-1,2} & \cdots & b_{n-1,n-1} - f_n(\overline{X}_n) \end{vmatrix}, \qquad \text{(VIII: 34)}$$

while $J_{r,r}$ is the cofactor of the element of the rth row and rth column of J.

Applying Lange's treatment and terminology as given in the Appendix to *Price Flexibility and Employment*, which may be referred to, it is easy to continue with a process like that above, putting successive $d\,y_s / d\,y_r = 0$ and simultaneously dropping analogous conditions (VIII: 28) $(s \neq r)$. Then we find that the condition for perfect stability of order m is that

$$b_{1,1} - f_n(\overline{X}_n) < 0, \quad \begin{vmatrix} b_{1,1} - f_n(\overline{X}_n) & b_{1,2} \\ b_{2,1} & b_{2,2} - f_n(\overline{X}_n) \end{vmatrix} > 0, \ldots$$

$$\ldots, \ \text{sign} \ \begin{vmatrix} b_{1,1} - f_n(\overline{X}_n) & b_{1,2} & \ldots & b_{1,m} \\ b_{2,1} & b_{2,2} - f_n(\overline{X}_n) & \ldots & b_{2,m} \\ \cdot\cdot\cdot\cdot\cdot\cdot\cdot\cdot\cdot\cdot\cdot\cdot\cdot\cdot\cdot\cdot\cdot\cdot \\ b_{m,1} & b_{m,2} & \ldots & b_{m,m} - f_n(\overline{X}_n) \end{vmatrix} = \text{sign} \, (-1)^m. \tag{VIII: 35}$$

It is evident that the quasi-equilibrium system may be perfectly stable of order $n-1$ at most.

If we wish to establish the conditions for stability in the special case in which the quasi-equilibrium is an equilibrium, and where consequently $\overline{X}_r = 0$ for all r, we only need to notice that $f_n(\overline{X}_n) = 0$, from which we have

$$J = f_1' \cdot f_2' \cdot \cdots \cdot f_{n-1}' \cdot \begin{vmatrix} \overline{X}_{1,1} & \overline{X}_{1,2} & \ldots & \overline{X}_{1,n-1} \\ \overline{X}_{2,1} & \overline{X}_{2,2} & \ldots & \overline{X}_{2,n-1} \\ \cdot\cdot\cdot\cdot\cdot\cdot\cdot\cdot\cdot\cdot\cdot\cdot \\ \overline{X}_{n-1,1} & \overline{X}_{n-1,2} & \ldots & \overline{X}_{n-1,n-1} \end{vmatrix}, \tag{VIII: 36}$$

where $f_1', f_2', \ldots, f_{n-1}'$ are all > 0. In this way the stability conditions are reduced to the form given by Hicks for the case of static equilibrium. But it is apparent that, since in this case we are all the time supposing p_n to be constant, the simplified expression obtained in (VIII: 36) cannot be used to set up conditions for perfect stability, and this agrees with Lange's result for a homogeneous Walras system.[1]

However, it has been pointed out that, in the static theory of equilibrium, Hicks's conditions of stability cannot be taken as a general expression for true dynamic stability. It may well be that something similar is the case here. We shall therefore go over to the other method.

3. *Conditions for stability: Samuelson's method*

Here we consider the system of differential equations

$$\frac{d\,y_r}{d\,t} = \frac{f_r(X_r) - y_r \cdot f_n(X_n)}{p_n}, \quad (r = 1, 2, \ldots, n-1). \tag{VIII: 37}$$

The solutions of this system will be called y_r^t and are functions of the time t and arbitrarily chosen initial values at time t_0 for the y's in a neighbourhood of the quasi-equilibrium position which may be regarded as the stationary solution

[1] Lange, *Price Flexibility and Employment*, p. 100—01.

of (VIII: 37). The system is then said to be stable if $y_r^t \to \overline{y_r}$, when $t \to \infty$, $\overline{y_r}$ being the solutions of the quasi-equilibrium system of equations.

In order to be able to solve (VIII: 37), the magnitude p_n, which appears explicitly on the right-hand side of (VIII: 37), may be considered to be written as a function of t and the y's, so that (VIII: 37) may be transformed to a system of differential equations of the second order. It would not, however, be possible to rewrite this system in a form homogeneous and having constant coefficients. Therefore, in order to facilitate the treatment we make use of the following device.[1]

As previously mentioned, in a quasi-equilibrium situation all absolute prices rise (fall) linearly with respect to time, that is, we have $p_n = f_n(\overline{X}) \cdot t$ (putting $t_0 = 0$ and $p_n^{t_0} = 0$). Our new assumption is that, although we introduce into (VIII: 37) certain initial values for the relative prices which do not coincide with the quasi-equilibrium values, this does not change the change of p_n with respect to time too much for us to be able to use, as an approximation, the expression

$$p_n = f_n(\overline{X}_n) \cdot t. \tag{VIII: 38}$$

This assumption is equivalent to the assumption made in Section 2 that $d\,p_n/d\,y_r = 0$, (VIII: 29).

So we have

$$\frac{d\,y_r}{d\,t} = \frac{f_r(X_r) - y_r \cdot f_n(\overline{X}_n)}{f_n(\overline{X}_n) \cdot t}, \quad (r = 1, 2, \ldots, n-1). \tag{VIII: 39}$$

Let us now introduce the auxiliary variable u, and confine ourselves to the case in which all $\overline{X}_r > 0$, that is, in which the quasi-equilibrium system is inflationary, so that $f_n(\overline{X}_n)$ is also > 0. u is defined by

$$u = \log_e(f_n(\overline{X}_n) \cdot t), \tag{VIII: 40}$$

from which

$$\frac{d\,y_r}{d\,u} = \frac{f_r(X_r) - y_r \cdot f_n(\overline{X}_n)}{f_n(\overline{X}_n)} = F_r(y_1, y_2, \ldots, y_{n-1}), \quad (r = 1, 2, \ldots, n-1),$$
$$\tag{VIII: 41}$$

What we now wish to derive is the conditions for y_r^u to approach $\overline{y_r}$ when $u \to \infty$, the y_r^u being the solutions of the system (VIII: 41). For, if $y_r^u \to \overline{y_r}$ when $u \to \infty$, then $y_r^t \to \overline{y_r}$ also, since $t = e^u / f_n(\overline{X}_n)$. If $u \to \infty$, $t \to \infty$ also, but much more rapidly.

We now expand the function F according to Taylor's Theorem, in a neighbourhood of the quasi-equilibrium position, and neglect the non-linear part of the expansion. Then, bearing in mind that $F_r(\overline{y_1}, \overline{y_2}, \ldots, \overline{y_{n-1}}) = 0$, we get

---

[1] This device was pointed out to me by Docent Göran Borg, The Institute of Mathematics, Uppsala.

$$\frac{d}{d\,u}\,(y_r - \bar{y}_r) = \sum_{s=1}^{n-1} F'_{r,s} \cdot (y_s - \bar{y}_s), \quad (r = 1, 2, \ldots, n-1), \quad \text{(VIII: 42)}$$

where $F'_{r,s}$ stands for $\partial F_r / \partial y_s$, evaluated in the quasi-equilibrium position.

Since equations (VIII: 42) are homogeneous and linear with constant coefficients, they have solutions

$$y_r^u - \bar{y}_r = \sum_{s=1}^{k} q_{r,s}(u) \cdot e^{\lambda_s \cdot u}, \quad (r = 1, 2, \ldots, n-1), \quad \text{(VIII: 43)}$$

where the λ_s's are the k distinct roots of the characteristic equation

$$\begin{vmatrix} F'_{1,1} - \lambda & F'_{1,2} & \ldots & F'_{1,n-1} \\ F'_{2,1} & F'_{2,2} - \lambda & \ldots & F'_{2,n-1} \\ \cdot \cdot \cdot \cdot \cdot \cdot \cdot \cdot \cdot \cdot \cdot \cdot \cdot \cdot \cdot \\ F'_{n-1,1} & F'_{n-1,2} & \ldots & F'_{n-1,n-1} - \lambda \end{vmatrix} = 0, \quad \text{(VIII: 44)}$$

and the $q(u)$'s are polynomials in u.

Then

$$\left.\begin{aligned} F'_{r,s} &= \frac{f'_r(\bar{X}_r) \cdot \bar{X}_{r,s}}{f_n(\bar{X}_n)}, \quad (s \neq r) \\ F'_{r,r} &= \frac{f'_r(\bar{X}_r) \cdot \bar{X}_{r,r} - f_n(\bar{X}_n)}{f_n(\bar{X}_n)}, \end{aligned}\right\} \quad \text{(VIII: 45)}$$

and, since we still write

$$b_{r,s} = f'_r(\bar{X}_r) \cdot \bar{X}_{r,s}, \quad \text{(VIII: 31)}$$

the characteristic equation becomes

$$\begin{vmatrix} \dfrac{b_{1,1} - f_n(\bar{X}_n)}{f_n(\bar{X}_n)} - \lambda & \dfrac{b_{1,2}}{f_n(\bar{X}_n)} & \ldots & \dfrac{b_{1,n-1}}{f_n(\bar{X}_n)} \\ \dfrac{b_{2,1}}{f_n(\bar{X}_n)} & \dfrac{b_{2,2} - f_n(\bar{X}_n)}{f_n(\bar{X}_n)} - \lambda & \ldots & \dfrac{b_{2,n-1}}{f_n(\bar{X}_n)} \\ \cdot \cdot \cdot \cdot \cdot \cdot \cdot \cdot \cdot \cdot \cdot \cdot \cdot \cdot \cdot \cdot \cdot \cdot \\ \dfrac{b_{n-1,1}}{f_n(\bar{X}_n)} & \dfrac{b_{n-1,2}}{f_n(\bar{X}_n)} & \ldots & \dfrac{b_{n-1,n-1} - f_n(\bar{X}_n)}{f_n(\bar{X}_n)} - \lambda \end{vmatrix} = 0. \quad \text{(VIII: 46)}$$

The condition that $y_r^u - \bar{y}_r \to 0$, that is, that $y_r^u \to \bar{y}_r$, or $y_r^t \to \bar{y}_r$, when $u \to \infty$, is that

$$R(\lambda_s) < 0, \quad (s = 1, 2, \ldots, k), \quad \text{(VIII: 47)}$$

where $R(\lambda_s)$ denotes the real part of the roots of (VIII: 46).

If the characteristic determinant is symmetric, a necessary and sufficient condition for (VIII: 47) to be valid is that (VIII: 35) is satisfied, where $m = n - 1$. But if there is such symmetry, then

$$b_{r,s} = b_{s,r}, \qquad (VIII: 48)$$

or,

$$f_r'(\overline{X}_r) \cdot \overline{X}_{r,s} = f_s'(\overline{X}_s) \cdot \overline{X}_{s,r}, \qquad (VIII: 49)$$

cf. Section 6 of this appendix.

The special case in which $\overline{X}_r = 0$ may be treated similarly, except that instead of putting $p_n = f_n(\overline{X}_n) \cdot t$, p_n is put equal to the constant p_n, and X_n is taken to be zero. The characteristic equation may now be written

$$\begin{vmatrix} f_1'(\overline{X}_1) \cdot \overline{X}_{1,1} - \lambda & f_1'(\overline{X}_1) \cdot \overline{X}_{1,2} & \cdots & f_1'(\overline{X}_1) \cdot \overline{X}_{1,n-1} \\ f_2'(\overline{X}_2) \cdot \overline{X}_{2,1} & f_2'(\overline{X}_2) \cdot \overline{X}_{2,2} - \lambda & \cdots & f_2'(\overline{X}_2) \cdot \overline{X}_{2,n-1} \\ \cdots & \cdots & \cdots & \cdots \\ f_{n-1}'(\overline{X}_{n-1}) \cdot \overline{X}_{n-1,1} & f_{n-1}'(\overline{X}_{n-1}) \cdot \overline{X}_{n-1,2} & \cdots & f_{n-1}'(\overline{X}_{n-1}) \cdot \overline{X}_{n-1,n-1} - \lambda \end{vmatrix} = 0. \qquad (VIII: 50)$$

which is entirely analogous to the characteristic equation given by Lange for the usual Walras system, except that (VIII: 50) is written in terms of relative prices whereas Lange's was given in terms of absolute prices.[1]

4. *The reactions of the system to changes of data*

An important question which now arises is how the quasi-equilibrium system reacts to changes in data, and we will investigate, *inter alia*, to what extent the results obtained in Chap. VII may be said to be valid when many goods are considered simultaneously and the system is more general. In order to do this, we introduce a parameter z into the excess demand equation for the ith good, so that this equation now becomes

$$X_i = X_i(y_1, y_2, \ldots, y_{n-1}, z). \qquad (VIII: 51)$$

a) First we consider the effect on the relative prices of an infinitesimal change in z.

The conditions of quasi-equilibrium,

$$f_r(X_r) - y_r \cdot f_n(X_n) = 0 \quad (r = 1, 2, \ldots, n - 1), \qquad (VIII: 22)$$

are differentiated totally with respect to z. X_n, and consequently $f_n(X_n)$ are regarded as constant (equal to $\overline{X}_n$ and $f_n(\overline{X}_n)$ respectively) during the differentiation, so that the market for the nth good is taken to be unaffected by the change in data. This approximation is made in order to include the following treatment in

---

[1] Lange, *Price Flexibility and Employment*, p. 96.

the same assumption of approximation as was used for the investigation of stability. Putting $X_{i,z} = \partial X_i / \partial z$, we get

$$
\left.
\begin{aligned}
&f'_r(\overline{X}_r) \cdot \sum_{s=1}^{n-1} \left\{ \overline{X}_{r,s} \cdot \frac{dy_s}{dz} \right\} - f_n(\overline{X}_n) \cdot \frac{dy_r}{dz} = 0 \qquad (r \neq i) \\
&f'_i(\overline{X}_i) \cdot \sum_{s=1}^{n-1} \left\{ \overline{X}_{i,s} \cdot \frac{dy_s}{dz} \right\} - f_n(\overline{X}_n) \cdot \frac{dy_i}{dz} + f'_i(\overline{X}_i) \cdot X_{i,z} = 0.
\end{aligned}
\right\} \qquad \text{(VIII: 52)}
$$

Here we have a linear non-homogeneous system of $n-1$ equations in dy_r/dz $(r = 1, 2, \ldots, n-1)$. If the system is solved for dy_i/dz we have

$$
\frac{dy_i}{dz} = -f'_i(\overline{X}_i) \cdot X_{i,z} \cdot \frac{J_{i,i}}{J}, \qquad \text{(VIII: 53)}
$$

where J and $J_{i,i}$ are defined by (VIII: 34). If the quasi-equilibrium system is dynamically stable and the characteristic determinant (VIII: 46) symmetric, then, as was mentioned in Section 2, $J_{i,i}/J < 0$, while f'_i is always > 0.

Obviously, if $X_{i,z} > 0$ then $dy_i/dz > 0$; and if $X_{i,z} < 0$ then $dy_i/dz < 0$.

If the system of equations (VIII: 52) is solved for dy_r/dz $(r \neq i)$, we get

$$
\frac{dy_r}{dz} = -f'_i(\overline{X}_i) \cdot X_{i,z} \cdot \frac{J_{i,r}}{J}, \qquad (r \neq i), \qquad \text{(VIII: 54)}
$$

where $J_{i,r}$ is the cofactor of the i, rth element of J; but no supposition has yet been made about the signs of $J_{i,r}/J$ $(r \neq i)$, and thus we cannot say anything about the signs of dy_r/dz $(r \neq i)$. However, as was shown by Mosak[1], if all the elements $b_{i,r}$, $(= b_{r,i})$, $(r \neq i)$ are positive, then each $J_{i,r}/J < 0$. Then obviously, $X_{i,z} > 0$ implies $dy_r/dz > 0$, for all dy_r/dz $(r \neq i)$ and for dy_i/dz; and $X_{i,z} < 0$ implies $dy_r/dz < 0$.

In words: if the change of data (dz) is such that it causes a partial increase in the excess demand for one good, the ith, (that is, $X_{i,z} > 0$), the relative price of this good will rise $(dy_i/dz > 0)$, when the quasi-equilibrium system is stable and symmetrical. If, furthermore, the assumption mentioned above $(b_{i,r} > 0, i \neq r)$ holds good, all the relative prices will exhibit a rise. And conversely, when the excess demand for a good partially decreases.

I think this result is a significant one. For, it will be recalled that the same result has been derived for the general static Walras system, and that that is one of the very few definite conclusions that it has been possible to draw from the Walras system. Also, it is a very important conclusion. What we have shown here is that this result does not depend on the fact that the Walras system is a *static equilibrium system*. Even if there is no static solution of the Walras system, this

---

[1] J. Mosak, *General-Equilibrium Theory in International Trade*, Appendix to Chapter II, "A Theorem in Determinants".

result continues to hold, if only the quasi-equilibrium system here has a solution and is stable.

If it is desired to go further and to compare the magnitudes of the rises (falls) in the various relative prices, especially between the relative price of the ith good and all the other relative prices, we have the equation

$$\frac{d\,y_i}{d\,z} - \frac{d\,y_r}{d\,z} = f_i'\,(\overline{X}_i) \cdot X_{i,\,z} \cdot \left(\frac{J_{i,\,r}}{J} - \frac{J_{i,\,i}}{J}\right). \qquad \text{(VIII: 55)}$$

We only know that, according to the assumptions made, both $J_{i,\,r}/J$ and $J_{i,\,i}/J$ are negative, but nothing about their absolute magnitudes, so neither do we know anything about the sign of $d\,y_i/d\,z - d\,y_r/d\,z$.

b) Now we consider the effect of changes of data on excess demand and the speed of the rise of the prices. We consider only the case in which all $\overline{X}_r > 0$.

$$\frac{d\,p_r}{d\,t} = f_r\,(X_r), \qquad (r = 1, 2, \ldots, n - 1). \qquad \text{(VIII: 20)}$$

Therefore

$$\frac{d}{d\,z}\left(\frac{d\,p_r}{d\,t}\right) = f_r'\,(\overline{X}_r) \cdot \frac{d\,X_r}{d\,z}, \qquad (r = 1, 2, \ldots, n - 1). \qquad \text{(VIII: 56)}$$

The conditions for quasi-equilibrium (VIII: 22) may be differentiated with respect to z and we get

$$f_r'\,(\overline{X}_r) \cdot \frac{d\,X_r}{d\,z} - f_n\,(\overline{X}_n) \cdot \frac{d\,y_r}{d\,z} = 0, \qquad (r = 1, 2, \ldots, n - 1), \qquad \text{(VIII: 57)}$$

assuming that the assumption still holds that the market for the nth good remains unaffected by the change of data.

From (VIII: 56) and (VIII: 57) we have

$$\frac{d}{d\,z}\left(\frac{d\,p_r}{d\,t}\right) = f_r'\,(\overline{X}_r) \cdot \frac{d\,X_r}{d\,z} = f_n\,(\overline{X}_n) \cdot \frac{d\,y_r}{d\,z}, \qquad (r = 1, 2, \ldots, n - 1). \qquad \text{(VIII: 58)}$$

In a) we found that $d\,y_r/d\,z \gtreqless 0$ according to whether $X_{i,\,z} \gtreqless 0$; also we have that $f_n\,(\overline{X}_n) > 0$ and $f_r'\,(\overline{X}_r) > 0$. So it follows at once from (VIII: 58) that

$$\frac{d\,X_r}{d\,z} \gtreqless 0 \quad \text{as} \quad X_{i,\,z} \gtreqless 0, \qquad (r = 1, 2, \ldots, n - 1), \qquad \text{(VIII: 59)}$$

and

$$\frac{d}{d\,z}\left(\frac{d\,p_r}{d\,t}\right) \gtreqless 0 \quad \text{as} \quad X_{i,\,z} \gtreqless 0, \qquad (r = 1, 2, \ldots, n - 1). \qquad \text{(VIII: 60)}$$

15

In words: if the quasi-equilibrium system is inflationary, (all $\overline{X}_r > 0$), and

(1) if a partial increase in the excess demand for the ith good occurs, ($X_{i,z} > 0$), this causes the excess demand for all the goods to rise (excepting the nth good, for which the excess demand is assumed to be constant), ($d\,X_r / d\,z > 0$, ($r = 1, 2, \ldots, n-1$)), and thereupon the speed in the rise in price for all the goods increases (excepting the speed of the rise in the price of the nth good, which is assumed to be constant); and

(2) a partial decrease in the excess demand for a good causes the excess demand for all the goods to decrease (excepting the nth), and thereupon the speed of the rise in the prices of all the goods decreases (excepting the nth).

It will be seen that a result of the change of data in case (1) is that the pressure of inflation definitely rises (quantitatively), since the excess demand rises in some markets (namely the first $n-1$) and does not fall in any market (the excess demand in the market for the nth good is constant). In case (2) the pressure of inflation definitely decreases (quantitatively).

Regarding the relation between the magnitude of the total change $(d\,X_i / d\,z)$ and the partial change $(X_{i,z})$ in the excess demand for the ith good, it is not possible to say anything more exact than that they have the same sign, if we only assume what has been assumed hitherto. For, since all $\overline{X}_r > 0$, upon substituting from (VIII: 53) in (VIII: 57), ($r = i$), we get

$$\frac{d\,X_i / d\,z}{X_{i,z}} = -f_n(\overline{X}_n) \cdot \frac{J_{i,i}}{J} > 0. \qquad \text{(VIII: 61)}$$

We know nothing about the absolute magnitude of $J_{i,i} / J$ (only the sign is known), so, with the assumptions made up to now, the ratio of $d\,X_i / d\,z$ and $X_{i,z}$ may be less than, equal to, or greater than 1. Yet (VIII: 61) shows that the greater the degree of inflation, that is, the greater $\overline{X}_n$ (and all other $\overline{X}$'s), the more likely it is that $(d\,X_i / d\,z) / X_{i,z} > 1$, unless some reason can be adduced that $J_{i,i} / J$ should fall (numerically) with the magnitude of $\overline{X}_n$.

Therefore, in order to show that $d\,X_i / d\,z$ is in general greater than or less than $X_{i,z}$, it is obviously necessary to introduce new assumptions. Let us differentiate $X_i = X_i(y_1, y_2, \ldots, y_{n-1}, z)$ totally with respect to z. Then we have

$$\frac{d\,X_i}{d\,z} - X_{i,z} = \overline{X}_{i,1} \cdot \frac{d\,y_1}{d\,z} + \cdots + \overline{X}_{i,n-1} \cdot \frac{d\,y_{n-1}}{d\,z}. \qquad \text{(VIII: 62)}$$

Since $d\,X_i / d\,z$, $X_{i,z}$ and $d\,y_r / d\,z$, ($r = 1, 2, \ldots, n-1$) always have the same sign (with our assumptions), it follows from (VIII: 62) that $\left| d\,X_i / d\,z \right| - \left| X_{i,z} \right| > 0$, if all $\overline{X}_{i,r} > 0$, which would be a quite untenable supposition, for one reason because it conflicts with the Hicks's condition for perfect stability in the special case when all $\overline{X}_r = 0$. Conversely, it follows from (VIII: 62) that $\left| d\,X_i / d\,z \right| - \left| X_{i,z} \right| < 0$, if all $\overline{X}_{i,r} < 0$, ($r = 1, 2, \ldots, n-1$), which implies that the ith good is complementary to all the other goods; but this would be a rather unsuitable assumption to work with, and would conflict with what we have already assumed, that all $b_{r,s} > 0$, ($r \neq s$).

However, we have discussed here only certain sufficient conditions that the sign of $d X_i/d z - X_{i,z}$ should be determinate, and, of course, that does not exclude the possibility that other conditions exist which are both necessary and sufficient, and which are economically reasonable without conflicting with the rest of the assumptions; but I have not been able to find them.

5. *Simultaneous changes of data*

In order to put the results in the general form most desirable for our purposes, we should now divide up the first n goods into groups, namely the first m goods which might be called commodities, and then goods $m + 1$ to n, which might be called factors. Then we may introduce m different parameters z_j, $(j = 1, 2, \ldots, m)$ into the excess demand equations for commodities, and find out the effects on prices, excess demands and speeds of the rise in price caused by simultaneous infinitesimal changes in these m parameters. Since these effects are additive, it is easy to see from our general assumptions, without further working, that, if all $X_{j,z_j} > 0 (< 0)$, $(j = 1, 2, \ldots, m)$, the total result is a rise (fall) in all relative prices, and increase (decrease) in all the excess demands and speeds of rise in price; but we can say nothing more. Therefore we confine ourselves to the case of only one parameter in one excess demand equation.

6. *The economic significance of the assumptions*

It will not be out of place now to say something about the economic significance of the more important assumptions in the analysis of Sections 2, 3, and 4.

The main one is the approximative assumption that the excess demand for the nth good may be regarded as constant for the whole of the investigation. This assumption obviously implies that we have to choose as the nth good one for which the reaction of the excess demand to a displacement of all relative prices, that is, for which $\overline{X}_{n,r}$, $(r = 1, 2, \ldots, n - 1)$, is very small—if such a good exists.

In order that (VIII: 35) may express true dynamic stability (assymptotic stability), it is assumed that

$$f_r'(\overline{X}_r) \cdot \overline{X}_{r,s} = f_s'(\overline{X}_s) \cdot \overline{X}_{s,r}. \qquad \text{(VIII: 49)}$$

This may be written as

$$\frac{\partial}{\partial y_s}\left(\frac{d p_r}{d t}\right) = \frac{\partial}{\partial y_r}\left(\frac{d p_s}{d t}\right), \qquad \text{(VIII: 63)}$$

or, taking the above-mentioned assumption of the constancy of X_n into account,

$$\frac{\partial}{\partial p_s}\left(\frac{d p_r}{d t}\right) = \frac{\partial}{\partial p_r}\left(\frac{d p_s}{d t}\right). \qquad \text{(VIII: 64)}$$

This is precisely the expression which Lange arrives at in his investigation of the Walras system. It means that the partial (marginal) effect of a change in the relative price y_s (absolute price p_s) on the speed of the rise in price of the rth good must be equal to the partial effect of a change in the relative price y_r (absolute price p_r) on the speed of the rise in price of the sth good.[1]

If the quasi-equilibrium system was stable and the above-mentioned assumptions were fulfilled, it followed that $d\,y_i/d\,z \gtreqless 0$, according to whether $X_{i,\,z} \gtreqless 0$. But to show in addition that $d\,y_r/d\,z \gtreqless 0$, $(r \neq i)$, according to whether $X_{i,\,z} \gtreqless 0$, it was further assumed that $b_{r,\,s} > 0$, $(r \neq s)$ that is, that

$$f'_r\,(\overline{X}_r) \cdot \overline{X}_{r,\,s} > 0, \qquad (r \neq s), \qquad \text{(VIII: 65)}$$

which implies, since f'_r is assumed positive (cf. (VIII: 20)), that all goods are substitutes.

7. *Summing-up of results*

The reason for carrying out this analysis at such length as we have done, on the basis of the assumptions just mentioned, is not that there is particularly good cause to call all of these assumptions economically reasonable. The assumption that all goods are substitutes for one another illustrates this. It was, however, intended to show which assumptions must be made in order to make the results from the one-commodity, one-factor analysis of Chap. VII applicable to a model with several goods, and to make the results more generally applicable, to non-inflationary as well as inflationary systems.

We may summarise the results from the one-commodity, one-factor analysis of Chap. VII in the following way:

(1) A quasi-equilibrium solution exists.

(2) This quasi-equilibrium is stable.

Regarding the reaction to changes of data, a partial increase (decrease) in the excess demand for the commodity causes:

(3) Both the excess demand for commodities and for factors to rise (fall).

(4) The resultant, or total, increase (decrease) in the excess demand for commodities to be less than the original, or partial, increase (decrease) in the excess demand for commodities.

(5) The commodity price to rise (fall) in relation to the factor price.

If we consider the results from the general quasi-equilibrium system, we have:

(1) The general quasi-equilibrium system may have a solution. The number of equations is the same as the number of unknowns.

(2) The general quasi-equilibrium solution will be stable (for small displacements) if (VIII: 47) applies.

----

[1] Lange, *Price Flexibility* . . ., p. 97 et seq.

(3) In the general quasi-equilibrium system a partial increase (decrease) in the excess demand for the first m goods (the commodities) leads to an increase (decrease) in the excess demand for all of the goods, assuming (VIII: 49) and (VIII: 65).

(4) It is not in general true of the general quasi-equilibrium system, when the assumptions are those we have made, that the resultant, or total, increase (decrease) in the excess demand for a good is necessarily less than the original (partial) increase (decrease), see (VIII: 61) and the remarks following it.

(5) We may divide up the n goods into the first m goods to be called commodities and then the $m + 1$th to nth goods, which are called factors. It is then possible to show that if a parameter z_j, $(j = 1, 2, \ldots, m)$ is introduced into the excess demand equations for each of the first m goods, and simultaneous changes in these parameters are considered, such that all $X_{j, z_j} > 0$, (< 0), $(j = 1, 2, \ldots, m)$, then all y_j, $(j = 1, 2, \ldots, m)$, will certainly rise (fall), when the assumptions are those given. But the same applies for all y_k, $(k = m + 1, \ldots, n - 1)$, and we cannot say whether the rise (fall) in y_j, $(j = 1, 2, \ldots, m)$, is greater or smaller than that in y_k, $(k = m + 1, \ldots, n - 1)$. Therefore we cannot either say with certainty that the prices of commodities rise (fall) in relation to the prices of factors, for to do so would require that we could show that each y_j, $(j = 1, 2, \ldots, m)$, rises (falls) in relation to each y_k, $(k = m + 1, \ldots, n - 1)$, for we do know that all p_j, $(j = 1, 2, \ldots, m)$ rise (fall) in relation to p_n. Only in the special case in which we call all the first $n - 1$ goods commodities and the nth good factors can we show that the prices of commodities definitely rise (fall) in relation to the price of the factors (i.e. to p_n), because here we have just the one factor price, p_n, and we know that all y_r (i.e., all p_r / p_n), rise (fall).

CHAPTER IX

MONETARY EQUILIBRIUM

1. *The concept of monetary equilibrium*

The reasoning of the previous chapters has been almost exclusively designed for the disequilibrium which occurs in those situations which in Chap. I were characterized by the existence of a monetary pressure of inflation. We have studied some of those factors which may be supposed to be significant for the magnitude of this monetary pressure of inflation, and for the changes in that excess demand for commodities and factors which were made the basis of the concept of monetary pressure of inflation itself. But, the results of the preceding chapters have also been derived with the intention of contributing to the solution of the problem which is taken up in this chapter, namely, the problem of monetary equilibrium. This is a problem much debated; the discussion can be traced throughout the controversy between Wicksell and Davidson, which lasted almost three decades, via the Stockholm School to the post-war discussions, inspired by the publication of Beveridge's *Full Employment in a Free Society*[1], about the possibility of maintaining the value of money at a stable level during full employment. A special off-shoot of the discussion was the debate during the twenties and thirties about what was called "neutral money".

We have already in Chap. I defined the concept of monetary equilibrium to be used here. That was in connection with the definition of the concept of the monetary pressure of inflation. Monetary equilibrium was said to exist, if at a certain instant, or in a certain period, and reckoned at the prices for the instant (period), the sum of the values of the excess demand in all the commodity-markets is zero, and the sum of the value of the excess demand in all the factor-

---

[1] William Beveridge, *Full Employment in a Free Society*, George Allen & Unwin, London, 1944.

markets is zero. Using the notation of Chap. I, where p and P are prices and x and X excess demands, and the small letters refer to the commodity-markets and capitals to the factor-markets, we say that monetary equilibrium exists if

$$\Sigma\, x_i \cdot p_i = 0 \quad \text{and} \quad \Sigma\, X_j \cdot P_j = 0, \tag{IX: 1}$$

where the summations are taken over n commodities and m factors.

It is this definition of monetary equilibrium which will be examined in this chapter. We first come to the problem of what these two summations of values of excess demand really imply in the development of prices of commodities and factors; and now we have the opportunity to consider the aggregation problem which was mentioned in Chap. I, Section 6, the problem of the relation between sums of excess demand and price-levels. The second problem which arises concerns the assumptions necessary for the simultaneous fulfilment of the two conditions (IX: 1), when considered as parts of a complete system.

The first of these questions is treated in Sections 2 to 5. In Section 6, Myrdal's concept of monetary equilibrium is briefly related to the concept used in this study, and in the following sections the second of the above-mentioned problems is dealt with.

2. *Conditions for the constancy of the price-level and the wage-level*

As was said in Chap. VIII, there are many different conceivable hypotheses which may be applied to the relation between the speed of the rise in prices and the size of the excess demand in an individual market. Let us begin with a case which leads to well-known price-indices.

a) We assume that the speed of the rise in price for an arbitrary commodity is the product of the price of the commodity and a function of the ratio of the excess demand x_i and the supply of the commodity q_i. That is,

$$\frac{d\, p_i}{d\, t} = p_i \cdot f_i \left(\frac{x_i}{q_i} \right), \qquad (q_i > 0), \tag{IX: 2}$$

for all commodities. We further assume that $f_i(0) = 0$ and $f_i' > 0$. Let us also assume that (IX: 2) has the simple form

222

$$\frac{d\,p_i}{d\,t} = p_i \cdot k \cdot \frac{x_i}{q_i}, \qquad (IX:3)$$

where k is a constant (> 0), the same for all commodities. Thus we have that

$$d\,p_i = p_i \cdot k \cdot \frac{x_i}{q_i} \cdot d\,t. \qquad (IX:4)$$

If we divide each side by p_i, it is seen that (IX:4) says, roughly speaking, that the percentage rise in price in a certain period is proportional to the excess demand expressed as a percentage of the supply of the commodity in question and to the length of the period. This relationship is not immediately unreasonable, and it seems to be rather similar to a hypothesis sometimes used by the theorists of the Stockholm School (cf. below).

In this connection we consider a Divisia price-index[1], π, which is defined by the equation

$$d\,\pi = \pi \cdot \frac{\Sigma\,q_i \cdot d\,p_i}{\Sigma\,q_i \cdot p_i}. \qquad (IX:5)$$

If (IX:4) is combined with (IX:5) we get

$$d\,\pi = \left(\pi \cdot \frac{k \cdot d\,t}{\Sigma\,q_i \cdot p_i}\right) \cdot \Sigma\,p_i \cdot x_i. \qquad (IX:6)$$

Since the expression inside the brackets on the right hand side of (IX:6) is always positive, it follows that

$$d\,\pi \gtreqless 0 \text{ according as } \Sigma\,p_i \cdot x_i \gtreqless 0. \qquad (IX:7)$$

The expression $\Sigma\,p_i \cdot x_i$ is the sum of the value of the excess demand for all commodities at the instant considered, so it follows that, if this sum is positive, the Divisia price-index will indicate an increase, and if negative, a decrease in the price-level, and if it is just zero, the Divisia price-index will be constant.

---

[1] For example, see Harold T. Davies, *The Theory of Econometrics*, The Principia Press, Inc., Bloomington, Indiana, 1941, p. 330 et seq. This price-index has also been derived independently by the Finnish statistician L. Törnqvist, "Finlands Banks Konsumtionsprisindex" ("The Price-index of Finlands Bank"), *Nordisk Tidsskrift for teknisk Økonomi*, Copenhagen, 1937.

If we consider two situations — 1 and 2 — which only differ in that the sum of the values of the excess demands is of different size in the two situations, it is not difficult to see that we can write for the first situation

$$d\pi' = \left(\pi \cdot \frac{k \cdot dt}{\Sigma q_i \cdot p_i}\right) \cdot \Sigma p_i \cdot x_i', \qquad (IX:8)$$

whereas for the second situation we have

$$d\pi'' = \left(\pi \cdot \frac{k \cdot dt}{\Sigma q_i \cdot p_i}\right) \cdot \Sigma p_i \cdot x_i'', \qquad (IX:9)$$

where ′ and ″ refer to situations 1 and 2 respectively. If we assume the expressions inside the brackets on the right-hand sides of (IX:8) and (IX:9) to be the same, it follows at once that

$$d\pi' \gtreqless d\pi'' \text{ according as } \Sigma p_i \cdot x_i' \gtreqless \Sigma p_i \cdot x_i''. \qquad (IX:10)$$

Thus, assuming (IX:4) to be valid, the criterion for the existence of a monetary pressure of inflation (deflation) which was stated in Chap. I (equations (I:1), (I:2), and (I:3)) may be interpreted as saying that there is a monetary pressure of inflation (deflation), if either a Divisia commodity price-index, as defined in (IX:5), or a Divisia factor price-index, defined analogously to (IX:5), or both, rise (fall), and neither of them falls (rises). Also, monetary equilibrium is identical with the case in which both the Divisia commodity price-index and factor price-index are constant at the instant considered.

In the same way, the criterion stated in Chap. I, of whether a pressure of inflation has risen or fallen quantitatively between two situations being compared ((I:7), (I:8), and (I:9)), may be interpreted as saying that the quantitative pressure of inflation has increased (decreased) from situation 1 to situation 2 if either the Divisia commodity price-index or the Divisia factor price-index, or both, rise more (less) steeply in situation 2 than in situation 1, and neither of them rise less (more) steeply; and an unchanged quantitative pressure of inflation coincides with the case when both the Divisia commodity and factor price-indices rise equally steeply in the two situations. Yet it should be noticed that this interpretation of equations (I:7), (I:8), and (I:9) is subject to the condition that q_i remains unchanged, despite the change in the excess demand from x_i' to x_i''. This means that the changes in the excess demand are actually taken to be entirely due to changes in demand, so that in this case the applicability of the stated criterion for changes in the pressure of inflation is considerably restricted. However, there is no such restriction for the case treated in c).

Of course, the indices relevant here—Divisia indices—are not at all usual, and the results will therefore now be transferred to a discontinuous analysis, where it is assumed that the changes of prices occur only at the beginning of each period and are such that the excess demand occurring in the preceding period determines the marking-up of the price at the beginning of the period considered. We will call the length of the period Δt, where $\Delta t = t_2 - t_1$, and the excess demand at t_1 (that is, for the period t_1 to t_2), x_i^1, and the supply, q_i^1, and prices for individual commodities p_i^1 and p_i^2 at times t_1 and t_2 respectively (that is, for the periods t_1 to t_2, t_2 to t_3), so that $\Delta p_i = p_i^2 - p_i^1$. Then we may write a relation corresponding to (IX: 4), which is

$$\Delta p_i = p_i^1 \cdot k \cdot \frac{x_i^1}{q_i^1} \cdot \Delta t.^1 \tag{IX: 11}$$

It is natural to consider the Laspeyres price-index when we are dealing with the discontinuous case, since this price-index may be derived from integration of (IX: 5), i.e. of the Divisia price-index. Using the Laspeyres price-index, we obtain

$$\frac{\Sigma q_i^1 \cdot p_i^2}{\Sigma q_i^1 \cdot p_i^1} = \frac{\Sigma q_i^1 \cdot (p_i^1 + \Delta p_i)}{\Sigma q_i^1 \cdot p_i^1} = 1 + \frac{\Sigma q_i^1 \cdot \Delta p_i}{\Sigma q_i^1 \cdot p_i^1}. \tag{IX: 12}$$

---

[1] If it is assumed that the supply of commodities is fixed and the elasticity of demand for a commodity = 1, and further, that the occurrence of an excess demand always causes an instantaneous price rise so large that supply is equal to demand, then we have that

$$q_i^1 \cdot (p_i^1 + \Delta p_i) = (q_i^1 + x_i^1) \cdot p_i^1,$$

from which we get

$$\Delta p_i = p_i^1 \cdot (x_i^1 / q_i^1),$$

which corresponds to (IX: 11). Such assumptions are implicit in some of the theory of the Stockholm School, cf. Palander, "Om 'Stockholmsskolans' begrepp och metoder", p. 120.

With the aid of (IX: 11), we get

$$\Sigma\, q_i^1 \cdot \Delta\, p_i = \Sigma\, q_i^1 \cdot p_i^1 \cdot k \cdot \frac{x_i^1}{q_i^1}\;\; \Delta\, t = \Delta\, t \cdot k \cdot \Sigma\, x_i^1 \cdot p_i^1. \qquad (IX: 13)$$

Since $\Delta\, t \cdot k > 0$ and $\Sigma\, q_i^1 \cdot p_i^1 > 0$, it follows at once from (IX: 12) and (IX: 13) that

$$\frac{\Sigma\, q_i^1 \cdot p_i^2}{\Sigma\, q_i^1 \cdot p_i^1} \gtreqless 1 \text{ according as } \Sigma\, x_i^1 \cdot p_i^1 \gtreqless 0. \qquad (IX: 14)$$

If, as before, two different situations, 1 and 2, with excess demands x_i' and x_i'', are considered, it follows immediately from (IX: 12) and (IX: 13) that

$$\frac{\Sigma\, q_i^1 \cdot p_i'}{\Sigma\, q_i^1 \cdot p_i^1} \gtreqless \frac{\Sigma\, q_i^1 \cdot p_i''}{\Sigma\, q_i^1 \cdot p_i^1} \text{ according as } \Sigma\, x_i' \cdot p_i^1 \gtreqless \Sigma\, x_i'' \cdot p_i^1. \qquad (IX: 15)$$

As in the continuous case previously considered, in this case also the criteria in Chap. I for the existence of monetary pressures of inflation, deflation, and monetary equilibrium, and of changes in them (quantitative) may be interpreted in terms of the development in certain price-indices, the particular ones used in this discontinuous case being the Laspeyres commodity price-index and factor price-index.

The sums of the values of excess demands which are used must accordingly have a quite central practical importance, since the price-indices introduced are indices of just the type used in practice. This is not directly true for the Divisia price-indices, but it is so for the Laspeyres indices. However, it should be emphasized once more that it is assumed that relations (IX: 4) and (IX: 11), where k is a constant, are valid for all commodities and for all factors (the k need not be the same for commodities and factors). In actual fact it is not possible to reckon that k—of which the reciprocal can be taken to express the inertia of prices with respect to "induced" changes—will in general be the same for all commodities and for all factors. Usually, different prices will have quite different resistances to "induced" changes, and we thus arrive at the cases which follow.

b) Here the equations of price-reaction have the form

$$d\, p_i = p_i \cdot k_i \cdot \frac{x_i}{q_i} \cdot d\, t \qquad (IX: 16)$$

in the continuous case, and in the discontinuous

$$\Delta p_i = p_i^1 \cdot k_i \cdot \frac{x_i^1}{q_i^1} \cdot \Delta t, \qquad \text{(IX: 17)}$$

where the k_is need not be the same for all commodities (factors).

For the sake of simplicity we now only consider the discontinuous case, and—since all k_i must be assumed to be greater than zero (more about this later)—it may be seen at once that the "relevant" price-indices must have the form

$$\frac{\sum \left(\frac{q_i^1}{k_i}\right) \cdot p_i^2}{\sum \left(\frac{q_i^1}{k_i}\right) \cdot p_i^1}. \qquad \text{(IX: 18)}$$

Thus we may still interpret the criterion of pressure of inflation, etc., as an expression of the immediate development in certain price-indices, provided that the weights in the relevant price-indices are the quantities supplied divided by the coefficients k_i—the price-reaction coefficients. However, such an index does not belong to those customarily used and calculated.

c) The simplest possible case we can think of is that the price-reaction equations are

$$\frac{d\,p_i}{d\,t} = p_i \cdot f_i\,(x_i), \qquad \text{(IX: 19)}$$

where $f\,(0) = 0$ and $f' > 0$. This corresponds to the hypothesis used in Chaps. VII and VIII (p_i was, it is true, omitted on the right-hand side, but that is not an essential point in this connection, for, if it is only the relations at a particular time which are considered, it is always possible to re-define the quantities of goods in such a way that all $p_i = 1$ at this time). Let (IX: 19) now take the special form

$$d\,p_i = p_i \cdot k_i \cdot x_i \cdot d\,t, \qquad (k_i > 0), \qquad \text{(IX: 20)}$$

or, in the discontinuous case,

$$\Delta p_i = p_i^1 \cdot k_i \cdot x_i^1 \cdot \Delta t. \qquad \text{(IX: 21)}$$

If we confine ourselves to the discontinuous case, it will be seen that the "relevant" price-indices are of the form

$$\frac{\sum \frac{1}{k_i} \cdot p_i^2}{\sum \frac{1}{k_i} \cdot p_i^1}, \qquad \text{(IX: 22)}$$

so that the weights are what we have called the price-inertia coefficients. If these price-inertia coefficients are the same for all commodities (factors) the index simply becomes an unweighted mean of all commodity prices (factor prices). This is not a customary index, either, although there are examples of unweighted price-indices.

d) It is clear that we can consider other forms of price-reaction equations, where the speed of the rise in the price of a good is considered to be a function of other things than the excess demand for the good in question, e.g. the excess demand for other goods, the excess demand for several periods in the past, and so on.[1] In Section 4, c), one further possibility will be discussed. I know of no empirical guide for choice between such hypotheses, so it seems reasonable to use the simple case presented in c), until such empirical guides are found. Actually, that is what we have done in the previous two chapters.

3. *A converse method of procedure*

Up to now we have proceeded by beginning with the value sum $\Sigma x_i \cdot p_i$ etc. and next asking what price-index the sign of this sum will give us information about. But, of course, it is possible to proceed the other way: to begin with a certain price-index and then to ask how the value sum of the excess demands must be defined in order to give us information about the development in this particular index. By way of illustration we shall consider a simple example.

Let us consider the commodity-markets and suppose that a Laspeyres price-index $\Sigma q_i^1 \cdot p_i^2 / \Sigma q_i^1 \cdot p_i^1$ is to be kept equal to 1, while, for example, the price-reaction equations have the form $\Delta p_i = p_i^1 \cdot k_i \cdot (x_i^1/q_i^1) \cdot \Delta t$, (IX: 17), where k_i is not necessarily the same for different commodities. Then it can be seen that the Laspeyres price-index is constant if $\Sigma (1/k_i) \cdot x_i^1 \cdot p_i^1 = 0$, the treatment being a

---

[1] P. A. Samuelson, *Foundations of Economic Analysis*, Ch. IX; Trygve Haavelmo, *The Notion of Price Homogeneity*, and Lawrence R. Klein, *Economic Fluctuations in the United States 1921—1941*, John Wiley & Sons, Inc., Ltd., London, 1950, p. 50—57, "The Market Equation".

sort of converse of that in Section 2. The monetary excess demand in the commodity-markets must therefore be defined as a *weighted* sum of the values of the excess demands in the individual commodity-markets, the weights being the coefficients of price-inertia.

If the monetary excess demand in the factor-markets is defined in a similar way as a weighted sum of the values of the excess demand in the individual factor-markets, we arrive at a different definition of the concept of monetary equilibrium than that given by equations (IX: 1). It is however clear that, even if the monetary excess demand for commodities and factors thus defined is zero, and the desired price and wage-rate indices therefore constant, this does not in any way imply that *ex ante* investment and *ex ante* saving are equal. So we shall continue with the "relevant" price-indices, that is, those indices for which the unweighted monetary excess demand in the composite commodity-market and composite factor-market give an unambiguous indication of the development tendency.

4. *Excess demand as the cause of changes in prices*

In the preceding sections it was shown what assumptions are necessary in order to give a simple interpretation of the meaning of value sums of excess demand in terms of the development of some "relevant" price-index. Now we will discuss these assumptions more thoroughly and try to discover whether it is possible beforehand to say that they may be taken as a reasonable picture of the world we live in.[1]

a) The characteristic thing about the examples which were given in arriving at "relevant" price-indices is that the price-reaction equa-

---

[1] In this connection, see in general Palander's criticism of Myrdal's *Monetary Equilibrium:* Palander, "Om 'Stockholmsskolans' begrepp och metoder", p. 132 et seq. Myrdal talks about a specially constructed price-index (see, Myrdal, *Monetary Equilibrium*, p. 136) which would express whether monetary equilibrium (in his sense) exists or not. Myrdal weights the prices in this index partly with some "coefficients of price-stickiness", partly with some "investment-reaction coefficients". Since Myrdal never gives this index precisely, as a formula, but only gives a very sketchy intuitive indication of its construction, and neither does Palander attempt to make it more precise or to show how it is derived, the discussion of it by both Myrdal and Palander rather ends in mid-air. The arguments in the text which follow put forward some defence of Myrdal's line of thought against some of Palander's critical remarks upon it. But much of Palander's criticism seems to be justified.

tions considered express the speed of the rise in the price of a good as a linear, homogeneous function of the excess demand for this good. There can hardly be any *a priori* ground for believing that this corresponds to reality[1], but this is not necessary, either, for our reasoning to hold good. For we are are now interested in the case where the state pursues a policy designed to maintain monetary equilibrium in the commodity and factor markets, that is, to maintain $\Sigma x_i \cdot p_i = 0$ and $\Sigma X_i \cdot P_i = 0$. In this case, it is likely that the partial disequilibria, which are permitted to exist—in general, of course, $x_i \cdot p_i \neq 0$ and $X_i \cdot P_i \neq 0$—will not be very marked, and this means that our assumption of a linear, homogeneous relation only needs to be approximately valid in a suitable interval around $x_i = 0$ and $X_i = 0$.

It must be emphasized, however, that the price-reaction equations may be such that a "bias" results from this approximation. For example, this will be the case if all the $d\,p_i/d\,t = f_i(x_i) = e^{x_i} - 1$; if these functions are replaced by the straight lines $f_i(x_i) = x_i$, a systematic exaggeration of tendencies of prices to fall will occur, together with a systematic underestimation of tendencies of prices to increase.

b) The reason that we concerned ourselves with homogeneous, linear relationships between the speed of the rise in prices and the excess demand in Section 2 was not that it is impossible in principle to find a "relevant" price-index when this relationship is not linear and homogeneous. It is possible to find such indices in other cases, but the simplest and most customary price-indices are those which occur when the relationship is linear and homogeneous.

However, it is not always possible, even in this homogeneous linear case, to construct a "relevant" price-index. It has been assumed that all the price-reaction coefficients k_i are positive. But if one of them is zero, the corresponding price p_i acquires infinite weight in the price-index, and the variations of the index are thus completely determined by the variations in this particular price. The price-index in this case is obviously meaningless. It is very probable that some of the price-reaction coefficients are zero, when the period considered is rather short and there is monopolism in the markets. Entrepreneurs who prefer stable prices for their commodities will experience a somewhat

---

[1] Lawrence R. Klein, "The Dynamics of Price Flexibility, Comment", *American Economic Review*, 1950, p. 607, says, however, "I know that I am on safe empirical ground in the linear case".

longer period of excess demand before they mark up their prices. What is to be done about this difficulty, which was pointed out by Palander in his criticism of Myrdal?[1]

One possible solution is to exclude such "inconvenient" commodities from the value sums of excess demand considered, and to introduce the supplementary criterion of equilibrium that the excess demand for each of these commodities and factors shall be zero. However, this is altogether too uncomfortable a course to take.

Another and better solution is the following: We consider a certain period and suppose that certain entrepreneurs have price policies according to which they only alter their prices if there has been persistent excess demand for their commodities at the current prices for a fairly long period. Then their price-reaction coefficients may well be zero within a period (or rather, between two periods), although, considered over a longer period, they will be positive.[2] However, it is possible to determine a short-term *potential* price-reaction coefficient from the long-term coefficient. Suppose it is known that an entrepreneur only increases his price by 10 units if there is a certain excess demand per unit period for three consecutive unit periods. Obviously the increase in price may be reckoned as 1/3 of its value to be added for each period, and in this way a potential price-reaction coefficient may be determined for the unit period, however short that may be. This price-reaction coefficient does *not* tell us that, if a certain excess demand arises during a period, the price must increase by a certain amount at the beginning of the next period; what this potential price-reaction coefficient tells us is that, if there is a certain excess demand in each of a sequence of periods, the price for this sequence of periods will *on an average* rise by an amount per period which is given by the potential price-reaction coefficient.

When the price-reaction coefficients are defined in this way—so that the assumption that $k_i > 0$ is always valid for all commodities and

---

[1] Palander, "Om 'Stockholmsskolans' begrepp och metoder", p. 138—9.

[2] The only prices which are completely resistant to changes in the long run are those prices fixed and held fixed by the state, e.g. the price of gold on the gold standard. But in this case the cause of the constancy of the price is not really price-inertia in the sense used here, since the price of gold remains fixed only because the state (through a central bank) always ensures that at the given price the supply of and demand for gold are equal (i.e. excess demand = 0).

for arbitrarily short periods—the value sums of excess demand obviously cannot be taken to denote the development of the *actual* price-level (expressed by the "relevant" index) from one period to the next, that is, the development of prices in the very short run. The value sums of excess demand now tell us about the tendency of the price-level from a more long-term point of view, as this tendency appears at the instant considered.

The suggested procedure for determining the potential price-reaction coefficients described above is therefore in no way meaningless or uninteresting, but quite the contrary. It should also be noticed that, in discussing effectively repressed inflation, when all price-reaction coefficients may be taken to be set at zero by the state so that all prices are made infinitely resistant to change, it is obviously such potential price-reaction coefficients which we have in mind when we talk in a general way about the monetary pressure of inflation as identical with an upward pressure on the price-level.

c) Now we come to a third assumption which is fundamental for the establishment of value sums of excess demand and the interpretation of these in terms of the development of price-indices, namely, the assumption that it is always just the *excess demand* for a good which determines the development of the price of the good. Actually, this is also an implicit assumption in the criteria of monetary equilibrium which are based on the investment-saving relation. Therefore we will investigate the question of whether or not it may be reasonably assumed that it is the excess demand for a good which decides the changes in price for that good.[1] The only way to settle this question definitely is by testing the hypothesis empirically, but as long as this has not been done, we have to try to discuss it more generally.

The first problem to be dealt with concerns what is to be understood by the concepts of demand, supply and the related excess demand. When we are concerned with the tendencies of prices to change, we must on principle regard demand as active attempts to purchase and supply as available quantity of goods (cf. Chap. I, Section 9 and Chap. III). But it is only when a monetary pressure of inflation exists

---

[1] To answer this question by saying that we are here interested only in "induced" price changes which are *by definition* caused by the excess demand for the good considered, would be to beg the question. For, then we would have to explain why so great importance has been attached to "induced" price changes.

that there is a serious need for the distinction between the various concepts of supply and demand. Here, where we are for the moment only interested in monetary equilibrium, we may certainly assume as a good approximation that planned purchases = active attempts to purchase = optimum purchases, and that expected sales = quantity available for sale (assuming that no unexpected changes in productivity occur).

Another problem which arises is this: As a natural corollary of the method of analysis (the disequilibrium method, cf. Chap. II, Section 2), we have characterized a disequilibrium situation by a disparity between the quantity in demand and the quantity supplied at a given price. However, it is quite possible to characterize the disequilibrium (assuming the price to be quoted by the sellers) by the disparity between the price quoted by the sellers (the supply price) and the highest price which the buyers are willing to pay for the given quantity (the demand price), if the quantity supplied is given; or, alternatively, the disparity between the price quoted by the buyers (the demand price) for a given quantity to be supplied and the lowest price (the supply price), at which the sellers are willing to supply this quantity. If the disequilibrium is described in this way, it is feasible to define the concept of *excess price* as the difference between the demand price and the supply price, and to question whether the speed of the rise in prices cannot be taken to be a function of the magnitude of this excess price. If the demand price is denoted by p^d and the supply price by p^q and the excess price by $p^x = p^d - p^q$, the equations of price-reaction might be taken to be, for instance, $dp/dt = F(p^x)$, $F(0) = 0$ and $F' > 0$.

Let us illustrate this with an example from the preceding chapters. Consider Fig. 1 (Chap. IV, Section 2). The supply of labour being given, the actually realizable production is Q_1, whereas Q_0 is the production which might be profitably carried out if there were sufficient labour-power. The excess demand for labour-power may then be taken to be expressed by the unrealizable production (cf. Chap. VII, Section 2), i.e. the magnitude $Q_0 - Q_1 = B_1 C_1$. The difference between the commodity price p_0 and the marginal costs for the quantity Q_1, i.e. the profit margin $B_1 B_2$, may obviously be taken as an expression for the excess price of labour-services. We may therefore say that the difference between the two types of hypotheses concerning the tendency of wages to rise is that in the one case (excess demand hypothesis) the magnitude of the unrealizable production is taken to be the determinant of the speed of the rise in wages, and in the other case (excess price hypothesis), the profit margin is taken to be the decisive factor.

However, it will be noticed that when the conditions of productivity are given, the two hypotheses are equivalent, since the excess demand and the excess price, for changes in commodity prices or wages, are functionally connected in such a way that it is possible to write $p^X = g(X)$, $g(0) = 0$ and $g' > 0$ (p^X being the excess price for labour). But if changes in productivity occur, the marginal cost curve may be displaced in such a way that the displacement leads to an increase in the excess demand and a decrease in the excess price (wage-rate and commodity price given). *After* such a change in productivity, the two hypotheses become equivalent again, of course; but, if the excess price is supposed to be the "true" cause of the tendency of price to change, there is a change in the equation of price-reaction, into which excess demand enters as independent variable.

This does not imply that it becomes impossible to work with the hypothesis that the speed of the rise in price depends upon the excess demand if the relation which actually turns out to be valid is the one between the speed of the rise in price and the excess price. What it does imply is that we must work with changing price-reaction equations and with sliding price indices; of course, this complicates the analysis and makes forecasting extremely difficult, but it does not make the excess demand analysis meaningless.

It is necessary to point out that, even if the above-mentioned relation between excess demand and excess price exists when demand curves and supply curves are "normal", it is possible to think of cases where this relation does not apply (e.g. when the curves of both supply and demand have positive slopes), and in such cases the excess demand analysis may break down altogether; fortunately, this eventuality may certainly be neglected as unlikely.

We can therefore conclude that because it is possible that the tendency of prices to rise may be best regarded as a function of the excess price, the excess demand analysis need not therefore be abandoned. With the modifications described above, the excess demand may still

234

be taken as an expression for the size of the tendency of prices to rise.

With perfect competition there are hardly any serious difficulties in taking the direction of movement of prices to be indicated by the excess demand, but as soon as we pass over to the more realistic situation of monopolism, or between perfect competition and monopolism, further difficulties crop up. For instance, if we consider equation (IX: 21) which was given in Section 2—$\Delta p_i = p_i^1 \cdot k_i \cdot x_i^1 \cdot \Delta t$— we see that it says that the excess demand, x_i^1, experienced by the entrepreneurs between times t_1 and t_2 is what determines how much they will mark up their prices at the beginning of the period commencing at time t_2. If we suppose that the entrepreneurs maximise their profits from a short-term point of view, i.e. per unit period, their fixing of prices for the period between t_2 and t_3 obviously depends partly on their estimation of their marginal cost curves for the period and partly on their estimation of sales possibilities for the period at various alternative prices. If the cost curves for the period t_2 to t_3 are precisely similar to those for the period t_1 to t_2 the entrepreneurs will in general only mark up prices at t_2 as a result of an observed excess demand in the period t_1 to t_2 provided that the sales in the new period at the prices of the previous period are expected to be the same as in the previous period, and assuming the expected sales curves for the two periods to be iso-elastic.

So, if we are to take the excess demand as the sole determinant of the development in prices, it seems that we have to adopt an assumption of what has been called "static expectations", that is an assumption that everyone expects what happened in one period to repeat itself in the next period.

An objection to taking the excess demand as sole determinant of the development of prices will therefore probably be that there is usually monopolism in the commodity-markets, and that the economic units which fix prices cannot be taken to be subject to static expectations. Expectations about sales may be so constituted that, for instance, a sequence of actual developments in the past is extrapolated into the future. Also, it might justifiably be emphasised that static expectations will hardly be predominant in an inflationary situation. It might be said against this that static expectations really seem to be characteristic of at least one phase of open inflation[1], and that the assumption of static expectations is in any case reasonable for repressed inflation. The analysis of Chaps. IV to VIII, which was carried out with this assumption, need not therefore necessarily be irrelevant for reality because of the above objections (cf. below, Section 9).

Last and most important comes the point that we are now interested in the question of *monetary equilibrium*, and the definition of monetary equilibrium we are using here is such that, in order to be generally fulfilled, given the usual functional relations in a system, e.g. as presented in Chap. IV, it implies the coincidence of the entrepreneurs' expected sales for a period and the planned purchases for the period. One of the results of the reasoning of Chap. IV was that, with given prices and costs, the entrepreneurs optimum purchases of factors will depend on the planned production, which, disregarding changes in stocks, is closely connected with expected sales. Therefore, if the planned purchases of factors are to equal the actual quantity of factor-services offered for sale, the expected sales must be equal to the production actually realizable. So, if it is ensured that the simultaneous set of conditions for monetary equilibrium is satisfied —that is, that planned purchases of factors equal the quantity of factor-services actually supplied and planned purchases of commodities equals production actually realizable,—at the same time it has also been ensured that the expected (by the entrepreneurs) sales of commodities equal planned (by buyers of commodities) purchases of commodities. The problem of whether it is the buyers' purchasing plans or the entrepreneurs' expectations of the buyers' purchasing plans which are decisive for the marking-up of prices by the entrepreneurs is accordingly not met with as a serious theoretical difficulty under these conditions of monetary equilibrium.[2] But the purely

---

[1] *The Course and Control of Inflation*, League of Nations.

[2] However, it should be noticed that it is assumed heré that the results of the one-commodity, one-factor analysis of Chaps. IV to VII may be carried over to the case of several commodities and several factors. We have not proved that this is permissible. It was this reasoning, among other things, which was referred to when, in Chap. I, Section 6, the aggregation problem to be solved here was said to be only a "partial" aggregation problem.

practical difficulty of ensuring that an actual policy will result in the simultaneous satisfaction of these two conditions is, of course, a problem of the first order.

5. *Monetary equilibrium a process in time*

It is reasonable to extend the concept of monetary equilibrium to mean a *process* during which both the value of the excess demand in the composite commodity-market and the value of the excess demand in the composite factor-market are kept zero (if necessary, by continual application of suitable measures), i.e., where the inflationary gap in the commodity-markets and the factor-gap are permanently kept at zero:

$$\Sigma x_i \cdot p_i = 0 \quad \text{and} \quad \Sigma X_j \cdot P_j = 0. \tag{IX: 1}$$

If the assumptions discussed in the preceding Section 4 are fulfilled, this is equivalent to a certain simple commodity price-index and a certain simple factor price-index being kept constant. The way in which the commodity price-index and the factor price-index are constructed depends on the form of the price-reaction equations as discussed in Section 2; very probably chain-indices must be used.

That the price-level (wage-level) will remain constant if the value sums mentioned are permanently kept at zero, must be understood as follows. Suppose that we have at the beginning of a period certain absolute prices which we wish to make the basis for the unchanging price-level. If an economic policy is now pursued such that $\Sigma x_i \cdot p_i = 0$ for the current period at the current absolute prices (x_i always corresponds to a particular price among alternatives), this will ensure, not that all the individual commodity prices will be the same for the next period, but only that a certain price-index of the prices quoted in the next period, with the prices of the first period as basis, is equal to 1. If we now, by means of an appropriate economic policy, take care that $\Sigma x_i \cdot p_i = 0$ for this next period also (at *this* period's actual prices), that will ensure that the third period's quoted prices, put into a certain index with the second period's prices as basis, give an unchanged price-index; and so on.

There can hardly be any doubt that the line of thought is in this direction when, for instance, expressions such as "balance of the social economy", or, "stability with full employment"[1], and the like, are used. However, there remains the question of whether the concept of monetary equilibrium really can be given this simple formulation, for it is not enough to set up certain desirable aims for economic policy. The aims set up must also be economically possible. Therefore we must ask if the two conditions (IX: 1) inserted in a plausible complete economic system can be simultaneously fulfilled over time; for, hitherto in this chapter we have in the main considered these two conditions dissociated from one another (i.e. partially).

Before we consider this question, we will say a little about the relation between the definition of the concept of monetary equilibrium which has been attempted here and Myrdal's well known concept of monetary equilibrium.

6. *Myrdal's concept of monetary equilibrium*

Myrdal's criticism of Wicksell's various criteria of equilibrium led him to regard monetary equilibrium as equivalent to the equality of *ex ante* investment and *ex ante* saving. If these two magnitudes are equal at a given point of time (or for a given period), there is monetary equilibrium. As has been stressed before (e.g. in Chap. II), the conditions that the monetary excess demand in the composite commodity-market and the composite factor-market are each zero, imply the condition, *ex ante* investment = *ex ante* saving, assuming (cf. Chap. I, Section 9), that we can identify demand with planned purchases and supply with expected sales; this assumption should usually be justified when both the inflationary gap in the commodity-markets and the factor-gap are zero. On the other hand the reverse implication is not valid. Therefore the definition of monetary equilibrium in Section 5 (equation (IX: 1)), implies monetary equilibrium in Myrdal's sense; but monetary equilibrium in Myrdal's sense does not imply the fulfilment of conditions (IX: 1). With the assumptions developed in Section 4, we can also say that equations (IX: 1) are equivalent to constancy of both a commodity price-index and a factor price-index, but Myrdal's monetary equilibrium corresponds only to the constancy of a combined commodity and factor price-index, which constitutes

---

[1] Full employment is thus defined by $\Sigma X_j \cdot P_j = 0$. This definition of full employment need not to be suitable for all purposes.

one of the deficiencies of Myrdal's concept of monetary equilibrium.

It is not clear what Myrdal himself considered to be the significance of his monetary equilibrium, but if we accept Palander's immanent criticism of Myrdal's immanent criticism of Wicksell, Myrdal seems to have thought that, with static expectations, the savings-investment relation at a given instant indicates not only the direction of motion of prices and wages at that instant—this is, as we have shown, a sound idea—but also their development over several future periods. If investment is greater (less) than saving, this is taken to denote that a cumulative, continuing, upward (downward) process is going on, whereas if investment is equal to saving, this denotes that no such cumulative process is going on, and will not arise, unless there is disturbance from outside. The criticism of this idea is well known; and we have not attempted to give any such significance to our concept of monetary equilibrium. Although, taking the given conditions into account, it is possible to deduce, from $\Sigma\, x_i \cdot p_i = 0$ at a certain instant (or, for a given period), that the price-level is constant at that instant, it is not possible to say that $\Sigma\, x_i \cdot p_i = 0$ will also automatically *remain* zero. Whether or not that is true will depend on the functioning of the economic system, of which the statement "$\Sigma\, x_i \cdot p_i = 0$ implies the instantaneous constancy of a certain price-index" is only one among many other relationships mutually governing each other. We have not taken the concept of monetary equilibrium to mean anything more than that if $\Sigma\, x_i \cdot p_i$ and $\Sigma\, X_j \cdot P_j$ are kept permanently at zero—by measures of economic policy, if necessary—then one or another commodity price-index and one or another factor price-index will remain constant; whereas Myrdal talks about "monetary equilibrium", we really ought to talk about "monetary equilibristics".

We have previously mentioned Myrdal's idea of constructing a price-index in which not only the coefficients of price-inertia (price-"stickiness") would be used as weights, but also certain investment reaction-coefficients. Like Palander, I am not able to see how this is to be concretely interpreted, but it is possible to understand this much, that it is connected with Myrdal's wish to find conditions for monetary equilibrium which are such that if only they are once fulfilled, the system will automatically remain in monetary equilibrium subsequently. However, as we have interpreted the concept of monetary equilibrium as a process through time, cf. Section 5, the need for this obscure method of weighting the index disappears. Furthermore, it is easily seen, that unless the coefficients of price-inertia are defined in another way than we have done [1], the idea of weighting with both coefficients of price-inertia and of investment-reaction must be fundamentally misleading. In our "relevant" price-indices there is not "room" for other weights than those made necessary by the form of the price-reaction equations.

7. *The institutional framework*

If we consider an economic system (a model) comprising both commodity and factor markets, and specify that in this model there is to be monetary equilibrium in the sense just defined, it is in no way certain that the model concerned can fulfil this specification. The models examined in Chap. IV to VIII were characterized by the circumstance that it was not possible to have monetary equilibrium without special intervention of economic policy. These models were inconsistent when regarded as static models, and static equilibrium is identical with monetary equilibrium in models with only one good and one factor. On the other hand, we demonstrated that it was possible to bring about monetary equilibrium in these models by means of suitable measures. The measures considered all belonged to the realm of financial policy—direct and indirect taxation and changes in public spending—but monetary policy might also be considered.

However, it is not possible to discuss more precisely the possibilities of keeping a system in monetary equilibrium unless we take into account the institutional framework within which the monetary equilibrium is supposed to be established. Among other things, it was control of prices and wages which was of interest in this connection. As we saw in Chap. V, it was possible to establish "controlled monetary equilibrium" where control of wages can be abandoned in certain situations while price control needs to be maintained in order that the state of monetary equilibrium may persist, in spite of the fact that the supply of and demand for commodities and factors were made equal at the given prices and wages; in other cases, control of wages

---

[1] Neither Myrdal nor Palander makes clear what they really understand by coefficients of price-inertia or price-stickiness.

needed to be retained while control of prices might be relaxed. Reference may be made to Chap. V, Sections 2 and 7. The decisive point was the question of what real wage was supposed to prevail when the monetary equilibrium was established. But even if control of both wages and prices is taken to be abandoned, it is still possible to establish monetary equilibrium with varying real wages (price-wage ratio's) by means of suitable manipulations of direct and indirect taxation (see in particular Chap. VII, Sections 5 and 6). Therefore, even if the concept of "monetary equilibrium" put forward here is taken as a norm for economic policy, we have not strictly bound ourselves in all respects to any particular economic policy. Monetary equilibrium as defined here covers a wide range of alternative economic policies, especially from the point of view of distribution of income.

8. *Financial policy and monetary equilibrium*

In Chapters V, VI and VII, and so far in this chapter also, we have only considered the possibilities of maintaining monetary equilibrium in a given system which is not subject to disturbances from outside. If the system is disturbed from outside, the question arises of the correct policy to counter this disturbance, and of whether it is possible to retain the given definition of monetary equilibrium. The disturbances which come to mind in this connection are changes in productivity. It was a special credit to Davidson that he brought the significance of changes in productivity into the discussion of monetary equilibrium; these disturbances are of vital significance and go on continuously in such a way that we have a good idea of their long-term trend. We know quite certainly that in the long run we can reckon with a "normal" yearly rise in productivity of some few per cent. Davidson pointed out that the effect of this disturbance is that we cannot expect to maintain both wages and prices constant when the productivity changes. Although quite correct within Davidson's assumptions, we shall show that his statement does not apply universally in the sense that it is not possible to carry out such a policy that equilibrium is maintained in both the commodity and factor markets with constant prices and wages despite the changes in production. This result depends exclusively on the fact that whereas the economic policies considered by Davidson (and Lindahl) only include monetary policies (Davidson's ideas were worked out at about

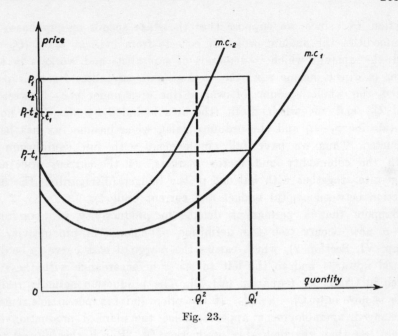

Fig. 23.

the beginning of the century, it should be remembered), we are including the possibility of using financial policies.

Suppose there is no control of prices and wages, and let us consider a simple case of perfect competition corresponding to the model
which was used in Chap. VI, Section 2. We suppose, for the sake
of simplicity, that the private economic subjects, workers and capitalists, save nothing, and that the state has a certain consumption,
consisting of purchases of commodities from the capitalists, which purchases are financed through taxation, both direct, in the form of taxes
on personal income, and indirect, in the form of a general excise on
all commodities produced. Suppose the following equilibrium is established (the manner of establishing it does not concern us here).

The market price is p_1 and the tax per article t_1 for the initial
equilibrium (the unbroken lines) in Fig. 23. The price *minus* tax, the
entrepreneurs' net price, is then $p_1 - t_1$. The marginal cost curve is
$m.c._1$, and the planned production coincides with the greatest realizable
production Q_1^1. The factor-gap is consequently zero. We assume the
demand in the commodity-markets to be such that, with the market
price p_1 and full employment, there is demand for just the total pro-

duction Q_1^1, since we suppose that the state spends on purchases of commodities the amount which it collects from indirect taxes ($Q_1^1 \cdot t_1$) and the amount which it demands of capitalists and workers in the form of direct income tax; the workers and capitalists for their part spend the whole amount of wages (the area under $m.c._{\cdot 1}$ between 0 and Q_1^1) and the whole profit (the area bounded by $m.c._{\cdot 1}$, the horizontal line $p_1 - t_1$ and the ordinate axis), when income tax has been deducted. Thus we have full employment with full equilibrium in both the commodity and factor markets, at the current price and wage-rate, together with balance of the budget (disregarding the distinction between capital budget and current budget).

Suppose that a permanent decline in productivity of magnitude $1 - a$ now occurs (see the definition of change in productivity in Chap. VI, Section 2), which causes the marginal cost curve to be displaced upwards and to the left to $m.c._{\cdot 2}$, in accordance with the rule given in Chap. VI (equation (VI: 2)). The production actually realizable is now only $Q_1^2 = a \cdot Q_1^1$. If the price and tax per article remain unchanged, unemployment appears, since the planned production becomes less than the realizable production Q_1^2. But if the indirect tax per article is lowered from t_1 to t_2, which latter is determined by the expression $t_2 = p_1 - (p_1 - t_1)/a^1$, the planned production will be just equal to the realizable production Q_1^2, and the factor-gap remains zero despite the unchanged market price and the fall in productivity.

What about the commodity-markets? Let us suppose for the moment that the direct taxes are unchanged and that the state continues to buy commodities with the revenue from these taxes. Then this part of the demand for commodities remains unaltered, both in quantity and value. The total income of the workers and capitalists is unchanged, *ex ante* and *ex post*, with the same value as before the fall in productivity, since substitution of the expressions just introduced for Q_1^2 and t_2 proves that $Q_1^1 (p_1 - t_1) = Q_1^2 (p_1 - t_2)$. The total income of the private individuals (and its division between workers and capitalists), being unchanged, and the direct income taxes as well, their total demand for commodities remains unchanged, in quantity and in value. The state's revenue from indirect taxation falls from $Q_1^1 \cdot t_1$ to $Q_1^2 \cdot t_2$,

---

[1] It will be seen that if $a < (p_1 - t_1)/p_1$, t becomes negative, that is, the indirect tax must be changed to a subsidy.

and, substituting the expressions given above for Q_1^2 or t_2, it is seen that $Q_1^1 \cdot t_1 - Q_1^2 \cdot t_2 = p_1 (Q_1^1 - Q_1^2)$. The decrease in the amount of indirect tax levied, necessary for maintenance of the equilibrium in the factor-market when market prices remain unchanged, is thus exactly equal to the value of the decline in the total production caused by the decline in productivity. Therefore, if the state diminishes its purchases of commodities by just the amount $Q_1^1 \cdot t_1 - Q_1^2 \cdot t_2$, the total demand for commodities will be equal to the total realizable production after the decline in productivity with market prices unaltered.

This method of maintaining equilibrium in the commodity and factor markets, with market prices unchanged, assumes that the state changes its payments for commodity purchases in accordance with the productivity. This is not very practical. We will assume that the state wishes to keep its real consumption unchanged despite the decrease in productivity, and, with the commodity prices as given, this means that the state wishes to keep the value of its consumption unchanged. This can only be achieved by increasing the amount of direct income taxes by the amount of the decrease in the indirect taxes, whereupon the total amount spent by workers and capitalists on the purchases of commodities decreases by just the amount of the decline in the value of the total production due to the decline in productivity.

The case of a rise in productivity is of course treated in a similar manner.

We thus come to a simple rule for the neutralization of changes in productivity, so that monetary equilibrium is maintained with prices, wage-rates and the state's consumption unaltered:

If there is a general decrease in productivity of magnitude $1 - \alpha$ (or, an increase of magnitude $\alpha - 1$), such that the total national product decreases by $1 - \alpha$ (increases by $\alpha - 1$), and if prices and wage-rates remain unaltered, monetary equilibrium may be maintained on both the commodity and factor markets, with the state's real consumption and the balance of the budget unaltered, by simultaneously: 1) decreasing (increasing) the indirect taxes, and 2) increasing (decreasing) the direct income taxes by the amount of the decrease (increase) in the total national product.

We shall not go into the question of the modifications of this rule necessary when the assumptions of the problem are less simplified than

244

those which have been the basis for the derivation of the rule. Neither shall we consider the important possibilities offered by such a financial policy for the solution of the intricate problems which have become acute in many countries of late years in connection with the policy of maintaining full employment.[1] The main thing in this connection is that such a financial policy as this provides an opportunity of maintaining monetary equilibrium in the sense that both prices and wage-rates are kept fixed, with full employment, despite the fact that the system is subject to changes of productivity.

It is thus evident that it is not necessary for the maintenance of monetary equilibrium to let the market prices of commodities vary in inverse proportion to productivity, or, assuming proportional changes in the marginal productivities of the various productive agents, the wage-rate in direct proportion to productivity. But, of course, this does not mean that the whole concept of monetary equilibrium should be bound up with the financial policy sketched above so that we should talk about monetary equilibrium only when this policy is actually carried out. We are in no way committed to such a point of view.

Let us look again at the definitions given in Chap. I, Section 4, for monetary pressure of inflation, and of deflation and monetary equilibrium (equations (I: 1), (I: 2), and (I: 3)); it has already been remarked there that certain open cases occur in which there is neither a monetary pressure of inflation nor of deflation, nor equilibrium. These open cases occur when there is either monetary excess demand in the composite commodity-market and monetary excess supply in the composite factor-market, or conversely, monetary excess supply in the

---

[1] A policy such as outlined here provides a basis for significant manipulations of the distribution of income. If increases in productivity are the normal, for example, it will be seen that the state is in this way able to divert every increase of the national product to the workers (and other recipients of small incomes), without increasing the direct taxation on larger incomes; moreover, the direct taxes paid by the low income groups gradually disappear. This means that it is possible in the long run to give the workers a rise in real income which, as a percentage, is larger than the increase in productivity, without this conflicting with the wish to maintain monetary equilibrium. There is thus a possibility of avoiding the spontaneous increases in wages due to the desire of the trade unions to obtain higher wage increases than productivity permits. See my article, "Finanspolitik og lønpolitik" ("Financial Policy and Wage Policy"), *Ekonomisk Tidskrift*, Stockholm, 1950.

composite commodity-market and monetary excess demand in the composite factor-market. It is just these open cases which become important when one regards the disturbances which changes of productivity cause in a policy designed to maintain equilibrium in the sense given in Section 5.

We may also call to mind the results of the investigations in Chap. VI and Chap. VII, Section 4. We found that, if no special economic measures are instituted, a rise in productivity with prices and wage-rates still unchanged leads to an increase in the excess demand for factors and a decrease in the excess demand for commodities; and conversely with a fall in productivity. Applied to the case where the changes in productivity occur in a situation where the monetary excess demand in both the composite commodity-market and the composite factor-market are zero, this means that when prices and wage-rates are unchanged, an increase in productivity gives rise to an excess demand for factors and an excess supply of commodities; and conversely when productivity declines. Hence, an increase of productivity leads to a falling tendency for commodity prices *and* a rising tendency for factor prices, and conversely, a decline of productivity leads to a rising tendency for commodity prices *and* a falling tendency for factor prices.

So, the disequilibrium which is caused by a (permanent) change of productivity obviously belongs to our open cases, and is neither inflationary nor deflationary. At the same time, it will be seen that this disequilibrium is of such a character that, normally, it will more or less tend to cancel itself, because of the change in the relation between prices and wages caused by the disequilibrium. The automatic reaction of the system is as a rule such that it tends to bring about a change in the relation between prices and wages in the direction which is necessary for the establishment of equilibrium. But, of course, the possibility exists that the change in productivity will shift the demand and supply relations in such a way that the system ends up in a serious disequilibrium, e.g. a quasi-equilibrium of the type discussed in Chaps. VII and VIII. During the process of transition from one state of monetary equilibrium to the other, we naturally do not have monetary equilibrium according to the definition of monetary equilibrium which we have chosen (disregarding the financial policy outlined in this section); but on the other hand, no process of inflation or deflation is going on.

So, it might perhaps not be unreasonable simply to extend the concept of monetary equilibrium to include transition processes of such a "harmless" character. The definitions in Chap. I would then be altered to say that monetary equilibrium exists not only when the excess demand in the composite commodity-market and in the composite factor-market are both zero, but also when the excess demands in these two groups of markets have opposite signs. In any case it is obvious that, so long as we concentrate upon the induced price changes, changes of productivity do not give rise to special difficulties with regard to the concept of monetary equilibrium, nor with regard to a policy designed to maintain monetary equilibrium.

9. *Final remarks*

Even if the system is in a state of monetary equilibrium in the sense given in Section 5, we are not sure that a continuous increase (decrease) in the levels of prices and wages cannot take place. It is only certain (by definition) that no induced increases in prices and wages take place. But spontaneous price and wage increases cannot be prevented merely by keeping demand equal to supply; this is due to the distinction made between induced and spontaneous price changes. However, if it is wished to maintain full employment with a stable value of money, the fact that at least the problem of induced price changes has been solved means a good deal. The way in which spontaneous changes can eventually be avoided will not be considered here. The causal factors involved belong for the greater part to the field of politics and social psychology (the "class struggle"), so that it is only possible to treat them economically to a minor degree. The problem is actually closely connected with that of abolishing monopoly in all its aspects. Probably the most unhappy thing to do would be to attempt to balance spontaneous tendencies to wage and price increases by the creation of induced decreases in wages and prices; for this would certainly lead to unemployment and would not in any way guarantee that the spontaneous tendencies could be held in check. The problem is well-known from the post war discussion of full employment; however, I shall only refer to the beautiful presentation of these problems by Keynes in *A Treatise on Money*[1], which antic-

---

[1] J. M. Keynes, *A Treatise on Money*, I, Chap. XI.

ipated most of the points of the present discussion of full employment.

In conclusion, we will just briefly mention a question which we have almost completely neglected up to now. It is the question of price expectations and their importance for the economic process. It is customary to accord these a foremost place in the explanation of the inflationary process. However, in general they do not affect the principle of the excess demand analyses used here. It is usually assumed that if people expect further price increases in the future a current process of price increase will be accelerated, compared with what would be the case if it were expected that current prices are to persist in the future. However, expectations of future price increases only accelerate the increases in current prices in that they increase the current excess demand; it is better to buy while prices are lower, and better to withhold supplies until prices are higher, and it is obviously the excess demand thus created which forces up prices at the moment. Because the expectations of price increases make themselves felt *via* the excess demand, we have hitherto been able to neglect them in our analysis. The price expectations form just one factor among many which contribute to the formation of the excess demand. This way of regarding price expectations may even be used in the special case where everyone is correct in his opinion about the development of prices and adapts himself accordingly, so that a process of "moving dynamic equilibrium" is set going, cf. Chap. I, Section 8.

Another thing is that general *changes* in price expectations give rise to difficulties for the excess demand analysis, since changed expectations with regard to the future price development may lead to changed sales expectations for the enterprises, and thus make unreasonable that assumption of "static expectations" with respect to quantitative relationships which we made in order to include the case of monopoly in those covered by the equations set up in Section 2. If, in a period analysis where price changes are taken to be determined by the excess demand in the previous period, we suppose that a certain period shows perfect equilibrium in all the markets, then all prices should remain unchanged in the next period, according to the assumptions set out in Section 2. If, for some reason or other, everyone at the beginning of the next period expects price increases in future periods, supplies will obviously be held back and purchases expanded if prices

17

really remain unaltered. Those who fix the prices will be clear about this and so will mark up the prices. Of course, it is still possible to consider this price increase as caused by the period's (expected) excess demand at unchanged prices, and the case does not therefore lie outside of the scheme of explanation of excess demand analysis; but it is obviously impossible to use the price-reaction equations given in Section 2. So the price expectations do disturb the analysis in so far as they can render the price-reaction equations unusable. The definition of monetary equilibrium (Section 5) is not disturbed by this, however, because if the state counteracts the (expected) excess demand arising during a period in such a way that those who fix the prices know that there will be no excess demand in spite of the changed price expectations, the prices will not be marked up. Monetary equilibrium still signifies unchanged price and wage levels, but the time-lag between excess demand and price increase may disappear.

Although price expectations and their changes in this way complicate the excess demand analysis to a considerable degree, no insurmountable difficulty is caused such as can only be solved by other types of analysis. Excess demand analysis may also be bent to this problem. But it is clear that in practical forecasting, price expectations and their changes are a difficulty of the first order, and that a policy which aims to maintain monetary equilibrium is forced to accord a great deal of weight to holding expectations in check.

CHAPTER X

CONCLUSIONS

This book has been given the title *A Study in the Theory of Inflation* to indicate that it is not in any way supposed to be an exhaustive treatment of the problems of inflation. Such a task as this latter would obviously be beyond the powers of one man, since it would have to cover the whole of the field of theoretical and empirical economic dynamics. It is not difficult to point to theoretical problems which have not been touched upon, and the relations with empirical facts are quite platonic, of course, in so far as this study is intended solely as a theoretical investigation. In this respect, the reasoning of the preceding chapters shares the fate of all other theory, in that it cannot be considered to be other than an aid, and possible an inspiration, to empirical investigation and so to the explanation of actual processes of inflation.

Much inflation theory is worked out in terms of supply of and demand for money; we have not made use of this approach and we have also shown why this type of analysis is not very suitable for the problems of inflation. Nearly all other inflation theory is expressed in terms of a difference between investment and saving. We have not found this approach very useful either. If we choose the pure *ex ante* definitions of the concepts of investment and saving, the saving-investment analysis implies that markets must be aggregated which it seems indispensable to keep apart; so the saving-investment analysis becomes too clumsy an instrument for the analysis of the disequilibria of a system in inflation. If, on the other hand, we choose other definitions of saving and/or investment the difference between investment and saving only becomes an indirect and, accordingly, bad way of describing phenomena which may just as well be described more directly. So, nothing seems to be gained, and, almost of necessity, something seems to be lost in applying the saving-investment analysis to the problems of inflation.

The models used as bases for the reasoning and conclusions drawn are, from the purely theoretical point of view, characterized by the explicit inclusion of disequilibrium in the labour-market in the analysis and by the fact that equilibrium between demand and supply in the labour-market is in general regarded as a necessary condition for total equilibrium; this means an addition to the more usual "Keynesian" condition that demand and supply of commodities (and services) shall be equal. This again means that the conclusions with regard to the effects of various changes in data and with regard to anti-inflationary policy are essentially different from the results of the more crude "Keynesian" models, where the labour market is not explicitly taken into consideration. Keynes's *General Theory* has, unfortunately, given rise to a habit of thought in inflation theory according to which "demand for commodities is also demand for labour". We have tried to remove this bad habit of thinking from our models.

If we turn to empirical considerations and ask in what fields it is particularly necessary to investigate factual connections—if the analysis presented here is taken as basis—it is what have been called "the price-reaction equations" which come to the fore. Is it possible to find measurable phenomena which can be taken as typical causes for upward or downward changes of prices? It is evident that the whole explanation of open inflation depends upon this question, and where repressed inflation is concerned, the problem occurs in implicit form. For, one of the questions which we must always be ready to answer when discussing repressed inflation is this: in what circumstances is it possible to remove the control on prices and wages without prices and/or wages changing as a result of this removal of control, and what happens if controls are removed anyway? This is in fact the cardinal problem of repressed inflation.

In this study, we have everywhere taken *the excess demand*, the difference between demand and supply at given prices, as decisive for the tendency to price changes. And it is far from being a matter of chance that this hypothesis was chosen. As Samuelson showed a decade ago, the classical and modern theory of static equilibrium is to a great extent based on implicit assumptions of this sort. It follows from the preceding chapters that the classical—and modern—monetary theory, the investment-saving analysis, must actually employ assumptions of this type if it is to be relevant for the explanation of changes in the value of money. A hypothesis which is so central for sections of economic theory as important as the analysis of static equilibrium and monetary theory is an obvious subject for empirical investigation, and there can hardly be any doubt that further progress in these fields must proceed by that road.

APPENDIX I

A SWEDISH ESTIMATE OF THE EXCESS OF PURCHASING-POWER FOR 1951

As was mentioned in Chap. III, estimation of "the excess of purchasing-power" in Sweden has been attempted each year since the beginning of the second World War. The calculations were started by Erik Lundberg at the Konjunkturinstitut in Stockholm, and were subsequently continued by the government's National Budget Committee. The results are published in the periodical surveys of the Konjunkturinstitut[1], and as a rule also in conjunction with the finance minister's submission of the budget to parliament.[2]

In Chap. III we have already given a description of what seems to be the view of the Konjunkturinstitut with regard to the principles for calculating the excess of purchasing-power if sufficient statistical information (and time!) were available. However, when it comes to the actual calculations, the methods used are very much more rough than the principles, and this is due to the lack of relevant statistical material. The Konjunkturinstitut (but apparently not the National Budget Committee) therefore usually prefer to call their calculations, "examples", and prefer to employ alternatives if there seems to be special uncertainty. Since Sweden is, by comparison with other countries, relatively advanced in statistical information, the difficulties experienced in Sweden with this type of forecasting may indicate a need for caution in similar attempts in other countries. Comparisons with the actual development, in so far as such comparisons are not made impossible because of measures of economic policy called forth by the very calculations, shows that the Swedish calculations for previous years have often been somewhat incorrect. In spite of that, they have proved to be so valuable as guides for economic policy that they have been continued.

As an example of the actual method of procedure used, we will give a synopsis of the calculations of the National Budget Committee for 1951. These calculations were made public in January 1951 and must therefore have been completed about the end of 1950. The methods are not quite the same as those used by the Konjunkturinstitut in previous years, cf. below.

[1] See *Meddelanden från Konjunkturinstitutet* (*Reports of the Konjunkturinstitut*), Serie A: 11 et seq., and Serie B: 2, 3, 8, 9, and 11, Isaac Marcus Boktryckeri Aktiebolag, Stockholm.

[2] Bilaga 1 till *Statsverkspropositionen* (The Treasury Proposals), 1951 and earlier years.

As in all other forecasting, the first thing to do is to give a review of the actual development in a previous period. The starting-point for the calculation becomes the following table[1], which shows the balance of supply in the national economy in the years 1947 to 1950, expressed in terms of the prices of 1949. The results for 1950 are also given in the prices of 1950.

TABLE 1. Balance of supply and realized demand 1947 to 1950.[2]

Mill. Sw. kronor	In 1949 prices				1950 in 1950 prices
	1947	1948	1949	1950	
Supply					
1. GNP (at market price)	27 330	28 480	29 910	$31\ 420 \pm u$	$31\ 450 \pm v$
2. Imports of commodities cif ...	5 530	4 980	4 330	5 330	6 100
3. Total supply (gross)..........	32 860	33 460	34 240	$36\ 750 \pm u$	$37\ 550 \pm v$
Realized demand					
4. Private home investment (gross)	5 860	5 350	5 180	5 450	5 610
5. Public home investment (gross)	2 140	2 520	2 720	2 930	3 000
6, Increase of stocks............	540?	400?	150?	$-100 \pm u$	$-100 \pm v$
7. Exports of commodities fob and foreign net balance of services	3 800	4 210	4 820	5 760	6 090
8. Private consumption	17 670	18 030	18 250	19 380	19 580
9. Public consumption..........	2 850	2 950	3 120	3 330	3 370
10. Total realized demand	32 860	33 460	34 240	$36\ 750 \pm u$	$37\ 550 \pm v$

The idea behind such a table is well-known. It may, perhaps, be pointed out that all figures in this table are entirely *ex post* magnitudes, and any "gap" of any sort cannot be read directly from the table, of course. All the same, it can be taken as a suitable basis for the calculations of the excess of purchasing-power for 1951, since the object of the calculations is just to show how these magnitudes should develop during 1951, if everyone were able to act as they wish to act (within the given framework of regulations). So each separate item in this balance is considered in turn, and an attempt is made to calculate the real development tendency (expressed in 1950 prices) during 1951 with the actual, *ex post*, results for 1950 as a basis, employing certain given premisses with regard to the government's policy, etc. A calculation like that in Table 2 is thus obtained.

---

[1] Bilaga 1 till *Statsverkspropositionen* 1951, Bihang 2, "Översikt över det ekonomiska läget 1951, Nationalbudget för år 1951." ("Review of the Economic Situation in 1951, The National Budget for 1951").

[2] The unknown magnitudes *u* and *v* are added because the calculations for 1950 are preliminary.

TABLE 2. Calculation of the excess of purchasing power for 1951 (in 1950 prices).

Factors increasing supply   Mill. Sw. kronor

Increase of GNP (at market price) .... + 1 000
Increase of volume of imports .... + 300

Total increase of supply + 1 300

Factors increasing demand

Increase of investments (excluding stocks)............................. +   300
Change from depletion of stocks to stocking-up........................ +   200
Increase of private consumption .... *at most* +   350

    increase of personal income .... + 2 600
    taxation .... — 750
    saving .... ±   0
    increase of prices .... *at least* — 1 500

Increase of public consumption.. +   150
Increase of exports .... +   300

Total increase of demand : *at most* + 1 300

According to this calculation, both supply and demand for 1951 should increase by about the same amount and there should thus be no excess of purchasing-power this year. However, in order to understand the meaning of this calculation and what conclusions may be drawn from the table, it is advisable to consider how each separate item is arrived at.

The increase in the gross national product is obtained by extrapolating the development of the real national product during the previous years. A 3 % rise has been used, which is less than the increase in preceding years; the steeper rise in previous years is actually fictitious in part. Moreover, it is worth noticing something which would hardly be expected: that (given full employment) the development of the national product has been one of the most difficult items in the forecasting.

The increase in imports. Part of the imports may be taken to be determined by the magnitude of the home production and its division with respect to various commodities; it is possible to estimate this part of the imports without any very great difficulties to the same degree of certainty as the gross national product. The rest of the imports are more difficult to estimate, as import speculation—because prices abroad are expected to rise, for instance—can be very important. Fortunately, miscalculations on this point are not catastrophic, because speculative imports will find expression in corresponding speculative intended increases in stocks, which enter into the demand. Therefore, such mistakes tend to some degree to disappear in the balance between the increase of supply and the increase of demand.

The increase in investments (excluding stocks) is made out partly from what is known of the state's investment plans and partly on a basis of the existing control of all new building and rebuilding. Investments in machinery and the like are partly reckoned with the help of information from the entrepreneurs as to their investment plans.

The change from depletion of stocks to stocking-up. This item is very uncertain and is best described as pure guesswork, using the general state of inflation abroad as a reason for the assumption of the intended increases in stocks.

The increase in private consumption is given as 350 million Sw. kronor, and this amount is arrived at from an expected increase of personal income of 2 600 million Sw. kronor, with a deduction of 750 million Sw. kronor increase in income tax, 0 Sw. kronor saving, and 1 500 million Sw. kronor as the effect of the price increases on consumer goods. The basis of these figures is an estimate of the rises in wages which may be expected to result from the general wage negotiations in February 1951 between employees on the one hand and employers and the public authorities on the other, as well as an estimate of such rises in prices which will be permitted by the price-control authorities, partly as an effect of rises in prices of imported commodities and the removal of certain subsidies, partly as a result of the increases in wage-rates. It is obvious that the incorporation of such "intended" (i.e. intended by the government) price increases in the calculation does not in any way conflict with the idea of a calculation of the excess of purchasing-power from the "equilibrium aspect" (cf. Chap. III, Sections 2, 3, and 6), but the results must of course be formulated in terms of the 1950 price level. Thus employing calculations of the increase in production and wages, the figure of 2 600 million Sw. kronor for the increase of personal income is obtained. The Swedish pay as you earn income tax causes about 750 million Sw. kronor of this to be paid directly to the state and to local authorities. The price increases which are reckoned on take another 1 500 million Sw. kronor of the nominal increase in income. Then there is saving, which is put equal to zero here. It would appear that this is to be taken to mean that the total voluntary saving from a nominal personal income which is expected to be 2 600 million Sw. kronor greater in 1951 than in 1950 will be the same as the *ex post* personal saving realized in 1950. This means that the intended average savings ratio should be lower in 1951 than the *ex post* average savings ratio in 1950. This point is undoubtedly the weakest in the whole calculation, and if anyone is inclined to do so, it is quite possible to reject the whole calculation as worthless because of this weakness alone.

The increase of exports is calculated on the basis of the production capacity of the industries producing commodities for export and on the possible absorption by the home market of commodities which would "normally" be sold to foreign countries. In periods when there are international seller's markets, the demand from abroad is not so important for the determination of the physical magnitude of the export. But in spite of that the calculation is very uncertain.

When the calculated changes are combined as in Table 2, the excess of purchasing-power with regard to commodities and services for 1951 is obtained. Of course, it is just a matter of chance, in no way connected with the principles of calculation themselves, that this is equal to zero.

As mentioned above, the calculation for 1951 of the National Budget Committee differs in some respects from the calculations of the Konjunkturinstitut for earlier years.

The calculations of the Konjunkturinstitut have always been more sophisticated than the calculation described in this appendix, e.g. in that the Konjunkturinstitut usually puts forward several alternative calculations of varying probability. More important is, however, that in previous years it was not the total change in saving which was estimated, but only that part of the change in saving which is dependent on changes in income. As has been pointed out in the publications of the Konjunkturinstitut, what is thus arrived at is only the *change* in the excess of purchasing-power, or rather, one of the factors which are important for the change in the excess of purchasing-power. The absolute magnitude of the excess of purchasing-power was, accordingly, not calculated. Therefore, the information which the calculations gave in previous years was very limited. Furthermore, it should be observed that whereas the Konjunkturinstitut attempts to calculate the excess of purchasing-power as a yearly rate based on the relationships at the beginning of the year, the calculation by the National Budget Committee seems to be intended to cover the calendar year 1951.

Calculations of the excess of purchasing-power in the labour-market, the factor-gap, has not been attempted; if the factor-gap is to be calculated, it is, of course, necessary to make the same assumptions with respect to the development of prices and wages as were made for the calculation of the excess of purchasing-power for commodities and services. For instance, if the excess of purchasing-power in the commodity-markets has been calculated on the assumption that wages are to rise by, say, 10 per cent in the middle of the year, but prices are to remain constant throughout the year, the factor-gap must naturally be calculated with the same assumptions. If the calculations are not synchronized in this way, they become meaningless when combined.

Although the excess of purchasing-power is not calculated for the labour-market, it is of interest to note that there seems to be a general idea that 1951—in spite of the equilibrium in the commodity-markets—will be marked by a severe shortage of labour-power; in other words, it seems that 1951 is to be a year with equilibrium in the commodity-markets but with a large factor-gap. That situations like this may arise was pointed out several times in the theoretical investigations of Chap. V.

APPENDIX II

LIST OF SYMBOLS USED

The symbols listed in this appendix are those which are used throughout the book. Symbols used only occasionally are not given here.

Symbols of the first of the two groups of symbols below are used when the argument makes it necessary to split up magnitudes of value into price and quantity. The precise meanings of these symbols and of their possible subscripts and superscripts are given in the text.

P and p Price of a good.

           y Ratio between two prices.

           w Wage-rate.

D and d Quantity in demand.

Q " q "   " supply.

X " x Excess demand, i.e. $D{-}Q$, or $d{-}q$.

When it is found unnecessary to split up values into price and quantity the following group of symbols is used (especially in Chaps. II, III, and IV). A more general explanation of this group of symbols was given in Chap. II, Section 5. If a superscript to the right is missing in the text, it means that the symbol concerned applies to the whole community. All symbols which are not appended with the superscript * refer to transactions wholly internal to the system. It should be observed that in Chaps. IV to VI the letters A, B, and C are also used to denote points in diagrams; however, no difficulties ought to arise from this.

$^{g}A_0^c$ and $^{g}A_1^c$ Capitalists' sales of commodities, expected and realized respectively.

$^{g}A_0^*$ " $^{g}A_1^*$ Capitalists' sales of commodities to foreign countries (exports), expected and realized respectively.

$^{l}A_0^w$ " $^{l}A_1^w$ Workers' sales of labour-services, expected and realized respectively.

$^{g}B_0^c$ " $^{g}B_1^c$ Capitalists' purchases of commodities for productive purposes, planned and realized respectively.

$^{g}B_0^*$ " $^{g}B_1^*$ Capitalists' purchases of commodities for productive purposes from foreign countries (imports), planned and realized respectively.

$^{l}B_0^c$ " $^{l}B_1^c$ Capitalists' purchases of labour-services, planned and realized respectively.

258

${}^{g}B_0^s$ and ${}^{g}B_1^s$		State's purchases of commodities for "productive" purposes, planned and realized respectively.
${}^{l}B_0^s$ " ${}^{l}B_1^s$		State's purchases of labour-services, planned and realized respectively.
${}^{g}B_0^w$ " ${}^{g}B_1^w$		Workers' purchases of commodities for productive purposes, planned and realized respectively.
C_0^{c+w} " C_1^{c+w}		Capitalists' and workers' purchases of commodities for consumption, planned and realized respectively.
E_0^c " E_1^c		Capitalists' income (gross profits), expected and realized respectively.
E_0^w " E_1^w		Workers' income, expected and realized respectively.
E_0^{c+w} " E_1^{c+w}		Capitalists' and workers' income, expected and realized respectively.
I_0^c " I_1^c		Capitalists' investments, planned and realized respectively.
I_0^s " I_1^s		State's investments, planned and realized respectively.
I_0^{c+s} " I_1^{c+s}		Capitalists' and state's investments, planned and realized respectively.
${}^{i}T_0^c$ " ${}^{i}T_1^c$		Capitalists' payments of indirect taxes, planned and realized respectively.
${}^{i}T_0^s$ " ${}^{i}T_1^s$		State's receipts from indirect taxes, expected and realized respectively.
${}^{d}T_0^{c+w}$ " ${}^{d}T_1^{c+w}$		Capitalists' and workers' payments of direct taxes (income taxes), planned and realized respectively.
${}^{d}T_0^s$ " ${}^{d}T_1^s$		State's receipts from direct taxes (income taxes), expected and realized respectively.
S_0^{c+w} " S_1^{c+w}		Capitalists' and workers' savings, planned and realized respectively.
S_0^s " S_1^s		State's saving, i.e. state's budget surplus, planned and realized respectively.
S_0^{c+w+s} " S_1^{c+w+s}		Capitalists' and workers' and state's savings, planned and realized respectively.

INDEX